Opinion Writing

Opinion Writing

The City Law School, City University, London

OXFORD
UNIVERSITY PRESS

OXFORD
UNIVERSITY PRESS

Great Clarendon Street, Oxford OX2 6DP

Oxford University Press is a department of the University of Oxford.
It furthers the University's objective of excellence in research, scholarship,
and education by publishing worldwide in

Oxford New York

Auckland Cape Town Dar es Salaam Hong Kong Karachi
Kuala Lumpur Madrid Melbourne Mexico City Nairobi
New Delhi Shanghai Taipei Toronto

With offices in

Argentina Austria Brazil Chile Czech Republic France Greece
Guatemala Hungary Italy Japan Poland Portugal Singapore
South Korea Switzerland Thailand Turkey Ukraine Vietnam

Oxford is a registered trademark of Oxford University Press
in the UK and in certain other countries

Published in the United States
by Oxford University Press Inc., New York

© City University, 2007

The moral rights of the author have been asserted
Database right Oxford University Press (maker)

Crown copyright material is reproduced under Class Licence
Number C01P0000148 with the permission of OPSI
and the Queen's Printer for Scotland

All rights reserved. No part of this publication may be reproduced,
stored in a retrieval system, or transmitted, in any form or by any means,
without the prior permission in writing of Oxford University Press,
or as expressly permitted by law, or under terms agreed with the appropriate
reprographics rights organization. Enquiries concerning reproduction
outside the scope of the above should be sent to the Rights Department,
Oxford University Press, at the address above

You must not circulate this book in any other binding or cover
and you must impose the same condition on any acquirer

British Library Cataloguing in Publication Data

Data available

Typeset by Laserwords Private Limited, Chennai, India
Printed in Great Britain on acid-free paper by
Ashford Colour Press Limited, Gosport, Hampshire

ISBN 978-0-19-921224-8

10 9 8 7 6 5 4 3 2 1

FOREWORD

I am delighted to write this Foreword to the manuals which are written by practitioners and staff of the Inns of Court School of Law (ICSL [now The City Law School]).

The manuals are designed primarily to support training on the Bar Vocational Course (BVC). They now cover a wide range, embracing both the compulsory and the optional subjects of the BVC. They provide an outstanding resource for all those concerned to teach and acquire legal skills wherever the BVC is taught.

The manuals for the compulsory subjects are updated and revised annually. The manuals for the optional subjects are revised every two years. In a new and important development, the publishers will maintain a website for the manuals which will be used to keep them up-to-date throughout the academic year.

The manuals, continually updated, exemplify the practical and professional approach that is central to the BVC. I congratulate the staff of the ICSL who have produced them to an excellent standard, and Oxford University Press for its commitment in securing their publication. As my predecessor the Hon. Mr Justice Gross so aptly said in a previous Foreword, the manuals are an important ingredient in the constant drive to raise standards in the public interest.

The Hon. Mr Justice Etherton
Chairman of the Advisory Board of the Institute of Law
City University, London
May 2007

OUTLINE CONTENTS

Foreword		v
1	Introduction	1
2	Qualities of good writing	4
3	Plain English	11
4	Introduction to opinion writing	19
5	Opinion writing	23
6	The use of law in an opinion	46
7	Getting started	55
8	An illustration of the opinion writing process	67
9	Examples of barristers' opinions	89
10	Advising for the purposes of public funding in civil cases	106
11	Advice on evidence in a civil case	117
12	Advice on evidence in a criminal case	135
13	Advice on evidence and quantum	151
14	Assessment criteria	160
APPENDIX A: Improving your writing skills		169
APPENDIX B: Exercises		183
APPENDIX C: Further exercises		188
APPENDIX D: Re Mr And Mrs Roberts		199
Index		203

DETAILED CONTENTS

Foreword v

1 Introduction 1
1.1 Written word skills 1
1.2 Objectives 1
1.3 Words and the barrister 1

2 Qualities of good writing 4
2.1 The qualities 4
2.2 Making choices 4
2.3 The English language 5
2.4 Clarity 5
2.5 A logical structure 6
2.6 Spelling 6
2.7 Grammar 6
2.8 Punctuation 7
2.9 Precision 7
2.10 Non-ambiguity 8
2.11 Conciseness 8
2.12 Completeness 8
2.13 Style 9
2.14 Appearance 9
2.15 The reader 10
2.16 Reading over 10

3 Plain English 11
3.1 Introduction 11
3.2 What is plain English? 11
3.3 Why use plain English? 11
3.4 What is the problem with legal language? 12
3.5 What is being done to promote plain English? 12
3.6 Recognising and rewriting legalese 12
3.7 Writing plain English 15
3.8 Basic rules of plain English 16
3.9 Further reading 18

4 Introduction to opinion writing 19
4.1 Summary of materials 19
4.2 The opinion writing course 20
4.3 Objectives of the course 20
4.4 Professional conduct 21

5 Opinion writing 23
5.1 Why learn to write opinions? 23
5.2 What is opinion writing? 23
5.3 The right mental attitude: the practical approach 25
5.4 The thinking process: preparing to write an opinion 27
5.5 The writing process: the opinion itself 33
5.6 How the opinion should be set out 35
5.7 Points of content 41
5.8 Style 44
5.9 When you have finished your opinion 45
5.10 Further reading 45

6 The use of law in an opinion 46
6.1 Introduction 46
6.2 Dealing with the well-known principle of law 47
6.3 Only cite authorities on points of law 47
6.4 How to cite cases 48
6.5 Show the relevance of the case 50
6.6 Which case(s) to cite 50
6.7 Using statutory materials 51
6.8 Which sources to cite 52
6.9 Apply the law to the facts 52
6.10 Producing sound conclusions 53
6.11 Summary 53
6.12 Examples 54

7 Getting started 55
7.1 The problem 55
7.2 The analysis 56
7.3 Writing the opinion 64

8 An illustration of the opinion writing process 67
8.1 Instructions to counsel 67
8.2 Preparing to write an opinion 69

8.3	Sample opinion	77
8.4	Feedback on sample opinion	82
8.5	An alternative opinion	84

9 Examples of barristers' opinions — 89

9.1	Liability and damages—personal injury	89
9.2	Liability—insufficient information	93
9.3	Quantum—personal injury	95
9.4	Opinion based on the law	99
9.5	Opinion following legal research	102

10 Advising for the purposes of public funding in civil cases — 106

10.1	Introduction	106
10.2	Advising for the purposes of public funding	108
10.3	Sample opinion—advice for the purpose of public funding	114

11 Advice on evidence in a civil case — 117

11.1	An approach to writing a civil advice on evidence	117
11.2	Sample advice on evidence	127
11.3	A more complex advice on evidence	130

12 Advice on evidence in a criminal case — 135

12.1	An approach to writing a criminal advice on evidence	135
12.2	Sample advice on evidence for prosecution	142
12.3	Sample advice for defence	144
12.4	A more complex advice on evidence	146

13 Advice on evidence and quantum — 151

13.1	Checklist for advice on evidence for assessment of damages in a personal injury case	151
13.2	Sample advice on evidence on assessment of quantum	155

14 Assessment criteria — 160

14.1	Assessment in opinion writing skills	160
14.2	Criteria for a typical opinion	161

APPENDIX A: Improving your writing skills	169
APPENDIX B: Exercises	183
APPENDIX C: Further exercises	188
APPENDIX D: Re Mr And Mrs Roberts	199
Index	203

1

Introduction

1.1 Written word skills

Before we start work on opinion writing and drafting skills specifically, we shall explore certain aspects of written word skills which are common to all the writing skills of a barrister, though particularly opinion writing and drafting. We call this first stage simply 'Written Word Skills'.

Although it is inevitable that anyone embarking on training for the Bar already has considerable skill in the use of the written word, nevertheless barristers do use words in particular ways that you will not have come across before and for purposes which are new to you. This part of the course is therefore intended to act as a bridge from the word skills you have already acquired to those that are specific to the barrister.

1.2 Objectives

By the end of this part of the course you should:

- appreciate the importance to a barrister of words and the way they are used;
- be able to identify weaknesses in your own written word skills and see how you might work to improve them;
- have begun to think more deeply about the precise meaning of the words you use;
- have started to use words in a way that will be useful in opinion writing;
- have started to use words in a way that will be useful in drafting;
- appreciate the need for clarity and the value of plain English at all times.

1.3 Words and the barrister

1.3.1 Tools of the trade

For the barrister, arguably more than for any other profession, words are the dominant tool of the trade. A barrister can do nothing of consequence without using words. Surgeons, architects, surveyors, accountants, soldiers and police officers can all carry out their professional functions to a greater or lesser extent without the use of words.

But virtually everything a barrister does involves speaking or writing. A barrister's performance will be judged almost exclusively on how well he or she speaks or writes.

1.3.2 Speaking and writing

Speaking and writing are two ways of communicating. Communication is the only purpose of either activity. Whenever we speak or write, either in everyday life, or professionally, we are trying to communicate some inner content: thought, idea, feeling, information or message. That inner content is largely expressed in words. The better we express ourselves, the better we choose our words, the better we put them together, the more effectively we communicate.

1.3.3 Communication

A barrister must communicate well; so a barrister must use words well. To explain something to your client, you must put it in such a way as to be sure your client understands. To make a point to a judge or jury effectively, not only must they understand it, you must express it in the most telling way. To get what you want from a witness, you must frame the question in exactly the right way. All this involves skill in the choice of words, the order in which they are put and in the structure of sentences, paragraphs and speeches. In the ideal world, a barrister's every word would be chosen, and every sentence composed, with great care.

1.3.4 The spoken word and the written word

There is no difference in essence between spoken word skills and written word skills: only the context changes. You may use different words in writing than you would orally, and your sentence structure may change, but you should still choose your words with care, putting them into the best order and composing the whole piece of writing or speech with a view to achieving perfection. The need to communicate effectively, to be clear in what you say, to be precise in what you mean is unchanged. In drafting, particularly, there is a need for precision and unambiguity in what you write that exceeds what is required in any other context.

1.3.5 Standards

A barrister is a specialist lawyer. No matter what kind of practice you have, you will be presumed a specialist in advocacy, in the provision of written advice and in drafting. All these skills are dependent on your word skills. A barrister is supposed to be an *expert* in the use of words and the use of language. You must not just speak and write well—by the standards of everyday life you must speak and write *exceptionally* well. You will be offering your services and charging a fee for which you undertake to speak and write better than those paying you could have spoken or written.

It follows that the standards of clarity, precision, grammar, punctuation and stylistic elegance that you need to set yourself throughout your professional career are almost certainly higher than the standards you have regarded as satisfactory up until now. And you need to set your standards even higher when you are writing than when you are speaking. In speech, the advocate is largely extemporising, having to compose sentences and thoughts even while speaking. Errors and stumbles can and do creep in. You don't always manage to think of just the right word. You don't always express something as accurately as you would like. But when you are writing, you have the opportunity to revise, correct and improve. There can be no excuse for errors and inaccuracies.

You should make up your mind that you will strive to reach these very high standards. With practice, you can attain them.

2 Qualities of good writing

2.1 The qualities

To write a chapter on the qualities of good writing takes some courage. There is a danger of being controversial, hypocritical and idealistic. Controversial because good writing is impossible to define, and so there will always be different views as to what constitutes good writing. Hypocritical, because one can only too often find in one's own writing the very faults one is criticising in other people's. Idealistic, because it is very rare to find a piece of writing with all the qualities described below in full measure. Nevertheless, some guidance as to what constitutes good writing is desirable, so that you can take steps towards improving your writing.

Rather than attempting to describe good writing it seems simpler to list some of its qualities. It goes without saying that the qualities described are those required of barristers, but doubtless many of these qualities are desirable in other contexts too.

2.2 Making choices

Everything that appears in the final version of what you are writing should be there because you intend it to be. Nothing should have crept in by accident, or thoughtlessness; nothing should have been left out by oversight. What you end up with should be exactly what you want. Every word you have used should be there because you have chosen to use that word as opposed to any other. The words should appear in the order you have decided upon. The sentences and paragraphs should be composed as you have designed them. The whole piece of writing should be structured in the way that you have decided works best.

In other words, you have choices. You can only write well by making choices. Those choices may be conscious, where you have weighed up two alternative words or phrases and chosen one rather than the other; or they may be subconscious, where a word or phrase has come into your mind and you have put it down because it is clearly right. But where a word or phrase comes to you intuitively, you still have a choice: whether to keep it, or to discard it and search for something better. Never, if you can avoid it, simply write down the first thing that comes into your head without examining it critically and *deciding* that it is just right.

When we speak, we frequently say things we do not mean to say, or we do not say them in the best possible way, or we forget to say things. This is the natural result of extemporising. A barrister must of course learn to minimise 'accidents' when speaking, but you will never eliminate them entirely. When writing, however, you have an opportunity you do not have when speaking: to go back over what you have written and improve it. Do not waste this opportunity. At every stage you have a choice: to leave what you have written or to improve upon it. Make that choice.

2.3 The English language

The English language is both your resource and your vehicle. Good writing involves drawing upon it and using it well. You should understand the language and the way it works, you should understand its vocabulary, so that you can make the language work for you rather than find it to be a hindrance or an obstacle that gets in the way of what you are trying to say.

Plain English is important: it has the qualities listed here. Try to write in plain English wherever possible. This means avoiding inappropriate jargon, archaic language, unnecessary verbiage, pedantic superfluities and antiquated sentence structures. 'Legalese' gives lawyers a bad name, creates barriers between you and your client and can narrow rather than broaden your thinking.

Nevertheless you are a lawyer and what you are writing may serve a specialised legal purpose rather than a general one. Plain English involves using the simplest and clearest language possible in the circumstances, not the simplest and clearest language available. A lawyer cannot sacrifice precision for simplicity, or clarity for the sake of shorter words. It is more important that what you are writing should fulfil its function than that it should make sense to someone who has no need to understand it.

There are times, therefore, when technical terms are preferable to lay terms; when uncommon words carry precisely the meaning you want while commonplace ones do not; when a long complex sentence gives the right emphasis while a short simple one distorts it. The rule is to use everyday language wherever possible but not at all costs.

2.4 Clarity

Good writing has total clarity. The meaning springs instantly from the words, which do not need to be pondered, reread or analysed. If you ever feel that a sentence you are writing is not expressing the idea behind it clearly, stop, and start writing it again.

The whole purpose of much of what a barrister writes is to clarify what would otherwise be unclear. An opinion may try to explain a complex situation so that it can be understood. A statement of case tries to define issues and bring them into the open. It follows that there is a great need for clarity in what a barrister writes. If it cannot be understood by those reading it, or if it is open to different interpretations, not only is it poorly written, but it has failed to serve the very purpose for which it was written.

Clarity of expression can never be achieved without clarity of thought behind it. In other words if you are not clear in your mind about what you think or what you want to say, you haven't the slightest chance of being any clearer in writing. So a barrister never, except in cases of extreme urgency, writes anything without long and careful thought first. Everything you set out to write must be planned and thought through.

Thereafter clarity will best be achieved through a logical structure, correct spelling, grammar and punctuation, precision, conciseness, completeness and style, which are dealt with below.

2.5 A logical structure

Clarity depends not only on the choice of words and word order, but also on the structure of what is being written. The whole piece of writing needs to be composed in a clear and coherent manner. This will almost always mean that the structure should be logical.

Whatever it is you are trying to say can be broken down into smaller pieces of content. You cannot make a point without explaining the point you are making and justifying it in some way. You cannot express an opinion without giving reasons for that opinion. So in most pieces of professional writing there will be a reasoning process that you need to set out. That process needs to be logical. The reasons you give must actually lead to the conclusion you express. If they do not, then what you write will lack clarity; it may even appear unsound.

The reasoning process is likely to be a series of small links in a logical chain. Each link must be placed in the right order, and be connected correctly to the other links. This involves logical thought, logical explanation and a logical structure to what you are writing. A piece of writing that has this structure is easy to read, clear and compelling in its persuasiveness. A piece of writing that does not is likely to be muddled, confusing and unprofessional.

Once again, clarity of thought is crucial to achieving this aim. You need not only to have clear thoughts, but to organise them logically as well.

2.6 Spelling

Good writing should be free from spelling errors. Spelling errors make you look unprofessional. Unfortunately they are very common. A barrister should take all reasonable steps towards eliminating them. The first step is to accept that spelling matters. So many people in ordinary life think it is unimportant.

In the modern age a great many spelling errors occur not because the writer cannot spell, but because he or she is clumsy on the keyboard, makes typographical errors, and then fails to correct them. If you care as much as you should about spelling, you will be constantly alert to this danger. A computerised spell-checker can pick up a great many of them, but never all, because all it can do is recognise whether a word exists in its dictionary or not. It cannot distinguish between commonly confused words, both of which exist. It is therefore your responsibility, not your computer's, to make sure your spelling is correct.

Of particular importance in the professional world is to spell names correctly, especially that of your client. Always study the spelling of any name you are given and make sure you reproduce it precisely. People called Emmet with one 't' get very annoyed indeed when they are addressed as Emmett with two 't's, especially if they know the writer has the correct spelling in front of them.

2.7 Grammar

A barrister's writing should be free from grammatical error. The rules of grammar dictate word forms, word order and sentence structure. If a verb is in the wrong tense, an adverb in the wrong place, or a sentence improperly composed, the only possible result is obscurity of meaning. You cannot write clearly if your writing is not grammatical.

Grammar is particularly important where you are using long sentences. If the structure of a sentence is not abundantly clear at first reading, almost certainly it suffers from being too long. Any grammatical inconsistency is therefore likely to destroy the value of the long sentence.

Good grammar is the grammar of clear usage, rather than the grammar of pedants. Beware of absolute rules of grammar, such as 'Never split an infinitive', 'Never put a comma before "and"'. In the end the best grammar is the grammar that makes the meaning clearest.

2.8 Punctuation

Good writing must be properly punctuated. This is often essential for clarity in all forms of writing. It can be crucial to the meaning of a legal document. Take care to use full stops, commas, semicolons and colons properly and in the right places. The sense of a sentence can be destroyed by a comma in the wrong place or the lack of a comma where one is needed. The structure of a sentence can become immediately unclear when a comma is used instead of a semicolon. A full stop in the wrong place can spoil the connection between two linked thoughts and result in a sentence with no main verb. Do not open a bracket and then fail to close it. Do not start a subordinate clause with a dash and end it with a comma. None of these common errors belongs to good writing.

Barristers need to take particular care over punctuation when drafting. Drafting can occasionally involve complex grammatical structures, long sentences and numbered subclauses. The wrong punctuation can easily destroy the whole relationship between various parts of the sentence, or detach a subclause from the main clause to which it belongs. The choice of punctuation marks is just as much a part of drafting as the choice of words.

2.9 Precision

Barristers need to write with precision. Everything you write should ideally say exactly what you want to say, neither more nor less. This is an essential part of clarity and is inevitably something you have always attempted to achieve whenever you have written anything. But there are degrees of precision. Whenever we communicate either orally or in writing, we always manage to say more or less what we mean, otherwise we would fail to communicate altogether. We are usually inclined to be rather more precise when we write than when we speak, because we have the opportunity to be (see **2.2**). But even then, we frequently express our thoughts and feelings in a vague or generalised way. Only occasionally do we attempt to write with exactitude.

As a lawyer you will need to write with a greater degree of precision than you would probably use in everyday life. This is true generally, particularly true of opinions and advices and quite fundamental in drafting. In statements of case there can be no room for anything less than absolute precision. The words you use must be chosen for their precise meaning; the sentences you write must be composed to convey a precise sense.

Lack of precision will at best result in a degree of confusion; at worst it may mean you are in effect telling lies.

The more precise what you are writing needs to be, the more carefully you will need to compose it. This takes time and thought. You need to ponder the words and phrases you are using. With experience you will learn to avoid the worst traps and become adept at spotting ambiguities. But it involves setting yourself standards of accuracy beyond those you would regard as sufficient for everyday communication.

2.10 Non-ambiguity

This is a special kind of precision which is of particular importance. Very often in everyday life we use words which mean precisely what we intend them to but which are capable of bearing another meaning if looked at from a different viewpoint or in a different context. We frequently do not notice this alternative meaning because both we and the person we are communicating with share the same fixed viewpoint. Even if we are aware of the possible ambiguity we frequently do not worry about it because we are sure that what we say or write can only be received in the context we intend.

But when you are writing in a legal context you must be aware of all the different viewpoints from which your words might be seen and ensure that what you write is genuinely unambiguous. You should reckon that if what you write could reasonably bear another meaning than that which you intend, someone somewhere will probably try to read it in that way. A quick glance through the law reports will show how many cases arise through an ambiguity in somebody's written words, an ambiguity that obviously never occurred to the person who wrote them. Learn to be aware of and avoid all possible ambiguities. Again, this is particularly important in drafting, but generally true of all a barrister's writing.

2.11 Conciseness

Good writing is concise. This does not mean it should be abbreviated, or even short; rather that it should be succinct and to the point. Try to avoid repetition, waffle, long-windedness or digression. Leave out what is unnecessary or that which obstructs your flow or meaning without adding anything. A good piece of writing should never be a word longer than it needs to be.

But beware of trying to be too concise. If what you are writing merely becomes a summary of what you mean to say, it will not do. Clarity is more important than brevity. Ideas are sometimes more accurately expressed in 20 words than 10. Arguably even style should be given a higher priority than excessive conciseness. Make sure that your writing, as well as being concise, is also always complete.

2.12 Completeness

This is the quality which must be balanced with conciseness. When you write you must express your ideas completely. If what you write has only partially expressed what you are trying to say, or has only set out half the story, or does not explain your full reasoning step by step, then it is incomplete. If incomplete, it is also almost certainly imprecise, ambiguous and unclear.

Just where you draw the line between completeness and conciseness is a matter of fine judgment. You will not always draw the line in the same place. Sometimes you will know that what you are writing will serve its purpose better if you err on the side of conciseness; on other occasions you will realise that it is essential to get everything down in full even if that means you are not as concise as you might have been. But always be aware of the balance that has to be achieved in a good piece of writing.

2.13 Style

Style may not be high on everyone's list of priorities, but it is not to be ignored. Good writing has good style. Style is very hard to define, since it is a matter of artistic impression, but good style is nevertheless something we recognise and appreciate when reading a piece of writing. It is certainly an important quality in anything we describe as 'well written'.

Good style is elegant. Elegance cannot be allowed to become the prime objective of a lawyer's writing: something that seems to have been written chiefly to impress the reader with its beauty and composition rather than for practical business purposes will look out of place in a legal context. If it is in conflict with precision, non-ambiguity or completeness, then clarity demands that elegance should to some degree be sacrificed. But it is usually possible, if enough care is taken, to achieve elegance as well as each of the other qualities of good writing.

No one can tell you how to write elegantly. You will decide what feels and looks elegant for yourself. But good style involves a creative rather than a pedestrian or awkward use of language. Avoid clumsy phrases, tortuous constructions and jarring words. Maintain variety: do not use the same words or structure of sentence over and over again. Use a wide vocabulary: do not be repetitive in your choice of words, unless for effect. But do not use obscure words merely to show off.

Elegance is also very much a matter of flow and rhythm. Elegant writing usually sounds good when read aloud, as well as carrying the reader easily along the printed page.

2.14 Appearance

Appearance is also important. What you write should look clear and neat on the page. That makes it easier to read. So do not pack the type too densely, nor space it too widely. Do not use a type-size that is too small or too large. Allow reasonable margins. Give your headings and subheadings appropriate weight, neither too heavy nor too light. Do not use enormous numbers of footnotes.

Be consistent in your formatting. This applies, for example, to subheadings (font, type-size, weight); the spacing and indentation of paragraphs, sub-paragraphs and bullets; and the use of bold and italic type and capitals. If there are more than two pages, number them.

2.15 The reader

You should always have the reader in mind when you write. Just as you only speak to communicate with a particular person or people, so when you write you should always be aware of the person you are writing for. A letter is addressed to a particular individual and must be written in a way that will communicate easily with him or her. Do not use legal terminology if you are writing to a non-lawyer. Do not write to a solicitor as if he or she were a lay client. Do not make jokes that will not seem amusing to the person concerned.

An opinion may be addressed to a solicitor, but frequently a lay client will wish to read it and it should be comprehensible to him or her. Statements of case need to be understood only by other lawyers, but they must make sense to a lawyer who has no other knowledge of the case. Always be aware of the characteristics and background of the likely reader of what you write and gear it to that reader.

2.16 Reading over

Usually, anything you write will come back to you in printed form, either from a typist or your computer. Never be satisfied with what you have written until you have read over and checked the printed version. If you care as you should about the quality of your writing, you will care enough to wish to correct typographical errors and to give yourself one final opportunity to improve in any small way you can on what you have written.

For further guidance on improving your writing, see **Appendix A**.

3

Plain English

3.1 Introduction

We have already mentioned plain English in **Chapter 2**. In one sense 'plain English' simply means English that is clear and well-written. But it has come to acquire a slightly narrower meaning, as the alternative to obscure legalistic jargon, or 'legalese'. This chapter looks at the differences between plain English and legalese, and how you can go about learning to write in plain English as a lawyer.

It goes without saying that plain English is just as important to oral communication as it is to written communication, so do not be misled into treating it purely as a part of Written Word Skills just because this is where we have introduced the topic. Use plain English whenever it is appropriate to do so, in advocacy, in conference, in negotiation, in opinion writing and in drafting, just as you probably use it in everyday life.

3.2 What is plain English?

Plain English involves the use of 'plain and straightforward language which conveys its meaning as clearly and simply as possible without unnecessary pretension or embellishment' (Richard Wydick, *Plain English for Lawyers*).

3.3 Why use plain English?

The Law Reform Commission of Victoria put it this way:

The language of the law has long been a source of concern to the community. It has been the subject of continuous literary criticism and satire. Critics have highlighted its technical terms, its convolutions and its prolixity. These faults have been noted by judges and by practising and academic lawyers as well. Calls have regularly been made for the use of a more simple and straightforward style. Some improvements have been made in response to those calls. But legal language remains largely unintelligible to most members of the community. It even causes problems for members of the legal profession. In some cases, the obscurity may arise from the complexity of the law and of its subject-matter. In other cases, however, it is due to the complexity of the language in which the law is expressed. Some lawyers do not take sufficient care to communicate clearly with their audience. Letters, private legal documents and legislation itself are still drafted in a style which poses unnecessary barriers to understanding. (*Legal Language*, para 14.)

The advantage of plain English is that it readily conveys its message to its audience.

3.4 What is the problem with legal language?

The Law Reform Commission of Victoria said:

Many legal documents are unnecessarily lengthy, overwritten, self-conscious and repetitious. They consist of lengthy sentences and involved sentence construction. They are poorly structured and poorly designed. They suffer from elaborate and often unnecessary cross-referencing. They use confusing tautologies... They retain archaic phrases... They use supposedly technical terms and foreign words and phrases. They are unintelligible to the ordinary reader and barely intelligible to many lawyers. (*Legal Language*, para 17.)

This kind of legal writing presents a barrier to effective communication. It is very easy to fall into the habit of writing like this, because such language is all around you, in precedents, forms, contracts, statutes and even the speech of some lawyers. You can pick it up without thinking about it. But if you do, you will not be writing efficiently, effectively or in the interests of your client. So you must learn to recognise legalese, to avoid it whenever possible and to substitute plain English instead.

3.5 What is being done to promote plain English?

The legal establishment, in particular the judges and to a lesser extent the parliamentary draftsmen, are becoming increasingly aware of the need to write in plain English and to insist that others do so as well (where they have the power to enforce this). More and more court orders, standard forms, statutes and regulations are being drafted in plain English. Reform is, however, a long process because old habits die hard, and there is resistance in some quarters.

A major revolution has, however, been brought about by the Civil Procedure Rules 1998 which came into force on 26 April 1999. These are all drafted in plain English and are specifically designed to enable a lay person to deal with a civil action in person. The ethos behind these rules is also likely to result in many more documents being drafted in plain English in future, particularly statements of case.

See also regulation 7 of the Unfair Terms in Consumer Contracts Regulations 1999:

7. *Written contracts*

    (1) A seller or supplier shall ensure that any written term of a contract is expressed in plain, intelligible language.

    (2) If there is doubt about the meaning of a written term, the interpretation which is most favourable to the consumer shall prevail...

This regulation is likely to have a very significant effect on the drafting of consumer contracts.

3.6 Recognising and rewriting legalese

The worst examples of legalese are never too hard to spot. Rewriting such passages may, however, present more of a problem. Consider the following examples.

3.6.1 First example—a letter

Consider the following (taken from *Yes, Prime Minister* by Jonathan Lynn and Antony Jay):

Dear Prime Minister, *Cabinet Office*

I must express in the strongest possible terms my profound opposition to the newly instituted practice which imposes severe and intolerable restrictions on the ingress and egress of senior members of the hierarchy and will, in all probability, should the current deplorable innovation be perpetuated, precipitate a progressive constriction of the channels of communication, culminating in a condition of organisational atrophy and administrative paralysis which will render effectively impossible the coherent and coordinated discharge of the functions of government within Her Majesty's United Kingdom of Great Britain and Northern Ireland.

Your obedient and humble servant,
Humphrey Appleby

Reproduced with kind permission of BBC Enterprises Ltd, London.

This is of course a spoof, but it contains the sort of language we are trying to avoid. The situation behind the letter is that the Prime Minister has locked a door which was previously unlocked and which allowed Humphrey Appleby immediate access from his offices to the Prime Minister's. Try rewriting the letter in plain English. 'Please unlock the door' is tempting, and it is plain English; but it will not do, because it gives no reasons for the demand and because it does not have the tone of a formal protest which is what the writer clearly intends. It is not particularly difficult to do, but you will probably lose the flavour of the original. This is because the original, for all its pomposity, is actually very fluently and elegantly written, and full of character.

3.6.2 Second example—a lease

The following subclause was in a lease which was the subject of the action in *Inglewood Investment Co Ltd v Forestry Commission* [1989] 1 All ER 1:

Subject to the provisions of the Ground Game Act 1880 the Ground Game (Amendment) Act 1906 and the Forestry Act 1919 all game woodcocks snipe and other wild fowl hares rabbits and fish with the exclusive right (but subject as aforesaid) for the Appointers and all persons authorised by them at all times of preserving the same (except rabbits) and of hunting shooting fishing coursing and sporting over and on the appointed hereditaments and premises *Provided always* that as regards rabbits the Commission shall have an equal right with the Appointers to kill the same and the Appointers shall not keep or permit to be kept any rabbit warren in or in the immediate vicinity of the appointed lands.

Can you understand it? What does it mean? It consists of over 100 words. It was one of a list of reservations in a schedule, which is why there is no main verb. The plaintiffs (the successors in title to the appointers) were contending that under this clause they had exclusive rights to shoot deer on the land. The court held however that they did not, because 'game' meant only those animals listed, and 'preserving...hunting shooting fishing coursing and sporting' also covered only the game listed. Can you rewrite it (a) to make it say what the plaintiffs were contending it said and (b) to give it unambiguously the meaning that the court gave it?

The difficulty is that the original is trying to say too many things all at once. Your aim will be to say one thing at a time. You will probably want to break it down into several sentences; maybe also into several subclauses. Even then it is very difficult to do. Do not expect what you draft to be shorter than the original. In situations like this the plain English version, though clearer, is often longer.

3.6.3 Third example—a statute

This is s 7(11) of the Small Landholders (Scotland) Act 1911:

The Land Court shall thereafter determine, with due regard to the provisions of the Landholders Acts, and by order or orders declare—

> (a) *In respect of what land, if any, specified in the scheme, one or more holdings for new holders may respectively be constituted, and up to what date the power to constitute them otherwise than by agreement may be exercised;*
>
> (b) *What is the fair rent for each new holding;*
>
> (c) *What land, if any, specified in the scheme is to be excluded therefrom; and*
>
> (d) *Whatever else may be necessary for the purpose of making the scheme effective and of adjusting the rights of all parties interested in or affected by the proceedings:*
>
> *Provided that, where the Land Court are of opinion that damage or injury will be done to the letting value of the land to be occupied by a new holder or new holders, or of any farm of which such land forms part, or to any tenant in respect that the land forms part or the whole of his tenancy, or to any landlord either in respect of an obligation to take over sheep stock at a valuation or in respect of any depreciation in the value of the estate of which the land forms part in consequence of and directly attributable to the constitution of the new holding or holdings as proposed, they shall require the Board, in the event of the scheme being proceeded with, to pay compensation to such amount as the Land Court determine after giving parties an opportunity of being heard and, if they so desire, of leading evidence in the matter: Provided always that, where within twenty-one days after the receipt from the Land Court of an order under this subsection a landlord or a tenant, as the case may be, intimates to the Land Court and to the Board that he claims compensation to an amount exceeding three hundred pounds and that he desires to have the question whether damage or injury entitling him to compensation as aforesaid will be done, together with the amount of such compensation (if any), to be settled by arbitration instead of by the Land Court, the same shall be settled accordingly; and, at any time within fourteen days after the said intimation, failing agreement with the Board as to the appointment of an arbiter, it shall be lawful for him to apply to the Lord Ordinary on the Bills for such appointment, and the Lord Ordinary shall, forthwith on receipt of such application, nominate a single arbiter to decide the questions aforesaid, whose award shall be final, and binding on the Board, in the event of the scheme being proceeded with; and, if no final award be given within three months from the date when the arbiter is nominated, the questions aforesaid shall be decided by the Land Court as herein-before provided:*
>
> *Provided that the Arbitration (Scotland) Act, 1894, shall not apply, and the Second Schedule to the Agricultural Holdings (Scotland) Act, 1908, shall apply to any such arbitration with the exception of paragraphs one, five, ten, eleven, and sixteen thereof, and with the substitution of the Lord Ordinary for the sheriff and the auditor of the Court of Session for the auditor of the Sheriff Court: And provided further that, in the event of the scheme not being proceeding with, the expenses of parties reasonably incurred in connection with the arbitration as the same may be allowed by the auditor of the Court of Session shall be paid by the Board.*
>
> *In determining the amount of compensation under any provision of this Act, no additional allowance shall be made on account of the constitution or enlargement of any holding being compulsory.*

This is perhaps a slightly unfair example: no modern statute would have a single subsection as long as this. The very length of it is daunting. Can you see how it might be rewritten and restructured today? It may well be you will want to turn it into ten or more separate subsections.

3.6.4 Fourth example—a court order

Before *Practice Direction* [1994] 1 WLR 1233; [1994] 4 All ER 52, a freezing injunction might have looked a bit like this:

UPON hearing Counsel for the Plaintiffs ex parte AND UPON reading the affidavit of MILES KING, sworn herein on 11th June 1994 AND UPON the Plaintiffs by their Counsel undertaking:

(1) To abide by any order this Court may make as to damages, in case this Court shall be hereafter of opinion that the Defendant should have sustained any loss and damage by reason of this order for which the Plaintiffs ought to pay.

(2) To indemnify any person (other than the Defendant, his servants or agents) to whom notice of this Order is given against any costs, expenses, fees or liabilities reasonably incurred by him in seeking to comply with this Order.

(3) To serve upon the Defendant as soon as practicably possible the Writ in this action, this Order and the affidavits specified above.

(4) To notify the Defendant as soon as practically possible of the terms of this Order.

(5) To notify and inform any third parties affected by this Order of their right to apply to this Court for this Order to be varied or discharged insofar as this Order affects the said third parties.

IT IS ORDERED THAT:

(1) The Defendant, whether by himself, his servants or agents or otherwise, be restrained until trial or further order from removing any of his assets out of the jurisdiction, or disposing of or charging or otherwise dealing with any of his assets within the jurisdiction so as to deplete the same below £44,809.

(2) Without prejudice to the foregoing, the defendant be restrained until further order from drawing from, charging or otherwise dealing with the account standing in his name at the Threadneedle Street branch of Barclays Bank at Threadneedle Street, London EC4, except to the extent that any credit balance on it exceeds £44,809.

(3) Provided nothing in this Order shall prevent the Defendant from expending:
   (i) up to £300 per week on living expenses;
   (ii) reasonable sums in respect of the legal expenses of this action;
   (iii) such sums as shall have been previously approved in writing by the Plaintiffs.

(4) Liberty to apply on 24 hours' notice to the other party.

(5) Costs reserved.

Would an ordinary lay person have much chance of understanding this? Would he or she know what was the effect of not complying with the order? Or what steps now needed to be taken? Probably not, without the help of a solicitor. Look now at the Annex to PD 25A under the Civil Procedure Rules 1998, which sets out the current standard form for a freezing injunction.

You will notice that the meaning and effect of the order is set out in plain English, such that a lay person who takes the trouble to read it would understand his or her position. But, not surprisingly, this takes much longer than the old fashioned order.

3.7 Writing plain English

Your aim in writing plain English is to write concisely and clearly so that the reader can understand easily what you are saying.

What is plain English and the extent to which you need to write in plain English does therefore depend on who your reader is. If your reader is another lawyer then you may use legal terminology and words that draw fine distinctions because your reader will understand them and appreciate them. If your reader is a lay person it may be unwise to use legal jargon and unnecessary to draw fine distinctions: you will not help, but cloud his or her understanding by using such words. Where you are writing for a mixed readership, as for example when you are writing an opinion, you will need to strike a balance. You want your opinion to be accessible to your lay client, while at the same time to be professional and precise for your instructing solicitor.

Most lawyers, even when they are trying to write in plain English, do not write as plainly as they could in their first draft. If you are determined to write plain English you will usually need to go through several drafts. The more you write, the more you can see how it could be made simpler and clearer. The more you simplify and clarify your words, the more precise and clear the thought behind them becomes, which in turn leads to even plainer language. It takes longer to write good plain English than it does to write legalese.

The biggest danger, certainly when drafting, is to sacrifice precision for the sake of simplicity. You must take great care to avoid this. Often what looks simple is only simple because it is more general and imprecise than what you started with.

3.8 Basic rules of plain English

It is not possible in this manual to cover all the rules of plain English, or all the good and bad words and phrases that exist. There are other books that go into this more fully. Especially recommended is *The Complete Plain Words* by Sir Ernest Gowers. See also **Appendix A**.

However, some very basic rules can be identified and they are these:

3.8.1 Use short sentences

Everyone has their own idea of how short a short sentence is, and what is short for lawyers may be long for journalists. We suggest you regard a sentence of 25 words and under as short. Try to write for the most part in short sentences. You can usually achieve this if you do not try to express more than a single thought in each sentence. But do not go out of your way to avoid longer sentences when they are appropriate. Good and elegant writing usually requires that sentences should vary in length rather than all have about the same number of words. Variety maintains the reader's interest.

3.8.2 Use correct grammar and punctuation

Although it may sometimes be more concise, or more like everyday speech, to use bad grammar, in written English grammatical errors can only mean a lack of clarity. For most people correct grammar is instinctive, and mistakes only occur when we do not conceive a sentence as a whole. Always read through whole sentences, trying to phrase them as you would if speaking them aloud, and any grammatical errors will probably leap out at you.

Punctuation is also important. It is essential to plain English that you should take care over punctuation, since it is part of the structure and clarity of your sentences. You can often spot the need for punctuation marks, or the need to remove them, if you speak or think your sentence through aloud.

3.8.3 Use everyday English

We have already seen that there is a place for legal terminology and a time to avoid it. Jargon, and other technical terms, should be dispensed with wherever possible. There are many occasions when there are perfectly clear and straightforward alternatives to jargon words. Only occasionally is the technical term the only suitable word.

Legalese at its worst goes beyond simply using legal terminology and uses totally obscure or archaic words and phrases that nobody uses in everyday English. There really can be no excuse for these in ordinary writing.

It is also important to resist all the other absurd jargons that creep into written and spoken English from time to time, and are known variously as, eg 'computerspeak', 'Haigspeak', 'Socialese', etc. Such language only makes what you are writing sound obscure and pompous. A student once complained in a letter that there was 'a comprehension dissonance' between his tutor and himself. He wanted to know why his written work had been marked down for lack of clarity!

3.8.4 Use simple structures

Avoid putting an idea in a complicated or roundabout way when it can be put in a simpler one. Almost everything you write at a first attempt can in fact be put more simply and in fewer words. Avoid in particular compound structures which use three or four words to express a single concept, double negatives and the passive rather than the active voice.

Of course this cannot be an absolute rule. The compound structure or the double negative may occasionally carry a shade of meaning or precision which the alternative does not. The passive voice may give the sentence the correct subject (eg 'The defendant was sued by the claimant' tells the reader that you are writing about the defendant. The alternative 'The claimant sued the defendant' introduces a sentence about the claimant).

Avoid word-wasting idioms and phrases like 'The fact that it was raining' (since it was raining) or 'In the region of' (about). Also make sure you get rid of redundant words, as in 'null and void', 'totally and utterly'.

3.8.5 Use the first and second person

Wherever appropriate it is always clearer to talk in terms of 'I' and 'You' rather than in the third person or in a wholly impersonal way. There are certain formalities in opinion writing and drafting that must be observed and do not allow for the use of 'I' and 'You', but these apart, never be impersonal when you can be personal. It is clearer, shorter and more honest.

3.8.6 Arrange words with care

A great deal of poor English can be improved simply by changing the arrangement of words and phrases. If you put clauses in a better order, the meaning of a sentence often becomes much clearer. If you reduce the gap between a subject and the verb or the verb and its object you can often make a sentence much easier to understand. Always try to arrange your material so that the reader is assisted through it and it is easy to absorb. If the reader ever has to stop, go back and re-read, then you have not written plain English.

3.8.7 Use a good layout

Although sometimes what a lawyer writes will be in conventional paragraphs, on most occasions a barrister writes in numbered paragraphs, clauses and subclauses. If these are well marked, they will be easier to read. If a contract term consists of 200 words for example, it will be more easily understood if broken up and subdivided than if it appears as a solid block of text. Even conventional paragraphs are often easier to read if they are numbered and subtitled; and it goes without saying that several shorter paragraphs are usually easier to read than a few very long ones.

3.9 Further reading

Gowers, Sir Ernest, *The Complete Plain Words*, 3rd edn, eds Sidney Greenbaum and Janet Whitcut, Penguin, 1986.

Rylance, Paul, *Legal Writing and Drafting*, Blackstone Press/Oxford University Press, 1994.

Trask, R L, *Mind the Gaffe—The Penguin Guide to Common Errors in English*, Penguin Books, 2001.

Wydick, Richard, *Plain English for Lawyers*, 4th edn, Durham NC: Carolina Academic Press, 1998.

Asprey, Michèle M, *Plain Language for Lawyers*, 3rd edn, Federation Press, 2003.

See also **Appendix A** for improving your writing skills.

4

Introduction to opinion writing

4.1 Summary of materials

In this, the main part of the manual, you will find materials for the opinion writing course. These materials explain how to go about writing an opinion, deal with specific aspects of opinion writing and cover several different types of opinion. You will find a large number of sample opinions taken from real cases in practice, which illustrate the skill and enable you to see what you are working towards.

Chapter 5 deals with the background, purpose and method of opinion writing as well as the content and style of opinions. It is concentrating largely on the opinion on the merits of a case. You should regard this chapter both as your starting point and your bible of opinion writing. Read it carefully before you start the opinion writing course, and re-read it several times again once you have gained some experience.

Chapter 6 goes into more detail on one important aspect of opinion writing—the use of law, especially case law.

Chapter 7 concentrates on the first steps you need to take in writing an opinion—the research and analysis phase. It contains a practical example of the complete reasoning process leading up to the writing of an opinion in a straightforward case. At the end of the chapter, you are invited to have a go at writing the actual opinion for yourself, guided by what you have read, and then to compare your version with the one printed in Appendix D.

Chapter 8 gives you a practical illustration of the process of writing an opinion. It begins with some instructions to counsel, then goes through the analysis of facts and law, the preparation and planning of the opinion, and finally sets out the completed opinion. There then follows a critique of the opinion and an alternative opinion in the same case by another author.

Chapter 9 consists entirely of sample opinions taken from real cases in practice, written by different barristers, which individually illustrate different aspects of opinion writing and types of opinion, and collectively give you an overview of the skill as it is practised in chambers.

Chapter 10 concentrates on a very specific type of opinion—the opinion produced largely for the benefit of the Community Legal Service Fund. It outlines counsel's duties when advising an assisted client and gives an example.

Chapter 11 introduces a major type of opinion—the advice on evidence. There is a full explanation of how to go about writing an advice on evidence in a civil case, together with practical examples.

Chapter 12 covers the advice on evidence in a criminal context, once again with text and examples, covering advice to the prosecution and to the defence.

Chapter 13 takes a very specific and technical type of civil advice on evidence—the advice on evidence relating to assessment of quantum in a personal injury case. This chapter should be read in conjunction with **Chapter 11** of the *Remedies* manual.

Chapter 14 explains the standard assessment criteria by which you should judge your opinion writing skills, and which will be applied as appropriate by assessors on the course.

4.2 The opinion writing course

To a very large extent, opinion writing is a skill learned by practice and experience. Most of the opinions you write during the course will be in the context of practical training exercises or assessments. However, we will not require you to write a full opinion immediately. There are numerous sub-skills involved in opinion writing, all of which can and should be isolated and developed separately before they are employed together. The course will therefore start by looking at the skills of:

- analysing instructions;
- thinking practically;
- ascertaining the needs of the client;
- getting to grips with the facts;
- identifying the issues;
- using the law in a practical way;
- giving advice;
- answering questions;
- reaching conclusions;
- exercising judgment;
- encapsulating a long thought process in a single paragraph;
- clear expression;
- structuring an opinion;

and maybe other sub-skills also. This will be done by means of a series of short exercises. Only then will you be asked to write a complete opinion for yourself.

4.3 Objectives of the course

By the end of the course you should:

- Understand the context of an opinion in a barrister's work and in a case.
- Understand the purpose of an opinion in different contexts.
- Appreciate the qualities of a good opinion.
- Know and be able to make use of the basic principles of opinion writing.
- Understand how to plan an opinion.
- Be able to write a clear structured opinion.

- Have developed some skill at exercising your judgment on legal and factual issues.
- Have developed some skill at giving reasons for your opinions.
- Have developed some skill at expressing both your opinions and your reasons for them clearly and in written form.

4.4 Professional conduct

4.4.1 Code of conduct

You should be aware of the following provisions of the Code of Conduct of the Bar of England and Wales.

Applicable to practising barristers

302 A barrister has an overriding duty to the Court to act with independence in the interests of justice: he must assist the Court in the administration of justice and must not deceive or knowingly or recklessly mislead the Court.

...

Drafting documents

704 A barrister must not devise facts which will assist in advancing the lay client's case and must not draft any statement of case, witness statement, affidavit, notice of appeal or other document containing:
  (a) any statement of fact or contention which is not supported by the lay client or by his instructions;
  (b) any contention which he does not consider to be properly arguable;
  (c) any allegation of fraud unless he has clear instructions to make such allegation and has before him reasonably credible material which as it stands establishes a prima facie case of fraud;
  (d) in the case of a witness statement or affidavit any statement of fact other than the evidence which in substance according to his instructions the barrister reasonably believes the witness would give if the evidence contained in the witness statement or affidavit were being given in oral examination;

provided that nothing in this paragraph shall prevent a barrister drafting a document containing specific factual statements or contentions included by the barrister subject to confirmation of their accuracy by the lay client or witness.

4.4.2 Written standards

You should also note the following extracts from the Written Standards for the Conduct of Professional Work issued by the Bar Council:

1. Introduction
1.1 These Standards are intended as a guide to the way in which a barrister should carry out his work. They consist in part of matters which are dealt with expressly in the Code of Conduct and in part of statements of good practice. They must therefore be read in conjunction with the Code of Conduct, and are to be taken into account in determining whether or not a barrister has committed a disciplinary offence. They apply to employed barristers as well as to barristers in independent practice, except where this would be inappropriate. In addition

to these General Standards, there are Standards which apply specifically to the conduct of criminal cases.

...

5   Conduct of Work

...

5.6 In relation to instructions to advise or draft documents, a barrister should ensure that the advice or document is provided within such time as has been agreed with the professional client, or otherwise within a reasonable time after receipt of the relevant instructions. If it becomes apparent to the barrister that he will not be able to do the work within that time, he must inform his professional client forthwith.

5.7 Generally, a barrister should ensure that advice which he gives is practical, appropriate to the needs and circumstances of the particular client, and clearly and comprehensibly expressed.

5.8 A barrister must exercise his own personal judgment upon the substance and purpose of any advice he gives or any document he drafts. He must not devise facts which will assist in advancing his lay client's case and must not draft any originating process, pleading, affidavit, witness statement or notice of appeal containing:

   (a) any statement of fact or contention (as the case may be) which is not supported by his lay client or by his brief or instructions;

   (b) any contention which he does not consider to be properly arguable;

   (c) any allegation of fraud unless he has clear instructions to make such an allegation and has before him reasonably credible material which as it stands establishes a prima facie case of fraud; or

   (d) in the case of an affidavit or witness statement, any statement of fact other than the evidence which in substance according to his instructions, the barrister reasonably believes the witness would give if the evidence contained in the affidavit or witness statement were being given viva voce.

Further ethical requirements will apply where counsel receives instructions directly from the lay client under the 'Bar Direct' scheme. Counsel should be aware of these additional requirements before accepting instructions from the lay client. For further details please contact the General Council of the Bar.

5

Opinion writing

5.1 Why learn to write opinions?

Opinion writing is something that all barristers do. It is a common misconception that a barrister's work consists solely of appearances in court, advocacy, or advising clients orally, in a face-to-face situation. In fact a considerable part of most barristers' work, for some the most part, is done in chambers and in writing.

Barristers usually think of their work as falling into two categories: court work and chambers work. For court work, they are using their interpersonal and expressive skills: their skill at advocacy, their communication skills, their ability to think and speak at the same time, their skill at questioning, and occasionally their negotiating skills. For chambers work they are using their writing and thinking skills: their ability to manage factual information, to carry out legal research, to draft, to advise. Before the introduction of the Bar Vocational Course, surprisingly few barristers used to identify opinion writing as a skill in itself.

But they were wrong not to do so. In reality neither a barrister's work nor a barrister's skills can be divided so neatly into those two categories. Giving advice to a client in conference, that is, in a face-to-face situation, may happen either at court or in chambers. A negotiation may be conducted anywhere, even by telephone. A barrister is just as likely to have to write an opinion on a train returning from court or at the kitchen table as at his or her desk. Communication skills form an important part of opinion writing; thinking skills, fact-management skills, even drafting skills are an important part of advocacy. In learning opinion writing, you are actually learning skills, aptitudes and a way of thinking that prepare you for all aspects of a barrister's work.

5.2 What is opinion writing?

5.2.1 Paperwork

As well as (rather mistakenly) dividing his or her work into court work or chambers work, a barrister will usually identify (more accurately) a specific category of chambers work: 'paperwork'. All barristers have paperwork to do. Some have more of it than others, depending on the nature of their practice, but none will ever get away from it entirely. 'Paperwork' is a relatively self-contained aspect of a barrister's work; it consists of two things: opinion writing and drafting.

5.2.2 Instructions

Paperwork arises in response to a written set of instructions. 'Instructions' come from solicitors, called your instructing solicitors, and look like a brief, tied up with red ribbon, but rather than containing instructions to appear before some tribunal (a brief) they contain instructions to advise in writing, draft documents or both. If you are instructed to draft a statement of case, or other documents, you do so. If you are asked to advise in writing, what you write and send back is called an 'opinion'. An opinion is therefore your written response to instructions to advise.

These instructions are likely to be your first contact with the case or dispute. Instructing solicitors have sent the papers to you because the time has arisen when they can no longer advise the client or handle the client's case without reference to counsel. It may be that they want a second opinion; it may be that the case is in an area in which you can give specialist advice; it may be that the case is bound to result in court proceedings and they consider it best therefore to bring in counsel at the earliest possible moment; it may be that a statement of case needs to be drafted: it does not make sense to ask you to draft without also advising; it may be that a favourable counsel's opinion is required in order for the client to be granted public funding. However, there are many other situations, and later stages, at which counsel's opinion may be sought.

5.2.3 Contents of instructions

Included in the instructions will be (a) a document from your instructing solicitor, setting out what you are asked to do, the background to the case, possibly a description and analysis of the issues, maybe even the solicitor's own answer to the problem; (b) all other relevant documents, plans, photographs, etc. These are likely to include copies of any claim form which has been issued, statements of case which have been served, documents which have been drafted; copies of any contract, conveyance, lease, will or other instrument out of which the dispute arises; copies of all correspondence which has passed between the parties and their solicitors and/or insurers; statements of any witnesses, including your client(s) or representatives of your client company; expert reports, medical reports, etc.

The instructions, when analysed, consist broadly of a question, or, more likely, a series of questions. These questions are asked by your instructing solicitor, on behalf of the client. Your opinion is your answer to these questions. An answer must always tell the questioner what he wants to know (not necessarily what he wants to hear!). Since your questioner is the solicitor, the answer is basically addressed to him or her. But since the solicitor is only asking the questions so as to be able to advise the client, the answer must also concern the client specifically and the advice given must be advice to the client, not just to your instructing solicitor.

Probably the most common questions asked in instructions are: 'Does the client have a good case? If so what remedies are available to him? How much would he recover in damages?' or 'Is there a good defence to this action? If not, how can liability be minimised? How much is the client likely to have to pay in damages?' Your opinion answers these questions, gives advice, and is returned to your instructing solicitors with the instructions.

5.2.4 Advisory character of opinions

Once again: an opinion is your response to instructions to *advise*. It follows that it must contain advice. In learning to write opinions, you are more than anything else learning to *advise*. Advising is not just an activity, something you do. You do not advise someone simply by telling them what to do. You do not advise someone by writing a lengthy essay and putting 'That is my advice' at the end of it. Nor is it just a way of saying things: you do not give advice simply by starting every third sentence with the words 'I advise that'. Advising is inextricably bound up with and is part of the mental attitude with which you approach opinion writing, with the thinking process that precedes the actual writing of the opinion, and with the writing process itself. We need therefore to look at opinion writing in these three aspects: the mental attitude, the thinking process and the writing process.

5.3 The right mental attitude: the practical approach

The mental attitude required to write a good opinion, or give good advice, is that of a practitioner as opposed to an academic. The approach required is a practical as opposed to an academic approach. Practical rather than academic thought is needed.

5.3.1 Abandoning an academic attitude

Whatever course in law you followed at the academic stage, and however practical it appeared to be, it is inevitable that your approach has been largely academic so far. This is because at the end of the course you were going to be examined not on what you did, but on what you knew. Practitioners are not much concerned with what they know, but with what they do. So long as your concern has been knowledge of the law, seeking to understand the law, considering what the law is or should be, rather than solving problems, advising people, deciding what to do next, your approach has been fundamentally academic.

The most academic academics tend to have a theoretical approach to the law, studying it for its own sake. If confronted with a legal problem they will regard the research and the analysis of the law as an end in itself and may even regard the reaching of conclusions or the answering of the problem as something of an irrelevance. To the academic, the problem is more important than its answer.

The practitioner abhors a problem with no answer. He or she will always seek to reach a conclusion, to provide the best possible answer to the problem. The practitioner will regard the law as relevant only insofar as it helps to find an answer. His or her mind will be focused on the client rather than the law. However academic or practical your approach has been hitherto, it must now become more practical.

None of this has actually defined the right mental attitude or the practical approach. Even if a definition is possible, it is probably not desirable. The practical approach is something to be developed and acquired, and defining it does not necessarily help. But it is possible to give some guidance on how you can develop the right mental attitude. Here are four fundamental principles to remember at all times:

- You are dealing with a real situation.
- The facts are more fundamental than the law.
- The law is a means to an end.
- Answer the question.

5.3.2 You are dealing with a real situation

It goes without saying that every case in practice involves a real situation. You must deal with every case in training as if it were a real situation too, even though it may not be easy: some of the problems can be slightly artificial, deliberately simplified; events may seem somewhat contrived. But you should treat the case as real.

In a real situation there is a real client with a real problem who wants your advice. Imagine, if it helps, that a client, Mr Smith, is sitting opposite you. What would you say to him? How could you help him? This focuses the mind on what Mr Smith actually wants, or the reason he is seeking your advice.

Mr Smith has not come to see you so that you can show off your knowledge. He has a problem and wants help in finding the right answer. He does not specifically want to know what the law says, but rather how he stands in relation to the law. He wants to know what his legal position is and what he ought to do about it. That's the problem. It's *his* problem. And it's a real problem.

But where does the reality of the problem lie? It does not lie in the questions of law that the problem raises, or even in the questions of fact which you will have to answer. It lies in the facts themselves. It is not because of the law that the problem exists, but because of the facts. The facts are the reality. So the second principle is:

5.3.3 The facts are more fundamental than the law

Because they come first. It follows that in dealing with a case, in advising a client, in writing an opinion, your starting point will always be the facts. This may seem obvious and you may protest that you have always taken the facts as your starting point. But have you?

During the academic stage, when confronted with a problem, what thoughts first ran through your mind? Quite possibly, thoughts like: 'Is this a tort case or a contract case?' 'What's the point of law in this case?'—legal questions, rather than factual questions.

The first thoughts that run through a practitioner's mind in reading instructions are questions like 'What's happened?' 'What's the situation?' 'What's the problem?' 'What does my client want?' 'What should be done?' 'What advice can I give?' Such questions address the facts, not the law. The facts are fundamental because they give rise to the problem and to any questions of law that may be answered in order to achieve a solution to the problem.

So if the facts are more important than the law, where does the law fit in? The answer lies in the third principle:

5.3.4 The law is a means to an end

And frequently a very important means, but not an end in itself. The law is what you consult, and use where appropriate, to help you produce a solution to the problem. The law provides a framework which enables you to shed light on the facts, organise the facts, analyse the facts, and interpret the facts, and within which you are able to form an opinion on the facts and answer questions of fact.

The golden rule is: use the law to help you form an opinion on the facts, not the facts as an excuse to form an opinion on the law. This becomes clear when you look at what your client is actually asking. For example, the claimant company in *Photo Production Ltd v Securicor Transport Ltd* [1980] AC 827 would not have asked its legal advisers, and did not want to know the answer to the question 'In what circumstances can a party in fundamental breach of contract rely on an exclusion clause?' The question it would have asked, and wanted an answer to, was 'Can Securicor, in the events which have happened, rely on this exclusion clause?' or even, quite simply, 'Is Securicor liable to pay this company the cost of rebuilding its factory?' So an answer expressed in the form of, 'In my opinion the decision of the House of Lords in *Suisse Atlantique* was correct' is quite meaningless. What your client wants is an answer expressed in the form: 'In my opinion Securicor can rely on its exclusion clause and the claimant will fail to recover damages'. In other words, since the question arises out of the facts of the case and not the law, the answer must address the facts and not just the law.

The lawyer who, when consulted by a client, investigates the law and answers only the questions of law, is like a doctor who, when consulted by a patient, investigates the symptoms, informs her what she is suffering from and packs her off without prescribing treatment. The law must also be used to help your client attain his or her objectives. This leads into the fourth principle:

5.3.5 Answer the question

Your instructions are a series of questions, all of which need to be identified and answered. Not only must you answer all the questions, you must answer the actual questions asked and not those which have not been asked, as illustrated above. You will not tend to answer the right questions if your mental attitude is wrong, and if you don't answer the right questions you will not be advising your client properly.

This is not as easy or as obvious as it sounds. It is very rare that you will be able to say yes or no, win or lose. But what the practitioner cannot do is say, 'I can give no answer'. There may be no *definite* answer, but there *must* always be *an* answer. Just how you do this is described below (see **5.4.6** and **5.7.1**). But as far as the mental attitude goes, the essential principle is that you should always be seeking to answer every question as clearly and as completely as you can, and this means not only questions where the answer is clear, but also those where it is unclear; not only questions of law, but questions of fact as well. Dealing with questions of fact is likely to be something you have not yet been asked to do, or have avoided doing, at the academic stage. A barrister, in writing an opinion, has to deal with questions of fact. All of them. As clearly and completely as it is possible to do. There may be no definite answer to them, but they must still be dealt with.

5.4 The thinking process: preparing to write an opinion

If you can appreciate and adopt the four principles of the practical approach, then you will be in the right frame of mind, an advising frame of mind, to start the first stage of writing an opinion, which is the thinking process.

The thinking process can be divided into seven stages, but you should note that these seven stages are not separate such that stage 2 only begins when stage 1 is complete, and so on. Rather they overlap, and your thoughts will be going on to later stages even while you are completing the early stages. They are set out here in the logical order in which they first come in to your thinking process. The first step, obviously, is:

5.4.1 Stage 1: read and digest your instructions

Surprisingly, this does not necessarily mean, at this stage, reading every word of them. In practice they could be hundreds of pages thick, and it will not be productive to plough through them page by page only to discover that half of them are irrelevant. What you are trying to do in reading your instructions is to find out exactly what your instructions are, what is required of you, what the case is about, what are the basic facts, and what your client actually wants to know.

In fact you will find that your instructions frequently set out quite expressly what you are asked to do. In reading your instructions, you will begin with that, but will start gathering the facts from whatever documents seem appropriate, referring back and forth through your instructions all the time. You will frequently find, for example, that if there are statements of case enclosed, that is the best place to start, because they will encapsulate the story; then you may find that your client's witness statement is the best thing to read next, followed by your solicitor's comments on it, but always referring to items of correspondence whenever they are mentioned. There is no best rule: you will quickly develop skill at assimilating your instructions fast. While you are doing this, you will in fact also have started stages 2 and 3: you are likely to discover the answer to the primary question fairly early on, and you will be absorbing and organising the facts even as you read. Stage 2 is:

5.4.2 Stage 2: answer the primary question: what does my client actually want to know?

This is very important. You must have a clear idea of what your client wants to know if you are to address your mind to the right issues and give proper advice. Your objective is, after all, to tell your client what he or she wants to know.

As we have seen, your client does not really want to know the law. He or she does not even primarily want to know the answer to questions like, 'Has there been a breach of contract?' 'Was the driver of the other car negligent?', though these are questions you will certainly have to address your mind to and give an answer to. Your client, at the end of the day, is interested in the *result* as it affects him or her and the questions he or she is seeking an answer to in reality are, for example:

Not	But
Will the claimant establish liability?	Will I have to pay damages to the claimant? If so, how much?
Will my claim under the Fatal Accidents Act succeed?	Can I get compensation for the death of my husband? Will it be enough to maintain my standard of living?
Is the restraint of trade clause valid?	Can I take my new job or can't I?
Is the gift in clause 3 of the will valid?	How much do I give to Mary and how much to John?

Until you have accurately identified what your client wants to know, you have no basis on which you can tackle stage 3, which is:

5.4.3 Stage 3: absorb and organise the facts

This is a process of fact management, a skill which is central to any lawyer's work and which you must acquire. It requires a clear, logical and incisive mind.

The facts must be absorbed: everything that is important or relevant in the case must be at your fingertips. You must make sure you have a comprehensive grasp and understanding of all the material facts. This cannot be done simply by absorbing or memorising facts: they must also be organised or marshalled. There are many different ways of doing this: note making, schedules, time plans, charts, diagrams, etc are all useful, both on paper and in your head.

As you organise the facts, you will discover that a great many facts included in your instructions—a lot of the information provided—will in the end turn out not to be relevant to the questions you have to answer or to the issues in the case. Such irrelevant material can be discarded from your thoughts. There will also, inevitably, be gaps in your instructions, facts that are not included, information or documents not provided. You will need to identify these and formulate the right questions to ask which will elicit precisely the further information you require.

Your instructing solicitor may well have expressed a view on what are the material facts. That view may well have affected his or her decision as to what information to provide. Your instructing solicitor may also have identified the issues which he or she thought were important in the case. If this has been done well, you will find your solicitor's work very helpful when you are organising the facts and identifying the issues for yourself. But do not regard your instructing solicitor's view as definitive. You may well take a different view of the case, and regard different facts and issues as important. You may even see different issues arising altogether. It is important to keep an open mind and not to assume that you have to agree with your instructing solicitor's view of the case.

The process of organising the facts must inevitably be coloured by, and therefore takes place to a considerable extent in parallel with, the next stage, which is:

5.4.4 Stage 4: construct a legal framework

At this point the law comes into your thinking. Eventually, you are going to apply the law at two stages and for two different purposes. The one you might think of first, to help you answer the question, or even to provide the answer to the question, comes later. At this stage you apply the law to help you to organise the facts and to discover the questions which need to be answered, to identify the issues of fact and law involved in the case and to put them into a proper order.

What you are in fact doing is constructing a framework for the case and for your opinion in the case. This framework consists of a sequence of issues, each issue basically encapsulating a single question. The issue arises, and the question needs to be posed, because, from your knowledge of the law or your research, you have identified it as an essential ingredient in the chain of questions of law and fact all of which have to be answered to determine the answer to the question your client is asking. Two examples of well-established frameworks may help to illustrate the point:

- In a personal injury action, based on negligence:
  - Did D owe C a duty of care?
  - Was D in breach of that duty (ie, was he or she negligent)?
  - What are C's injuries and losses?
  - Were they caused by D's negligence?
  - Was C contributorily negligent?
  - Is the damage reasonably foreseeable?
  - Did C mitigate?
  - What is the quantum of damage?

- In a claim for damages for breach of contract:
  - Was there a contract?
  - What were its terms?
  - Has D acted in breach of the contract?
  - What damage has C suffered?
  - Was that damage caused by D's breach?
  - Was it within the parties' contemplation?
  - Did C mitigate?
  - How much is it in financial terms?

Every case has such a framework, either a standard one, like these examples, or a standard one adapted to exclude issues that do not arise or include other issues that do arise, or a framework specially constructed for the unique facts of the case.

Such a framework can only be constructed by an application of the law. You may know the law, or you may have to research it. If research is required, this may be a lengthy process, involving reading many cases, textbooks and statutes. Inevitably, when you are doing that research you will not only have in your mind the sequence of issues you are trying to construct, but also the search for an answer to them. However, identifying the issues logically comes first.

It is very important when looking up or researching the law to do so with the facts of the case that you have absorbed and organised clearly in your mind. You should never, ever conduct legal research without knowing what question you are seeking the answer to, otherwise it will be without purpose or direction. In constructing your framework, you will have in mind such questions as: What must be established before the claimant can succeed in this case? In what circumstances will I advise the executor to give the money to John, and in what circumstances to Mary? Research without such questions in your mind is likely to be lengthy, disorganised, academic and fruitless.

Identifying your sequence of issues and constructing your framework will also help you in the process of organising facts. It will tell you which facts are relevant and what is the relative importance of various pieces of information. It will show you how the facts fit together, what depends on what.

As well as identifying the specific issues upon which your client's case depends, you must also identify all the questions upon which an answer is required. Some of these questions will have been specifically posed in your instructions. But other questions are only implied. Some examples of the sort of implicit questions you might find are:

- Do I have a good case?
- What are the chances of success?
- How strong is the evidence?
- Is it worth proceeding in this matter?
- Is any further evidence required?
- What's the procedure?

And one question which you should regard as implicit in every set of instructions:

- What is the next step?

Every implied question must be identified and given a place in your sequence of issues to be answered.

A place will very probably also have to be found in your framework for issues relating to the case for the other side. You cannot consider your client's case without considering the likely opposing case. Possible defences that might be raised give rise to additional issues. The likely evidence that the other side will produce will give rise to evidential issues. These evidential issues belong in your structure just as much as legal or factual issues.

By the time you have organised the facts and produced your legal framework, you should have arrived at stage 5, which is:

5.4.5 Stage 5: look at the case as a whole

Before you can go further, it is important that you should be able to see the case as a whole, see how everything hangs together, where each question leads. You will see the starting point in your line of reasoning and where your reasoning will lead. All the issues involved in the case, and all the material facts, interrelate. The case is a unity which you understand and can find your way around. It has shape and structure. This structure will, incidentally, almost certainly provide the skeleton plan for your written opinion.

It is at this point, also, when you should clearly see what gaps there are in the information and evidence available to you. You must identify these gaps and make a request for any additional material required to be provided, bearing in mind what it is realistic to expect your solicitor to provide. You must also be ready to answer the issues you have raised in alternative ways, depending on how any additional evidence or facts turn out.

You may have started on the next stage already, even while you were organising the facts and constructing your framework, but you can only really deal with it when you have seen the case as a whole.

5.4.6 Stage 6: answer all the questions

Every question in your sequence of issues must now be answered. Every question has an answer. The answer may not yet be clear, it may have to be determined by a court, but nevertheless you can give your answer. You do this by forming an opinion.

A few of the issues that need to be dealt with will have a clear answer, yes or no, A or B. Such an answer can only be given where the facts and law are so clear that there can be no real doubt or where there is only one answer in law. If, for example, you are dealing with a case involving a collision between two motor vehicles on a public highway, you can state categorically that the defendant driver owed a duty of care to the claimant; that is not a matter for your opinion. Where you have a written contract between two parties, neither of whom has challenged its validity, you can state that that is the contract; to express the 'opinion' that it is 'probably valid' would be ridiculous.

But it is unlikely that you will be able to answer many of the issues in this way: certainly not major issues around which the dispute turns, unless your research into the law provides a definite answer. If the overall answer, or the answer on a central issue were so clear, it is unlikely that instructing solicitors would have sought your opinion at all. Most of the issues will not be able to be answered in a definite way. There can be no conclusion of certainty on a question of fact. Rather, you will have to reach a conclusion of uncertainty, where you exercise your judgment to form an *opinion*.

You may have to exercise your judgment to form an opinion on questions of law or fact, questions of mixed law and fact, or all three. Your research into the law may have provided a clear legal answer to any question of law, but more likely you will have to form an opinion on the law itself, or its applicability to the facts of the case. Hence the necessity only to carry out your legal research knowing what question you are trying to answer. The judgment you use in forming an opinion on the law is your lawyer's judgment, using your skill at legal understanding and interpretation.

But more importantly you will use your judgment to form opinions on questions of fact as well. There can be no certain answers to questions like, 'Was the driver negligent?' 'Did the claimant behave reasonably?' 'Is this piece of evidence convincing?' 'Is this version of events credible?' No statute or reported case can ever answer such questions. And yet you must answer them. You must reach your own conclusion insofar as the law and facts allow, even though your conclusion is a conclusion of uncertainty. You exercise your judgment to form an opinion. The judgment you use in answering such questions is not just a lawyer's judgment, but your judgment as an experienced practitioner, as a man or woman of the world, as a decision-maker. One of the qualities that is most respected in good barristers is their ability, when exercising their judgment, almost always to be right. It is a quality you should cultivate.

It is important to emphasise at this point that you are exercising your judgment, not giving judgment. You are not the final judge of the case, deciding who should win and lose, resolving questions of fact with findings of fact which cannot thereafter be challenged. In exercising your judgment you are weighing up all the information you have before you, and forming an opinion about what would be the likely decision of a judge on *that information* alone. You are exercising your judgment for the purpose of giving advice, not for the purpose of determining the case. You cannot see yourself as the final judge; and you must remember that there is a case for the other side that must in the end go into the balance as well.

It follows that you cannot answer all the questions asked simply by looking at your instructions and the facts as presented to you and exercising your judgment on them. You will need also to use your powers of inference or even your imagination to examine the likely case for the other side. Just because your client appears to have a good case does not mean your client will succeed. The other side doubtless think they have a good case as well. In the end a court is likely to have to resolve disputes of fact; there will be a conflict of evidence. There can only be a clear case when the facts are virtually certain or agreed between the parties. A good *answer* to a claimant's or the prosecution case does not mean the *defence* will succeed. Your client may turn out to be an unreliable or an incredible witness. It is important therefore to look at what the other side may say in court and take this into account in exercising your judgment.

Your instructing solicitor may have expressed a view as to what the answer to one or more questions is. While you should have due regard for his or her opinion, you must not substitute it with your own. You may disagree.

So you must answer all the questions in your sequence of issues, exercising your judgment where necessary, deciding what your opinion is, what you think. This is all part of advising your client. Having answered all the questions in your sequence of issues, you will have found your answer also to the central question of what it is your client actually wants to know, and you can come on to the final stage, which is:

5.4.7 Stage 7: consider your advice

In other words, you do not just form an opinion on your client's case or problem, you also advise your client what he or she should or could do. If your client has a problem, he or she does not only want to be told the solution, he or she wants to be shown how to go about obtaining that solution. What your client needs is good practical advice, so you should consider also the practical steps that you advise your client to take. This will be a very important part of the written opinion.

5.4.8 The seven stages

These seven stages of the thinking process are not, to a practising barrister, conscious stages which he or she goes through. But they are all logically present in the thinking process and every competent barrister goes through them subconsciously, bringing them in in the order set out above, even if he or she has never actually thought about them! They are all necessary in order to be prepared for the actual writing of the opinion.

5.5 The writing process: the opinion itself

You have now been through the thinking process: everything is clear in your mind. You know what your answers are, what advice you are going to give. You have to: you cannot possibly write an opinion until you know what your opinion is. But simply knowing your opinion, knowing the answer, does not mean the writing process is a mere formality. You have to know how to express yourself in an opinion, how to transfer the thinking process on to paper. What you do *not* do is simply write out the thinking process itself. Rather, you set out the *fruits* of the thinking process. We need to look a little more closely at what an opinion is and what it is for.

5.5.1 The purpose of the opinion

We have already seen what your opinion is in essence: it is your response to instructions. Your response has, however, three different aspects, all of which we have touched on, but which we can now state more clearly ((a), (b) and (c)), and an objective ((d)):

(a) *Your opinion is your answer* to a series of questions asked of you by your instructing solicitor on behalf of your client. Therefore every question must be identified and answered. We have already seen the necessity of this, and discussed how you identify issues and answer them as part of the thinking process. We shall shortly consider how you actually express your answers in writing.

(b) *Your opinion is a kind of interim judgment* on your client's present position as you see it. You must be objective, as a judge would be. Although, at the end of the day, if the case is to proceed, it will be your duty to do the best you can for your client, to fight the case on his or her behalf, to show his or her case in the best possible light, to win the case so far as the law and facts allow, you have not reached this stage yet. At this point you are not trying to fight a case, win it or show it in the best possible light: that would be to mislead your client. You may consider *how* the case may be fought and won, and assess the chances, but nevertheless you must judge the strength or weakness of your client's case coolly and accurately. We have already considered the importance of exercising judgment. This is always an objective process. The only subjective element is that you are judging the case put to you by one side only, rather than the case put to you by both sides, as a judge would at trial. But, again remember, you are *not* the judge. You are not *deciding* the case.

(c) *Your opinion is a piece of advice* to your client regarding his or her position and what he or she should do. This *is* subjective: you are obviously trying to help your client as opposed to anyone else and to solve that client's particular problem. Advising is not just a matter of advising someone what to do, but is closely bound up with the whole process of answering questions and exercising judgment.

(d) *Your objective in writing the opinion* is to lead your client to the clearest possible understanding of his or her position, so that he or she can decide, on your advice, what to do about it. So your opinion should be clear, complete, unambiguous, easy to read, easy to follow, and an accurate representation of what you actually think. It should be definitive, rather than discursive, but it must be a *reasoned* opinion. An opinion is incomplete if no reasons are given. It must also look to the future and indicate the way forward.

5.5.2 Some things that an opinion is not

(a) An opinion is not an *argument*. Arguments seek to persuade somebody of something and there is no element of persuasion in an opinion. You are not arguing your client's case, presenting it to a court, or trying to prove anything. You may well *rehearse* the arguments for and against your client's case: but that is part of the reasoning for your opinion, which is your view on those arguments.

(b) An opinion is not an *essay*. An essay discusses, explores, considers; it is discursive rather than definitive. An essay, typically, sets out the thinking process, rather than the fruits of the thinking process. Your opinion should never resemble an essay.

(c) An opinion is not a *submission*. When making a submission, you are putting forward an argument, or a theory for someone else's judgment. In an opinion you are exercising your own judgment, giving your own advice. Your opinion should *never* contain the words 'It is submitted that' or 'I submit that'. Such words betray a fundamental misunderstanding of the whole concept of opinion writing. If you find yourself writing them, cross them out and write what you really mean, which is, 'It is my opinion that' or 'I think that'.

(d) An opinion is not an *instruction*. Although your opinion is definitive, and you are giving judgment, in layman's terms 'laying down the law', you cannot go too far. You can tell your client what his or her position is and advise your client what to do; you can tell him or her how to go about things and give instructions about the conduct of a case. But you cannot *tell* your client to bring a claim or abandon one; *tell* him or her whether to enter into a contract or not; *tell* him or her to plead guilty or not guilty. Decisions such as these are your client's to make (except in very rare circumstances): your task is not to make the decision for your client, but give him or her all the information and advice needed in order to make the right decision.

We can at last come on to the questions of how you actually set out the opinion and express yourself in it.

5.5.3 For whom is the opinion written?

One thing you will find quite hard to sort out in the early stages of learning to write opinions is whether you are really writing for the instructing solicitor or for the lay client. The strict answer is that you are writing for the instructing solicitor. He or she has sent you the instructions and posed the questions; it is to him or her that you are replying. A more complete answer is that you are writing for both the solicitor and the lay client, but in different ways and to a different extent in different cases. You should ask yourself 'Who is going to act on this advice?'. If it is the solicitor, then you are writing primarily, or occasionally exclusively, for his or her benefit. But if it is the lay client, you must make sure that your opinion is written in such a way as to be intelligible and helpful to him.

However, writing for the lay client does *not* mean that you should avoid legal terminology or explain legal principles in layman's terms. To the extent that you are giving legal advice, you are writing as one professional lawyer to another, and you should assume that your instructing solicitor has the same knowledge of general principles as you do. Just take care to avoid unnecessary obscurity and jargon. It is where you are giving practical advice which will affect your lay client that you should make sure the lay client can understand the advice you are giving, and the reasons for it.

There is a balance to be struck, which is not easy to explain, but which comes quite naturally once you have read a few opinions and had some practice.

5.6 How the opinion should be set out

The first thing to be clear about is that there is absolutely no correct or incorrect way to write an opinion. You may do it however you wish. Every barrister has to a greater or lesser extent their own individual style. However you write your opinion, there will always be a barrister who will say 'I don't like your style, I wouldn't write it like that'. During your training you will probably hear contradictory views forcefully expressed.

Nevertheless, there are undoubtedly such things as good opinions and bad opinions. We have already examined quite thoroughly the qualities that a good opinion should have and the functions it should serve, and you cannot give it those qualities or fulfil those functions simply by writing it any old way that happens to take your fancy. In the interests of clarity, it *must* have a clear structure; in the interests of completeness, it must have full reasoning; in the interests of readability it must follow a clear line. In the end, you will discover your own style and write your own opinions as you wish, but it is good to have a starting point.

The following structure is therefore a suggested starting point. It is safe, mildly conventional and unoriginal: but if followed it should lead to a good rather than a bad opinion.

5.6.1 Skeleton plan

Before you start writing your opinion, you must have a skeleton plan. This plan will have evolved during the process of thinking and analysing the issues. Without such a plan (which may be on paper or in your head) your opinion is bound to be disorganised, rambling and poorly structured. Having prepared that skeleton plan, try as hard as you can to stick to it. Do not wander off at a tangent, or allow yourself to drift into discussing an issue you had decided to take at a later stage, unless it is clear to you that this is an improvement on your original plan.

A good skeleton plan should actually save you time. You should find it is quicker to write the opinion after you have constructed your skeleton than it would have been without it. It is important therefore to draw up your skeleton in a helpful way. Your skeleton will not save you time if it is just the barest of bare bones: a few words, maybe a few paragraph headings. You need more flesh on the bones. It should tell you not just what you are going to write *about*, but what you will actually *say*. So it should give you a clear indication of the issues you will deal with, in what order, and roughly how much space you will devote to each. It will list the points you want to raise in relation to each issue. It will tell you what your conclusion on each issue is going to be. It may even tell you exactly how many paragraphs your opinion will contain, and what will go into each paragraph.

On the other hand, you will also not save yourself time if your skeleton is too full, amounting to the entire opinion in note form, or even containing some half-written paragraphs. This will lead to much duplication of your efforts.

5.6.2 Backsheet and heading

Your opinion has a backsheet on which should be printed the title of the case as it appears in your instructions. This may be a full court heading (as in statements of case) or it may just be the name of the client. Use whatever your instructing solicitors have used. Underneath appears, in capitals, in tram lines, 'OPINION' or 'ADVICE' as the case may be. Thus:

<u>Mary Smith v International Pancakes Ltd</u>

OPINION

The same heading, or an abbreviation of it, will usually appear also on the inside, immediately above your first paragraph.

Your opinion may be called 'Opinion' or 'Advice'. There is not a hard-and-fast distinction. Traditionally, it is an opinion when you are advising on law, questions of fact, liability, merits, quantum of damages, etc; and an advice where the emphasis is on evidence or procedure or the practical steps to be taken. Try to differentiate, but do not worry too much if you cannot. As a rough guide, call it an opinion in civil matters (except for an advice on evidence) and an advice in criminal matters. But many barristers will disagree with this.

After the heading, there follows the body of the opinion, written in numbered paragraphs. You write in the first person, that is to say, you refer to yourself as 'I' not as 'counsel'. But you refer to your client and your instructing solicitor in the third person, 'he, she, it or they', rather than in the second person, 'you'.

5.6.3 The opening paragraph(s)

The opening paragraph(s) should contain a brief statement of what the case is all about, and your objectives. In other words, you identify the fundamental facts, the key issues and what you are asked to advise about.

Some barristers will say that the opening paragraph(s) should contain all the material facts. There are good reasons why this may be useful in some instances, but generally speaking the facts are well known to the client and the instructing solicitor and little purpose is served by setting them all out. What you should certainly not do, is simply copy out your instructions at great length or regurgitate all the facts unselectively and uncritically. The introduction to the opinion should be concise.

Next, you may decide to state your main conclusions and give your overall opinion on the case. Most barristers actually put their conclusions at the end of the opinion, but you are encouraged to put them at the beginning while learning the skill. It is helpful to both the solicitor and client and an aid to clarity. If the overall conclusion is already stated one can read the subsequent reasoning knowing where it is leading. It is also a very good discipline to make yourself state the opinion at the outset, as it ensures that you cannot start writing without having decided what your opinion is.

If the conclusions are not stated at the beginning, they must be clearly stated at the end of the opinion.

5.6.4 Subsequent paragraphs: your reasons

5.6.4.1 Setting out your reasons

Use however many paragraphs you need. This is where you set out the reasoning that has led you to your overall conclusions. You do this by taking each issue in its logical order, saying what you think on that issue and why; that is, stating your opinion and reasons, and giving advice.

The logical order should be clear once you have applied the correct legal framework and put the problem into shape (as part of the thinking process). So, for example, if your overall conclusion is that in your opinion Mary Smith has a very good chance of establishing that International Pancakes Ltd is liable to her for her injuries and that she is likely to recover damages in the region of £25,000, your reasoning might go like this:

1. International Pancakes owed her a duty of care, because... [identify the specific facts and why they gave rise to a duty, applying the appropriate law].
2. The company was in breach of duty, ie, negligent, because... [identify the acts and omissions that constitute negligence and if necessary explain why].
3. There is some difficulty about causation, but in my view this can be overcome because... [give reasons].
4. Most of the loss and damage suffered by Mary Smith is recoverable but one or two small items were not reasonably foreseeable, because... [give reasons].
5. The heads of damage are... [set out] and in my opinion they will be quantified as follows... [give your quantification and reasoning on each head].

This is a very simple example. Many of the above issues may well subdivide, in which case you might state your overall opinion on the issue of negligence before going on to deal with each sub-issue in turn, indicating the reasoning that has led you to the opinion that International Pancakes was negligent.

On any issue where your opinion is required, you should state it. Do not leave it to be deduced or inferred; do not hint at it or obscure it. Ten pages of waffle with the words 'That is my opinion' at the end will not do. Use phrases such as 'I think that' 'It is my opinion that' 'I have come to the conclusion that'. And whenever you express an opinion, you must always give your reasons for it. This applies not just to your overall conclusion, but to each separate issue as well. For the reasons explained above, it is a good idea to state the opinion first and give the reasons for it second.

Giving reasons is not always something which comes easily. It may be relatively straightforward to give reasons for an opinion on the law, because the reasons will then be reasons of law. But when you express an opinion on a question of fact, you cannot use the law as your reason. It is nonsense, for example, to say 'The defendant was negligent because he owed the claimant a duty of care' or 'Clause 6 is unreasonable because the Unfair Contract Terms Act 1977 applies'. Your reasons for an opinion on a question of fact can only come from the facts themselves. For example, 'The defendant was negligent because he had read the instruction manual which stated quite clearly that the machine should never be switched on without the safety guard in place and nevertheless he did so'; or 'Clause 6 is unreasonable because in effect it makes the claimant responsible for checking the quality of the defendant's workmanship, which she would have neither the skill nor the knowledge to do'.

Another common fault is the reasoning which simply repeats the conclusion. It is meaningless to write an opinion which states, expressly, or in effect, 'The defendant was negligent because he failed to take reasonable care for the claimant's safety' (ie, he was negligent because he was negligent); or 'Clause 6 is unreasonable because it fails to satisfy the test in section 11 of the Unfair Contract Terms Act 1977' (ie, it's unreasonable because it's unreasonable). Make sure you avoid such circular statements.

Giving reasons actually constitutes the bulk of your opinion. It can be a lengthy process, especially if the issues are complex or there is a lot of law involved. It is important therefore that your reasoning should be easy to follow. It must follow a clear line; the reader should always know where that line has come from, where it is going to, and what stage along the line he or she has reached. This is why it is impossible to write a good opinion without having prepared a skeleton plan first, and why you should stick to it.

It is to help you stick to your plan that it is suggested you write in numbered paragraphs. It is a useful discipline and recommended, at least while you are learning to write a good opinion. Other helpful aids are subheadings: put a title to each section of your opinion, as some judges do to their judgments in the law reports. Subheadings tell the reader at once what issue you are dealing with at each stage, and help you to stick to it. Also useful are short linking sentences explaining the structure of your opinion, for example, 'So for the reasons stated I think that clause 2 was a valid term of the contract and I shall now consider whether the defendants were in breach of it'.

5.6.4.2 Avoid irrelevance

The worst enemy of clear reasoning, apart from muddled thinking, is irrelevance. Your opinion must of course be complete, so everything relevant must be included; but it should also be as concise as possible, and so it should contain nothing irrelevant. It should be fairly easy to identify what is relevant and irrelevant if you ask yourself three questions:

- Is it part of my opinion in this case?
- Is it a necessary step along my line of reasoning?
- Is it part of the advice I am giving to this client?

If the answer to any of these questions is yes, then it is obviously relevant. You may get more than one yes, but if you get no three times, then it is almost certainly irrelevant.

Irrelevance is likely to creep in if you fall into the trap of setting out your thinking process or all your research into the law rather than the fruits of your thinking process or legal research. Other common examples of irrelevance are:

(a) Simply setting out the facts of the case or copying out your instructions without comment. You may well need to examine and analyse the facts with great care and in some detail, but only as part of the reasoning process.

(b) Giving an elementary law lecture; eg 'A person owes another a duty of care if there is a sufficient relationship of proximity between them and it is reasonably foreseeable...etc'. This makes you sound like a first-year undergraduate, not a professional lawyer.

(c) General exposition of the law in a particular area, quite irrespective of whether it actually touches on the facts of the case you are dealing with.

(d) Detailing all the case law you have researched. You may well have read a lot of cases, and having read them, come to a conclusion on the facts of this case. But it is most unlikely that every single case you have read forms part of your reasoning. You do not need to mention every case just because you read it. A general examination of case law is part of the thinking process, not part of your opinion. Do not describe your research in writing. State the conclusion you have come to and set out your reasons.

(e) Following blind alleys of reasoning. Do not take an issue, discuss it for several paragraphs and come to the conclusion at the end of it that it is irrelevant or makes no difference to your opinion. Such a discovery should have been made before you started writing, so you can simply state, 'Such and such is irrelevant because...'.

(f) Seeking to distinguish cases that are so wholly different that nobody would ever have thought of comparing them in the first place; similarly, discussing statutory provisions which obviously do not apply.

(g) Wasting time on hypothetical cases: 'If the facts were not as they are but something else', followed by several paragraphs of irrelevant discussion, concluding 'but that is not the case here so I do not need to concern myself with this possibility'.

(h) Advising your client of what he or she already knows.

Overall: keep your reasoning clear, sharp and to the point.

5.6.5 'Rules' of structure

5.6.5.1 Liability and quantum

One 'rule' of structure that should never be broken is that liability is dealt with first, then quantum. Do not mix the two together, or jump between them unless you have a very good reason to do so.

So, for example, if you are considering the liability of two potential defendants arising out of the same facts, the correct order of issues is usually:

(1) Liability of D1

(2) Liability of D2

(3) Quantum against D1

(4) Quantum against D2

and NOT, as students frequently attempt, (1), (3), (2), (4). Only do it this way round if D1 and D2 are potentially liable for completely different damage.

5.6.5.2 Separate parties

If you are considering the liability of two defendants, take each of them in turn, and consider possible causes of action against each of them separately. The correct order of issues, for example, might be:

(1) Liability of D1 for breach of statutory duty

(2) Liability of D1 in negligence

(3) Liability of D2 for breach of statutory duty

(4) Liability of D2 in negligence.

It might possibly, but rarely, be more appropriate to take the issues in the order (1), (3), (2), (4). But in no circumstances should you merge (1) and (2) or (1) and (3) into a single issue.

5.6.6 Subsidiary points

Having stated your overall conclusions, set out your reasoning and given advice, the main part of the opinion is complete. However, there may well be some subsidiary points to deal with and your next paragraph or paragraphs will deal with these. There are quite possibly some specific questions put to you in your instructions, which, while not being part of the overall opinion, must nevertheless be answered. There are also likely to be some implied questions to be dealt with. Every implied question must be identified and given a clear and complete answer, just as express questions must be. Some may be answered as part of your overall opinion, but others will be answered when you are dealing with subsidiary points. Remember that one question is always implicit and must be dealt with: What is the next step?

A major matter which may well need to be dealt with at this stage is evidence. Sometimes you will be asked specifically to advise on evidence, in which case you will either write a separate 'advice on evidence' or deal with it fully in your opinion. Even if you are not asked specifically to advise on evidence, however, it would be odd to make no mention of it in your opinion. You cannot consider your opinion on the strength of a case, or your advice to your client on what you think he or she should do without reference to evidence. It is in the end on the evidence that a case is won or lost. So you should be addressing your mind to what can be proved and cannot be proved on the evidence you have; and to what further evidence is required. Anything important must be mentioned in your opinion. It is no good advising your client that he or she has a good case if, say, a piece of machinery was not properly serviced, if in fact you do not have any evidence to show that it was not properly serviced. Indicate what evidence is missing, and from where it might be obtained.

Points of procedure may need to be dealt with. You may, for example, want to advise that a request for further information should be made, or that an application should be made to the court. You may want to advise for or against making a Part 36 offer, or accepting a Part 36 payment. You may want to advise that an attempt should or should not be made to settle the action. All these are examples of matters that should properly be dealt with in your opinion.

Also important is reference to any issue involving costs. In your client's mind there will always be an overriding question: 'How much is all this going to cost me?' You should make sure you are aware of your client's financial position, eligibility for public funding, etc. You should *never* advise that any step should be taken which might have implications in terms of costs, without advising your client what those implications are.

5.6.7 Further advice

It may well be that having dealt with all the issues, having answered all the questions and advised your client, there will still be other helpful advice you can give, in which case give it. Only give it if it is relevant and helpful. To decide whether it is helpful, remember your overall objective: to lead your client to the clearest possible understanding of his or her position, so that the client can decide, on your advice, what to do about it. Any advice which fulfils this objective, whether by clarifying the position or advising on the steps to be taken, is likely to be helpful.

5.6.8 The conclusion

The most common way to conclude the opinion is to have a paragraph headed 'summary of advice' or 'summary of conclusions', setting out the main points of advice once again in shortened form. This is certainly essential if you have not stated your overall opinion at the outset of the opinion, because it is important that your client and instructing solicitor should be able to extract your advice easily. Your advice should always be plain to see, not buried. It may also be a good idea if, for example, you have a corporate client and it is likely that your opinion will be summarised for a board or committee rather than presented in its entirety. In such a case it is wise that the summary should be yours rather than anyone else's. A summary of conclusions at the end may also serve a stylistic purpose.

Your final paragraph should round your opinion off in some way. This is actually more a point of style than of content. Barristers like to think that a good opinion is not just a functional piece of writing, but a work of good literature as well. In the same way as no good literature just suddenly stops, but rather rounds itself off neatly or tellingly, so should an opinion. It needs an end as well as a beginning and a middle. You can do this in any way you like, according to your literary abilities, but if you can think of nothing better, a conventional solution is to finish with the summary of advice mentioned above. This may be unnecessary, if you have already stated your conclusions at the outset, but it does at least solve the stylistic difficulty. You may alternatively finish with a restatement of what the solicitor and/or client should do next.

If you have also produced some other piece of writing, usually a statement of case, note this also in your final paragraph.

5.6.9 Counsel's signature

At the bottom of the opinion, counsel's name and signature appear, with date, and usually chambers address.

5.6.10 Variations in practice

Please remember that the above description of the structure and content of an opinion is only given as a starting point. You will probably not find a single barrister who agrees with every word of it. Do not expect every opinion you see to follow it precisely. Different opinions serve different purposes and their structure and layout will vary as the content varies.

There remain a few points of content and style to be dealt with.

5.7 Points of content

5.7.1 Answering questions that have no definite answer

The importance of answering questions is something we keep coming back to, and we have seen how most questions do not have a definite answer, a conclusion of certainty, but can only be answered by a conclusion of uncertainty, where you exercise your judgment to form an opinion. We must now look at the difficulty of expressing an opinion when you cannot be certain. The answer you give has got to be clear and complete. It is quite possible to give such an answer, and be helpful, without being definite. You must reach *conclusions*, ie, you must be conclusive, but you do not need to be definite in your answer. It is understood by all concerned that the barrister's opinion is only an opinion: infallibility is not expected. The rule is to be as definite as you can be but no more than you can be. It is a difficult balance to strike. The most common complaint of pupil masters is that their pupils tend to be too definite: to say 'The case will succeed' when they should say 'The prospects are good'. On the other hand, another common failing of beginners is not to be definite enough: to say 'The claimant may or may not succeed in his claim, depending on how things turn out'. Sometimes this vagueness is couched in definite terms: the opinion which, on close analysis, in effect states: 'In my opinion the claimant will succeed in this claim if the judge finds in his favour'!

You have to strike the right balance between certainty and uncertainty. If the question is 'Will the claimant succeed in his action?', do not answer 'yes' when you mean 'probably'; 'probably' when you mean 'possibly'; 'possibly' when you mean 'unlikely'; 'good chance' when you mean 'fair chance', 'reasonable chance' when you mean 'remote chance'; 'some chance' when you mean 'no'; or 'no' when you mean 'slight chance'. What you do is find a form of words which seems to you exactly to express your feeling about the strength of the case. For example:

I do not think that Mrs Jones has any good prospects of establishing liability in this case, but there is enough evidence before me to justify sending a letter of claim to the other side to see what response it provokes.

There are numerous obstacles to be overcome in establishing liability in this case, but on balance I think they can be overcome and once they are, Mrs Jones's prospects of success are good.

Take care, also, when expressing your opinion on a subsidiary question of fact. For example, 'In my opinion the driver of the car was negligent' sounds very definite. In this case it would probably not be understood as being quite so definite, because what you really mean is 'In my opinion a court would find him to have been negligent'; but take care. Phrases like 'In my opinion he was negligent' can appear in opinions, but they can mislead others and even you into treating as definite a question of fact which has yet to be decided. It is much better to say 'I think a court would find him liable'. Beware also of saying 'I would award the claimant damages of £50,000', when all you mean is that £50,000 is your estimate of a likely award by a court.

But, of course, a conclusion of uncertainty must not only be expressed, it must also be reasoned. This may be a lengthy process: probably the less certain you are able to be, the more reasoning you will need to justify your conclusion. To give your reasons for a conclusion of uncertainty, and to give advice in so doing, you will probably need to go through the following points. You will need to set out fairly fully the client's position as you see it, not just the legal position but the factual position, the position the client finds himself or herself in in the light of the law; you will need to consider the pros and cons, weigh up the evidence, assess the chances (not necessarily numerically); you should certainly make clear the circumstances in which your client would succeed and the circumstances in which he or she would not. You may well need to explain your view of what the other side's case is likely to be and the strength of it. All in all you identify and explain everything that has gone into the balance as you have weighed up your opinion, and let your client know exactly where he or she stands.

5.7.2 Citing cases and other authorities

Cases are mentioned, discussed, applied and distinguished in your opinion, just as they are in a judge's judgment. But whereas judges are obliged to deal with the arguments they have listened to and so need to discuss most of the cases they have been asked to read, in your opinion you should only cite a case where it is relevant to your opinion, reasoning or advice. Do not try to get in as many cases as you can. Do not mention every case you have read. Apply the relevancy test. Not every opinion needs to have cases in it. In practice a great many opinions are written which mention no case law at all. If no case is relevant, put none in.

Cases may be properly cited where they are authority for a point of law, where they form part of your reasoning or where they have helped you to reach your conclusion. They should not be cited just to show you know them. You should not, for example, put '(*Donoghue v Stevenson*)' every time you write the word 'negligence'. When you cite a case, cite it in the proper manner. If you simply put a case name at the end of a sentence, you are citing it as authority for what you have just said. Make sure you do not cite a case like this as if it were authority on a question of fact: for example, 'In my opinion the defendants were in fundamental breach of contract (*Photo Production Ltd v Securicor Transport Ltd*)'. If the case is simply being cited as the source of a proposition, or as an illustration or as part of your reasoning, this should be made clear. Cases that form part of your reasoning, either because they have led you to your conclusion, or because they need to be distinguished in order to justify your conclusion, can and should be cited for this purpose: use them in such a way that their relevance is clear. Otherwise do not cite them at all.

It will usually be sufficient simply to mention the name of the case in an appropriate and relevant way. It will only occasionally be relevant to set out the facts and *ratio* of a reported case, in which case try to make it part of your reasoning, rather than simply setting it out descriptively, like a chunk from a textbook. Never copy out headnotes of cases in your opinion.

Wherever you cite a case, or refer to a textbook, give the full reference, so that your instructing solicitor can look it up, and for your own future use.

5.7.3 Dealing with lack of information

You will never receive a set of instructions that contains every single point of information you could possibly want. There will always be some gaps. What you cannot do is use lack of information as an excuse for not advising. You must *never* say, 'I cannot advise on this point because I have not been told whether...' and then go no further.

You must always advise as fully as you can on the information you have. Even if there is something absolutely central to your opinion missing, you can still follow this rule. Sometimes the less information you have, the longer your opinion needs to be, because you will have to advise in such a way as to cover several eventualities. If your opinion depends on whether the claimant did or did not know that he had a flat tyre, you must say what your opinion would be if he did know and what it would be if he did not.

Where there are gaps in your instructions, it is essential that you should identify them and point them out to your instructing solicitors in your opinion. If there is information you need, you ask for it. In practice, if you could obtain it by telephoning your instructing solicitor, you should do so. Otherwise ask for it in your opinion. But do not ask for further information just for the sake of it. Always make it clear what you want that information for and how it will affect your opinion. If it will not make any difference to your opinion, do not ask for it.

5.7.4 Length

The question of the right length for an opinion is a tricky one. Some barristers write at greater length than others. Excessive length and excessive brevity are both common faults in students' opinions.

The aim must be to write an opinion that is just the right length in all the circumstances. A balance must be struck between completeness and conciseness, both as a matter of content and as a matter of style. But in fact the right length for an opinion is more an issue of content. Differences simply of *style* do not affect the length of an opinion all that much.

An opinion that is too short is usually too short because of inadequate analysis of the issues, inadequate thought or inadequate reasoning. In other words it is superficial. Only rarely is excessive brevity the result of over-enthusiastic pruning. More usually an opinion which is too short fails to say all that needs to be said and does so because the writer has failed to identify what needs to be said.

An opinion that is too long is usually too long because of an over-academic approach by a writer who has failed to distinguish between an opinion and an essay. The essence of an opinion is that it sets out the fruits of the research and thinking process, not that process itself. You should not bring in to the opinion every avenue of thought and reasoning that you have pursued. You should set out the conclusions you have reached at the end of the day and the advice you accordingly wish to give. If the case is complex, you do not 'do it justice' by writing a complex opinion, but rather by penetrating to the core of the matter, stripping it down to its bare essentials, unravelling all the complexities and encapsulating the result in a clear and concise opinion.

For this reason, if for no other, opinion writing is a skill in a way that essay writing is not.

5.8 Style

It goes without saying that your opinion should be written in clear, stylistic, fluent English. This will, however, inevitably be of your own individual style. Some barristers tend to write in short, punchy sentences; others prefer immaculately constructed, mellifluous sentences of 100 words or more. Either will be fine, if the opinion has all the qualities of a good opinion. Short, punchy sentences must not result in inaccuracy, or incomplete reasoning; long sentences must still be grammatical and easy to read. Your opinion ideally should be complete, but not a word longer than necessary. If you have the ability to be concise, brief and snappy without any sacrifice of content, this is ideal.

Within the opinion, try to stick to ordinary, everyday language, and avoid archaisms and pomposities like 'the said motor vehicle', 'the matters aforementioned', 'hereinafter referred to as the relevant date'. Phrases like this are derived from statements of case, and even there they are out of date. They have no place in an opinion, where there is no need for excessive formality or pedantic accuracy. Use the plain English you would use to write a letter. Perhaps not any kind of letter, but the kind of letter you would write, say, to your bank manager. You would not say, 'I am enquiring about the balance of my account (hereinafter referred to as my overdraft)'. Don't say it in an opinion either.

The one and only formality which remains conventional and which you should adopt is to refer to your instructing solicitors as 'Instructing Solicitors', usually with capital initials, and in the third person rather than the second person throughout. But do not refer to yourself in the third person: write 'I advise that', not 'Counsel advises that'.

Be polite, both to your client and to your instructing solicitor. Address your client as you would address him or her face to face: 'Mr Jones', not 'Jones' or 'Jack'; it is preferable to call him or her by name rather than to refer to him as 'the claimant'. Do not suggest that your client may be lying. Do not pass moral judgments upon him or her. Do not start an argument with your instructing solicitors, or accuse them of incompetence. Treat them with respect, as fellow professional lawyers.

Finally remember what has already been said: there is no one right way to write an opinion. Strive for perfection, but do not expect you will ever achieve it, or that there can ever be such a thing in reality. No two barristers will agree about the perfect opinion.

5.9 When you have finished your opinion

When your opinion has been typed, sign the typed copy, put a cross through the title of the action on the backsheet of your advice and on the backsheet of your instructions. Endorse the backsheet of your instructions 'Opinion enclosed', and sign it.

Then hand your opinion, tied up in the red tape on the outside of your instructions, to your clerk, who will (a) note the fee that you are going to charge for your opinion, and (b) let your solicitors know that the papers are ready and take their instructions as to whether they will collect the papers or would like them to be sent back by post or document exchange.

Remember also that the instructions may come back to you in the future. If so your original opinion should be included. But it may not be: so make sure you keep a copy just in case!

5.10 Further reading

Blake, Susan, *A Practical Approach to Effective Litigation*, 6th edn, Oxford University Press, 2005.

6

The use of law in an opinion

6.1 Introduction

The purpose of this chapter is to explore further the part played by law in an opinion.

It is in the use of law that the difference between writing an essay and writing an opinion becomes clearest. In essay-writing the main object is to write about the law. In opinion writing the main object is to advise a client what to do next. In opinion writing, the law is simply a means to an end; it is never an end in itself. The law is merely part of the reasoning process.

Whilst it is impracticable to draw up a list of hard-and-fast rules, this chapter is intended to provide some guidance on how law should be used in opinion writing.

6.1.1 Do not give a law lecture

Even though an opinion may require legal research and will have to contain advice given within a legal framework, the opinion must not give abstract advice. It must, in other words, be firmly anchored in the facts of the case with which you are dealing. It follows that the law must be related carefully to the facts of the case.

The opinion must be written in a way which is practical, not academic. Neither your instructing solicitor nor your lay client wants to read a legal treatise. They want advice which is specific to the instructions with which you are dealing. It is therefore important that you do not try to give a law lecture in your opinion. If you find yourself setting out the law in the sort of detail to be found in textbooks and articles, you will almost certainly be writing an essay, not an opinion.

For example, if you are advising on damages in a case involving breach of contract, the following text would need considerable pruning:

The object of the award of damages in a case of breach of contract is to put the claimant in the position, so far as money can do so, he or she would have been in had the contract been properly performed. It was held in Hadley v Baxendale *(1854) 9 Exch 341 (followed in* Victoria Laundry v Newman *[1949] 2 KB 528) that loss would only be recoverable if it was within the contemplation of the parties at the time they entered into the contract. This will be the case in either of two circumstances:*

>   *(1) the damage is such as may fairly and reasonably be regarded as arising naturally, ie in the ordinary course of things, from the breach; or*
>
>   *(2) the defendant was aware that this particular type of loss would flow from the breach of the contract because of special knowledge which he had at the time of making the contract (usually derived from something the claimant has said to the defendant).*

For example, if A contracts with B that A will repair a piece of machinery belonging to B and A fails to repair the machinery properly and B thereby loses an exceptionally lucrative contract, A would only be liable for the resulting loss of profit, insofar as it exceeds the loss of profit which could be expected to arise in any event, if he knew of its existence.

In tort, on the other hand, the test of remoteness (see The Wagon Mound *[1961] AC 388 and* The Wagon Mound (No 2) *[1967] 1 AC 617) is whether the type of loss sustained by the claimant was a reasonably foreseeable consequence of the tort committed by the defendant. If the type of loss is a reasonably foreseeable consequence, it does not matter that the degree of loss is much greater than expected* (Smith v Leech Brain *[1962] 2 QB 405).*

The law is set out in too much detail (especially in light of the fact that the principles being set out would be well known to your instructing solicitor already). The paragraph about tortious damages is of course irrelevant to a case where the only possible liability is contractual. It would have been much better to write something like this:

The first loss which the company sustained was the loss of profit on its contract with Widgets Ltd. The repairer had visited the company's premises on three occasions before the contract was finalised and must have seen that the company had only one moulding machine. It must therefore have been within the contemplation of the repairer that if this machine were to be out of action for longer than anticipated, the company would be unable to manufacture goods produced by that machine. The consequent loss of profit must therefore have been within the repairer's contemplation.

This advice is of course clearly based on the relevant legal principles but focuses on the facts of the case in which advice is sought, not on those legal principles.

One way of making sure that you are not writing a law lecture is to ensure each principle of law you refer to is related to the facts of the case in which you are advising, so that each statement of law is followed by a reference to the facts.

6.2 Dealing with the well-known principle of law

There is no need to set out basic principles of law with which instructing solicitors will be familiar.

EXAMPLE

Suppose that you are writing an opinion in respect of a claim arising from a road accident. To write, '*Following the neighbour principle established in* Donoghue v Stephenson *[1932] AC 562, one road user owes a duty of care to another road user' is unnecessary*. It is obvious that one road user owes a duty of care to another, and so the point does not have to be made expressly. The appropriate starting point would be to say that the defendant was (or was not) in breach of the duty of care owed to the claimant because...

6.3 Only cite authorities on points of law

Do not make a statement of fact and then cite a case to support it.

EXAMPLE

Suppose that you are writing an opinion in respect of a claim arising out of the alleged negligence of a doctor. It would be wrong to include a sentence which reads, '*In my view, the court will find that the doctor was in breach of the duty of care he owed the patient: see* Bolam v Friern Hospital Management *[1957] 1 WLR 582*'.

The relevance of the *Bolam* test is that it establishes that a doctor is to be judged according to the standard of what a reasonable doctor would do. It follows that this authority should be dealt with like this:

In Bolam v Friern Hospital Management *[1957] 1 WLR 852 it was held that a doctor is to be judged according to the standard of what a reasonable doctor would do. In the present case, the doctor failed to do what a reasonable doctor would have done in the circumstances in that ...*

6.4 How to cite cases

Where it is necessary to cite a case, you should always give a citation for that case, for example *Caparo v Dickman* [1990] 2 AC 605. For recent cases, the 'neutral' citation will precede the reference to a particular set of law reports, for example, *Chester v Afshar* [2004] UKHL 41.

The rest of this section is concerned with deciding which case or cases to cite.

6.4.1 Dealing with a minor point

Where you wish to refer to a point of law with which your instructing solicitor may well be familiar but where you also wish to show that there is support for the proposition of law you have just set out, it is usually sufficient to set out the proposition of law and then cite the authority for that proposition. In this instance, you are summarising the effect of the earlier decision, not relying on a specific dictum. Here, it is sufficient to set out the proposition of law and then give the name of the case, together with its citation.

EXAMPLE

*An accountant is only liable for negligently prepared accounts if reliance by the claimant on those accounts was reasonably foreseeable (*Caparo v Dickman *[1990] 2 AC 605).*

6.4.2 Dealing with a more important source

Where the source plays a more important role in your reasoning process, you generally need to deal more carefully with that source. In this instance, you should set out the basis of the decision you are relying on. Then apply the law you have stated to the facts upon which you are asked to advise.

EXAMPLE

You are asked to advise someone who was prosecuted by the police because the police had been given incorrect information by an informant who bore a grudge against your client. One of the possible causes of action you consider is a claim for malicious prosecution. Your legal research reveals a case called *Martin v Watson* [1996] AC 74, decided in the House of Lords.

That part of your advice might read as follows:

In Martin v Watson *[1996] AC 74 it was held by the House of Lords that, for the purposes of a claim for malicious prosecution, the person who supplied the information on which the police acted may be regarded as the prosecutor. However, this will only be so where the prosecution is brought by the police as a result of information received from the informant, the informant agrees to give evidence against the accused, and the informant is the only person who could give evidence against the accused (there being no other witnesses).*

In the present case, the evidence of the informant was supported by that of another witness. Thus, the prosecution in this case did not result exclusively from information supplied by the informant; there was other evidence upon which the police were able to base their judgment to arrest the accused. It follows that the informant in the present case cannot be regarded as the prosecutor, and so a claim for malicious prosecution against her would be bound to fail.

6.4.3 Set out the facts of the case and then paraphrase or quote part of a judgment

In many instances, it is sufficient to refer to the overall effect of the case without referring to a specific dictum. If a case is central to your reasoning, however, it may well be appropriate to quote from the judgment(s) in the report of the case. The words you are relying on will only make sense if the context of those words is made clear and so some of the background to the case has to be set out. When setting out the words you rely on you should paraphrase rather than quote from your source if you can shorten the text by so doing.

EXAMPLE

You are asked to advise someone accused of murder. Your client admits killing the victim but wants to rely on the defence of provocation. At the time of the incident, your client was suffering from the effect of an hallucinogenic drug and was taunted by his wife for allowing himself to be in such a state. One of the cases you find in your legal research is *R v Morhall* [1996] AC 90. When dealing with this authority, you need to make it plain that the defendant in that case acted under the influence of glue-sniffing, rather than hallucinogenic drugs. You might say something like this:

In R v Morhall [1996] AC 90 the defendant had been glue-sniffing. The deceased chided him about his glue-sniffing and a fight ensued in which the deceased was fatally stabbed with a knife by the defendant. It was held by the House of Lords that the general rule is that the effect of intoxication (whether alcohol, drugs or glue) is to be disregarded in assessing whether the accused acted as a reasonable person might have done. However, where the accused is 'taunted with his addiction or . . . even with having been intoxicated (from any cause) on some previous occasion . . . it may where relevant be taken into account as going to the gravity of the provocation' (per Lord Goff at pp 99–100).

In the present case, the provocation was closely connected with the fact that the accused had been taking an hallucinogenic drug. The jury should therefore be directed that the effect of the drug is to be taken into account when considering whether the accused responded to the provocation in a way that a reasonable person might have done.

If you wish to paraphrase rather than quote, then you could do so thus:

In R v Morhall [1996] AC 90 the defendant had been glue-sniffing. The deceased chided him about his glue-sniffing and a fight ensued in which the deceased was fatally stabbed with a knife by the defendant. The House of Lords affirmed the general rule is that the effect of intoxication (whether alcohol, drugs or glue) is to be disregarded in assessing whether the accused acted as a reasonable person might have done. However, Lord Goff (at p 667) held that intoxication may be taken into account where the accused is taunted with the fact of his intoxication or with the fact that he is addicted to drink or drugs as the case may be. Lord Goff said that such taunts could be relevant to the gravity of the provocation.

6.5 Show the relevance of the case

Whichever of the methods suggested in **6.4** you decide to adopt for a particular case, it is essential that you make it clear *why* you have chosen to cite a particular case. In other words, you must make clear what statement or principle of law you have derived from that case.

This is good discipline. If you are unable to show why you have cited the case, then either that case is irrelevant or you have not properly understood the effect of that case. In either situation, it has no part to play in the chain of reasoning which leads to the conclusions you have reached.

6.6 Which case(s) to cite

If there are several cases which appear relevant, you do not need to cite them all. Certain general principles may be applied:

(a) Cite the case which is the most authoritative: if a House of Lords decision is on point, you should cite that in preference to a later decision of the Court of Appeal which merely applies the law stated in the House of Lords case.

(b) Where a later case interprets, or seeks to resolve an ambiguity in, an earlier case, you will need to cite both if the later interpretation is relevant to the case in which you are advising.

(c) You should generally cite only the case which lays down the general principle; do not cite cases which merely apply that general principle without adding to it in any way. For example, when dealing with the requirement of confidentiality which is implied into contracts of employment, it is usually enough to cite the leading case, *Faccenda Chicken v Fowler* [1987] Ch 117.

However, there will be instances where one case sets out a general principle and a later case then applies that principle to a set of facts which are very similar to those of the case in which you are advising. For instance, *Caparo v Dickman* [1990] 2 AC 605 sets out the general principle that liability for economic loss due to negligent advice is usually confined to cases where the advice has been given for a specific purpose, of which the giver of the advice was aware. In *Spring v Guardian Assurance plc* [1994] 3 All ER 129 the House of Lords had to consider whether a person who supplies a character reference to a prospective employer owes a duty of care to the job applicant to ensure the accuracy of the reference. If you were to be instructed in a case involving an inaccurate employment reference, or something analogous to such a reference, it would be appropriate to cite *Spring*, rather than *Caparo*.

(d) Do not cite earlier cases if a later case sets out authoritatively the principle to be applied. So, where one House of Lords case restates a principle set out in an earlier decision of the House of Lords, you need only refer to the later decision. For example, in the provocation example (above), *R v Morhall* may be cited in preference to the older case of *DPP v Camplin* [1978] AC 705.

(e) In some instances, the law which is relevant to the opinion you are writing is based on a series of cases. This will be so where an area of law is being developed by the courts, so that each of a series of cases adds something new to the case which preceded it. Sometimes, it is appropriate to refer to the cases all together; sometimes you should deal briefly with each case, showing what each case adds to the principles established by the earlier cases. But remember that you must always focus on the principles that are relevant to the specific case in which you are advising.

(f) You must avoid giving a history lesson, for example by referring to a source which no longer represents the law. An example of this fault would be to write:

In Hollington v Hewthorn *[1943] 1 KB 587 it was held that evidence of a conviction in a criminal court could not be tendered in evidence in a civil case based on the same facts. The effect of this decision was reversed by the Civil Evidence Act 1968, s 11, which states that evidence of a conviction is admissible in civil proceedings if it is relevant to an issue in those proceedings.*

The effect of *Hollington v Hewthorn* is irrelevant (since it was reversed by the statute) and should be omitted: you should set out the law as it is, not as it was.

It would have been much better to write:

Civil Evidence Act 1968, s 11, states that evidence of a conviction is admissible in civil proceedings if it is relevant to an issue in those proceedings.

(g) It follows from these general guidelines that some of the law which you find in the course of your legal research should be omitted from your opinion. The following summary should help to remind you of some of the pitfalls:

   (i)   Do not cite several cases which all say the same thing.
   (ii) Do not go off at a tangent (ask yourself whether you are writing things which are relevant to your instructions).
   (iii) Remember that all the law you cite must be relevant to the case in which you are advising. It will often be the case that you spend a considerable length of time finding some law, only to decide that it is not sufficiently relevant to merit use in the opinion you eventually write.

6.7 Using statutory materials

Much of what has been said about the use of case law applies equally to statutes. In particular:

(a) Only cite a statutory source if it is an integral part of the reasoning which supports your conclusions.

(b) Only cite the statutory source which is in force at the time when the facts of the case in which you are advising took place.

(c) If you can paraphrase the statutory wording, so as to make it shorter or clearer, then you should do so.

EXAMPLE

The Theft Act 1968, s 6 says that:

A person appropriating property belonging to another without meaning the other permanently to lose the thing itself is nevertheless to be regarded as having the intention of permanently depriving the other of it if his intention is to treat the thing as his own to dispose of regardless of the other's rights; and a borrowing or lending of it may amount to so treating it if, but only if, the borrowing or lending is for a period and in circumstances making it equivalent to an outright taking or disposal.

It would be better to paraphrase this fairly long and convoluted provision:

Theft Act, s 6, provides that a person can still appropriate property even if he does not intend the owner to lose the property permanently. This will be the case where the appropriator treats the property as his own, regardless of the other person's rights. If a person borrows property belonging to someone else, the borrower can still intend to deprive the owner of the property permanently if the borrowing in fact amounts to an outright taking.

If you decide to paraphrase rather than to quote from a statute, you should take care that your paraphrase is accurate.

Statutes should be referred to by their short titles: for example, the Criminal Appeal Act 1995. Statutory instruments should be cited with both their title and number: for example, the Road Vehicles (Construction and Use) Regulations 1986 (S.I. 1986/1078).

Where a statute (or statutory instrument) has been amended, you should only cite it in its amended form (assuming that the amendment was in force at the relevant time). For example, it would be appropriate to write: 'The Children and Young Persons Act 1933, s 49(5) (as amended) provides that....'.

6.8 Which sources to cite

Usually, you should cite only primary sources (that is statutes, statutory instruments and cases). However, the citation of textbooks and articles is acceptable in some instances. For example, where there is no authority on a point, academic opinion may be a useful guide to the answer; similarly if there are conflicting decisions and the conflict cannot be resolved by applying the doctrine of precedent (*stare decisis*), as where the only relevant decisions are conflicting decisions of the High Court, academic opinion may well be of assistance.

6.9 Apply the law to the facts

A common fault is to cite a case but not show how the case supports the proposition for which it is cited. If a source (such as a case) is worth citing, the relevance of that source should be made apparent. You should show how any source you have cited helps you to reach your conclusion.

There is a technique which you can apply to make sure that you are doing this. After you have made a statement of law, apply it to the facts. This is a good way of ensuring that you are not writing an essay.

EXAMPLE

In Alcock v Chief Constable of South Yorkshire *[1992] 1 AC 310 the House of Lords held that one of the preconditions to a claim for nervous shock by a bystander who suffered psychiatric illness as the result of injuries negligently caused to someone else, was that the bystander should witness the accident or its immediate aftermath. In the present case, Mrs Jones did not see the injuries sustained by her son until she saw him in hospital some six hours after the accident. In my view, this was not sufficiently close in time to the accident to satisfy this requirement.*

6.10 Producing sound conclusions

If you are writing an essay, there is often no need for that essay to set out a firm conclusion; it is enough for there to have been a wide-ranging discussion of the law. In an opinion, of course, the same does not hold true. Conclusions must be expressed; otherwise your instructing solicitor and your lay client will not have been advised what to do next.

If the result of your legal research is that there is clearly a right answer to a particular question, that answer must be stated and the reason why it is the right answer must be made apparent. If the result of your legal research is that there is no single right answer, as where there is no statutory provision or case law directly on point, the possible answers should be set out and the opinion should suggest which answer is most likely to be right and must give reasons for that view.

For an opinion to be of an acceptable standard, the conclusions it contains must be sound and must be supported by sound reasoning. In this context, the word 'sound' may be taken to mean 'the right answer or, if there is no single right answer, an answer which may be argued with a reasonable prospect of success'.

When you are writing an opinion, you must remember that you are no longer writing an essay for a law tutor but you are learning to write an opinion for a real client with a real problem. This means that your advice must be realistic. It is not appropriate to advise a client that they have a strong case if the weight of authority goes against your client's case but you think that the House of Lords may ultimately support it. So it would in the vast majority of cases be wrong to say that your client has a good case on the basis that a previous decision of the Court of Appeal is incorrect. It follows that you should not base your opinion on a dissenting judgment in the Court of Appeal, even if you think that the dissenting judgment would ultimately be approved by the House of Lords; similarly, dissenting speeches in the House of Lords should not form the basis of your conclusion.

6.11 Summary

In a *Practice Direction* [2001] 2 All ER 510, Lord Woolf CJ gave directions on the citation of cases in civil courts. Although these directions are aimed at advocates in court, they serve as useful guidance on the use of case law in opinions. The Practice Direction states that, where a case is cited, courts will pay particular attention to any indication given by the court delivering the judgment that it was seen by that court as only applying decided law to the facts of the particular case, or otherwise as not extending or adding to the existing law. Advocates who seek to cite such a judgment will be required to justify their decision to cite the case. Similarly the opinion writer ought not to cite cases which do not add anything substantive.

The Practice Direction goes on to say that advocates will be required to state, in respect of each authority that they wish to cite, the proposition of law that the authority demonstrates, and the parts of the judgment that support that proposition. Similarly, it is important for the opinion writer to be able to identify the specific principle to be derived from the case. Furthermore, the Practice Direction says that if the advocate seeks to cite more than one authority in support of a given proposition, he or she must state the reason for taking that course; likewise, the opinion writer should not cite two cases where one will do. The Practice Direction also requires the advocate to demonstrate the relevance of the authority or authorities to the argument he or she is putting forward, and that citation of the authority is necessary for a proper presentation of that argument. The same principle applies equally to opinion writing: if you cannot show the relevance of the authority to the point you are making, the authority is redundant.

6.12 Examples

For some examples of opinions involving law in their reasoning, see **9.4** and **9.5**.

7
Getting started

The preceding chapters should have equipped you with the theory that you need in order to be able to write an opinion. In this chapter, we put some of the advice to use in the context of a fairly straightforward problem. **Chapter 8** illustrates the process using a slightly more complex case.

The focus of this chapter is on the analytical process which precedes the writing of an opinion. It is worth emphasising at the outset that, although it is vital to be thorough and painstaking in your analysis, a lot of your analysis will not be included in the opinion that you ultimately write.

7.1 The problem

In real life, a brief received by a barrister will usually be a fairly substantial document. It is likely to contain:

(a) Instructions to counsel, usually summarising the key issues in the case and invariably seeking counsel's advice (sometimes asking for advice on specific points, sometimes seeking general advice);

(b) together with a number of enclosures, such as:
   (i) a proof of evidence (or witness statement) from the lay client;
   (ii) proofs of evidence (or witness statements) from potential witnesses;
   (iii) other documentary evidence, such as contracts, correspondence, maps/plans.

Note that a proof of evidence only becomes a witness statement once it complies with the requirements of the CPR on witness statements (for example, including a declaration of truth by the maker of the statement): CPR r 49.1. Once the evidence of a witness has been put into the form of a witness statement it will (at the appropriate stage in the timetable of proceedings and assuming that the evidence is to be used as part of the client's case at court) be disclosed to the other side and will stand as the evidence-in-chief of that witness at the trial.

To put the writing of an opinion into context, you may find it helpful to read **Chapter 12** of the *Case Preparation* manual, which provides an overview of the stages of a civil case.

For detailed guidance on the Civil Procedure Rules you should consult the *Civil Litigation* manual or *Blackstone's Civil Practice*.

In this chapter we will assume that the problem can be summarised very briefly as follows (and in the form very similar to the summary of facts which usually appears at the start of an opinion):

> Mr and Mrs Roberts own a large house. The top floor comprises a self-contained flat, which they let to tenants. At the beginning of March 2007, Mrs Roberts engaged Mr Cork, a painter and decorator, to re-decorate the flat. It was agreed that the work would be done during the week 20 to 24 March and that Mr Cork would be paid £1,500. The flat was due to be let to a Mrs Heller for 6 months from 1 April 2007 at a rent of £200 pw. Mr Cork carried out the work at the agreed time but the standard of workmanship was very poor. Indeed it was so bad that Mrs Heller refused to move into the flat and went to live somewhere else. Mr and Mrs Roberts had to get the flat re-decorated (at a cost of £1,200) and had to find a new tenant. They had to instruct an agent to find a new tenant. Eventually, a new tenant was found; he moved into the flat on 1 September 2007.
>
> Counsel is asked to advise Mr and Mrs Roberts whether Mr Cork is liable to them, and if so what damages they can expect to recover.

7.2 The analysis

In this part of the chapter, we work through the analytical process which has to be carried out in order to decide what your opinion will say.

It is vital that you go through the analysis step-by-step. That is not to say that all the matters you consider during the analysis stage have to appear in the final opinion. But your advice is likely to be incomplete and unsound if you have not adopted a very systematic approach to the analysis. It can be very tempting to get straight to the question of whether there has been a breach of duty—but if you do this you may miss out important matters that have to be examined to see whether there was a duty in the first place, and to whom that duty was owed. If you adopt a systematic, step-by-step, approach, you can be sure that your analysis will be complete, and that important matters have not been left out.

The structure of the analysis naturally varies a little depending on the nature of the cause of action. **Chapter 5** at **5.4.4** gives guidance on the structure to adopt when analysing the legal issues raised by your instructions. The structure will depend upon the nature of the cause of action.

In a contract case, you should use this structure for the purposes of analysis:

- Was there a contract between the parties?
- What are the terms of the contract in so far as they are relevant (dealing first with express terms and then with implied terms)?
- Has the defendant acted in breach of those terms?
- What loss or damage has the claimant suffered?
- Each head of damage should then be considered separately:
  - Was that damage caused by the breach of contract?
  - Was that damage within the contemplation of the parties at the time when the contract was made?
  - Has the claimant acted reasonably to mitigate the loss?

In a tort case, you should use this structure for the purposes of analysis:

- Did the defendant owe the claimant a duty of care?
- Was the defendant in breach of that duty?
- Was the claimant contributorily negligent?
- What injury, loss or damage has the claimant suffered?

- Each head of damage should be considered separately (but not necessarily in this order):
  - Was it reasonably foreseeable?
  - Has the claimant acted reasonably to mitigate the loss?
  - What is the quantum?

You therefore need to decide whether the present case is a contract case or a tort case, or a case where both causes of action have to be considered.

At each stage, it is necessary to consider how the facts of the case in which you are advising relate to the legal principles that apply. It is also necessary to consider which matters are likely to be in dispute between the parties. If you are advising in a case after the defence has been filed, you will be able to tell from the defence what matters are/are not in dispute. If you are advising before proceedings have been issued, there may well have been correspondence with the intended defendant in which he or she responds to the points made on behalf of the intended claimant, and so you will be able to work out (at least to some extent) where the areas of dispute are. Where matters are (or are likely to be) in dispute, it is important that the case analysis process includes consideration of what evidence might assist the claimant to prove the disputed matters (or evidence which might be called to rebut evidence adduced on those matters by the defendant).

With that in mind, let us now start to analyse the case against Mr Cork.

7.2.1 What is the cause of action?

It is pretty obvious that this is a breach of contract claim.

7.2.2 Was there a contract?

It is highly unlikely that there will be any dispute over the existence of the contract. Mr Cork has done the work, so it is almost inconceivable that he would assert that there was no contract.

7.2.3 Parties: does it matter that it was only Mrs Roberts who had dealings with Mr Cork?

Our instructions state that 'Mrs Roberts engaged Mr Cork', suggesting that the contract was between Mrs Roberts and Mr Cork. However, we are also told that 'Mr and Mrs Roberts own' the house where the work was done (in other words that the house is owned jointly by Mr and Mrs Roberts).

Two legal principles are relevant here: first, there is privity of contract. A person who is not a party to a contract cannot (subject to the provisions of the Contracts (Rights of Third Parties) Act 1999) sue on that contract. Secondly, loss should be claimed by whoever has suffered that loss. It is easy to get bogged down in this sort of issue. Suggesting that Mr Roberts could sue in tort and Mrs Roberts in contract over-complicates things. It is much simpler to argue that Mrs Roberts entered into the contract not only on her own behalf but also on behalf of her husband (that is, acting for herself and as his agent). It is very unlikely that the other side would bother taking issue on this point, or that a County Court judge would not readily accept your argument on this point. Taking this straightforward approach means that the opinion will not have to deal at great length with the question of parties.

7.2.4 Terms: which terms of the contract are relevant?

The most important terms of the contract are those which we will allege to have been breached. We therefore need to identify which terms may have been breached. In considering the terms of the contract, one should consider express terms first and then go on to consider implied terms.

7.2.4.1 Express terms

There may be express terms that are relevant to the quality of the work done by Mr Cork. For example, the contract might specify the materials to be used. Can you think of any other express terms about the quality of the work that might have been expressly agreed between the parties?

It is unclear whether the contract was oral or in writing. Counsel should ask whether the contract was in writing (or, if oral, whether there is any documentary evidence of the terms of the agreement). It is important that any written agreement should be checked (for example, there may be an exclusion clause in the contract). Who should check the contract or documentary evidence? In cases where a substantial amount of money is at stake, it would be appropriate for counsel to look at the documents. However, in a case where less money is at stake, the added cost of seeking further advice from counsel would not be proportionate; in a case such as this, it would therefore be appropriate for the solicitors to check the documents themselves.

The solicitors should, of course, have included any written contract (or written evidence) in the brief if they had it (assuming the lay client to be in possession of the paperwork—bear in mind that people have an annoying tendency to lose important bits of paper!). Unless your brief makes it clear that the contract was oral, and that there was no written evidence of its terms, you should ask your instructing solicitor to check with the lay client to see if there is any relevant paperwork.

In the present case, it may be that the contract was an oral one and that there is no relevant paperwork. In that case, Mrs Roberts will have to be asked for her precise recollection about exactly what was said between her and Mr Cork.

7.2.4.2 Implied terms

The present case is about poor workmanship, so (assuming there are no relevant express terms) we need to find a term that relates to the quality of the workmanship. Some types of contract contain specific terms, for example because of statutorily implied terms. We are concerned with a contract for the supply of services. Such contracts are governed by the Supply of Goods and Services Act 1982 ('the 1982 Act').

Section 13 of the 1982 Act provides that 'in a contract for the supply of a service where the supplier is acting in the course of a business, there is an implied term that the supplier will carry out the service with reasonable care and skill'.

In other words, provided that the work was done in the course of a business, it should be done to a reasonably competent standard. It is highly unlikely that Mr Cork will dispute that he entered into the contract in the course of a business. But can you think of ways in which you might satisfy yourself, or if necessary, the court, that Mr Cork was acting in the course of a business when he entered the contract?

It is important that, where you are relying on a statutory provision, you read the provision carefully and check to see if there are any statutory exceptions to the provision you are relying on and whether there is any case law interpreting the provision or defining its ambit.

Section 16(1) of the 1982 Act provides that:

'where a right, duty or liability would arise under a contract for the supply of a service by virtue of this Part of this Act, it may (subject to subsection (2) below and the [Unfair Contract Terms Act 1977]) be negatived or varied by express agreement, or by the course of dealing between the parties, or by such usage as binds both parties to the contract'.

Subsection (2) states that 'an express term does not negative a term implied by this Part of this Act unless inconsistent with it'.

Where the agreement expressly states that the obligation to provide the services is to be judged subjectively by the supplying party, this express provision for a subjective standard in the agreement itself overrides the s 13 implied term which would otherwise be implied: *Eagle Star Life Assurance Co Ltd v Griggs* [1998] 1 Lloyd's Rep 256. So it is very important to ascertain whether there is anything in the contract (or, if the contract was wholly oral, whether anything was said) that might override the effect of s 13.

All of this underlines the importance of checking whether the contract made any specific provision for the quality of the work, and of reading the relevant statutory provisions.

7.2.4.3 Is Mr Cork likely to dispute the existence of an implied term of reasonable care and skill?

Unless he argues that something was said which would have the effect of removing or modifying the statutorily implied term, it is unlikely that Mr Cork could deny the existence of the implied term. It seems unlikely that he will seek to argue that he was not acting in the course of a business.

On the basis that it is unlikely that Mr Cork will deny the existence of the implied term, the opinion is not going to have to set out the basis for implying the term in great detail. Merely stating the term and its statutory basis will suffice.

7.2.5 Breach: have any relevant terms been breached?

This is where the case becomes a little more controversial. It is possible that Mr Cork will admit that his work was sub-standard. However, it is perhaps more likely that he will deny this.

It follows that one of the main issues that the opinion will have to deal with is the question whether or not Mr and Mrs Roberts can prove that Mr Cork acted in breach of contract.

7.2.6 How can Mr and Mrs Roberts prove the breach?

As we have already seen, the standard of workmanship to be expected of Mr Cork under s 13 of the 1982 Act is that of a reasonably competent painter and decorator. Since Mr Cork may well dispute the allegation that his workmanship fell below the appropriate standard, Mr and Mrs Roberts will need evidence to establish, on the balance of probabilities, that the work fell below that standard.

So the opinion will have to point out the need for proof and to identify possible sources of appropriate evidence. In particular, an opinion should consider whether there is a need for expert evidence (in other words, opinion evidence from someone with special knowledge of the subject-matter of the claim). In deciding what evidence is needed, and especially whether expert evidence is needed, regard must be had to the value of the claim. It must always be borne in mind that expenditure must be proportionate to the amount being claimed, since this is one of the requirements of the Civil Procedure Rules, and is expressly included in the Overriding Objective set out in Part 1 of the Rules.

In some cases, it may well be that expert evidence is in fact unnecessary. It may be that the court can draw the necessary inferences from the factual information that is put before it, without the need for opinion evidence from an expert. In the present case, it is likely that the physical evidence of the poor workmanship will have been obliterated by the remedial work done by the second builder, so there may be little that an expert could do in any event.

7.2.7 Evidence

In this section we therefore look at some of the evidence which may help Mr and Mrs Roberts to prove their case.

The lay client is usually a very important source of evidence. In most cases, when counsel is asked to write an opinion, the solicitors will include a statement from the client (usually called a 'proof of evidence') in the brief. Even so, it will often be necessary to ask the client to provide more detailed information on specific points. In the present exercise, the opinion will have to identify all the matters which Mr and Mrs Roberts should deal with in their proof of evidence. For example, they should be asked describe in as much detail as possible what was wrong with the work done by Mr Cork.

There might also be supporting evidence—so they should, for example, be asked if they took any photographs of Mr Cork's work. This would be useful evidence to supplement the oral evidence of either or both of them.

The second decorator is likely to be a very important source of evidence. He is in a good position to identify what is to be expected from a reasonably competent painter/decorator and to enumerate the ways in which Mr Cork's work fell short of that standard. However, it is important to distinguish between two types of evidence so far as this potential witness is concerned. First, there is his purely factual evidence as to what he saw when he first attended the newly decorated flat. Secondly, there is evidence as to the standard reasonably to be expected of a painter/decorator, and as to whether or not the work of Mr Cork fell below that standard. As regards the second, care is needed as this sort of evidence is likely to stray into the giving of opinion evidence.

A witness can only give opinion evidence if he or she is an 'expert' (and so within the ambit of Part 35 of the CPR and the Practice Direction related thereto). The value of the present claim is just above the £5,000 limit for small claims, and so it will be allocated to the fast-track (and so the parties will almost certainly be expected to try to agree on a jointly instructed expert). It is highly doubtful that the decorator would have the necessary independence to be regarded as an expert. Given the relatively low value of this claim, the opinion can deal with this fairly briefly. Opinion evidence may even be unnecessary, in that it is possible for the court to infer from the factual evidence given by the second decorator whether or not Mr Cork's work was of an appropriate standard.

It may be that Mrs Heller might be able to give evidence about the decorative state of the flat, assuming she can be located and assuming she is willing to cooperate, both matters which cannot be taken for granted. She might be unwilling to cooperate for a number of reasons, not least because she might suffer a degree of inconvenience if she agrees to help Mr and Mrs Roberts (for example, having to provide a statement to your instructing solicitor and later to attend court would be quite time-consuming). People are often reluctant to get involved in other people's disputes, and so you should never assume that a witness will be willing to cooperate.

7.2.8 Losses: what were the results of the breach of contract?

Mr and Mrs Roberts can claim for each of their losses provided that the loss in question:

- was caused by the breach of contract (ie, it resulted from the breach);
- was in the contemplation of the parties at the time the contract was made (ie, it is not too remote), and
- is not something that could reasonably have been avoided (ie, the claimants have mitigated their loss).

These principles are well-known and so do not need to be set out at length in an opinion. However, in our analysis of the case, each of these principles does have to be applied to each of the losses sustained by Mr and Mrs Roberts.

The first stage is to list the losses sustained by the claimants. In the present case, the list comprises:

- the cost of re-decoration;
- loss of rent;
- cost of finding a new tenant.

At the analysis stage, each item of loss has to be considered separately. When it comes to writing the opinion, it may be appropriate to deal with some losses together.

7.2.9 Re-decoration

7.2.9.1 Causation

The need to re-decorate (remember that Mr and Mrs Roberts will have to prove that re-decoration was appropriate) clearly flows from the poor workmanship of Mr Cork.

7.2.9.2 Remoteness

This is loss that is almost certain to be regarded by the court as having been within the contemplation of the parties at the time of the contract because it is loss which flows naturally from the breach (ie, it falls under the first limb of *Hadley v Baxendale* (1854) 9 Exch 341).

7.2.9.3 Mitigation

If the work done by Mr Cork was sub-standard, there remains the question of what was the appropriate remedial action. For example, was complete re-decoration of the flat a reasonable response to the condition in which Mr Cork left the flat? Or could the problems reasonably have been remedied by something less drastic?

In an opinion it is important to suggest solutions, as well as identifying problems. So there should be advice on how to decide whether the Roberts mitigated their loss appropriately. This will have to include advice on likely sources of evidence on the question of mitigation.

The second decorator would be ideally placed to give evidence on this (though it has to be borne in mind that he may have had a vested interest in that he may have earned more money by doing a total re-decoration).

Can you think of other evidence that might be available on this issue?

7.2.10 Lost rent

7.2.10.1 Causation

The loss of the tenant probably flows from the poor decorative state of the flat, although the case could be strengthened on this point. Again, the opinion should indicate how. For example, by evidence from Mrs Heller—if her evidence is available—that she rejected the flat because of its decorative state.

What if Mrs Heller's evidence is not available? Mr and Mrs Roberts will have to explain to the court why they were unable to let the flat to Mrs Heller.

7.2.10.2 Remoteness

Whether this loss is too remote depends on the state of knowledge of the parties at the time when they entered into the contract. This loss is unlikely to fall under the first limb of *Hadley v Baxendale*. However, it may fall under the second limb, namely such loss as may reasonably be supposed to have been in the contemplation of both parties, since this is dependent upon the actual knowledge of the parties.

Again, the opinion must give practical advice. How might Mr Cork have known that the flat was to be let for profit? In answering this sort of question, you should consider who might have told him and what he might have observed for himself.

A key question, of course, is whether he was told by Mrs Roberts about the intended use of the flat. If not, was there anything else that might have led him to realise that the flat was to be let for profit? The proof of evidence supplied by Mrs Roberts will have to set out what information she gave Mr Cork about the intended use of the flat.

Think about whether there might have been any other way that Mr Cork could have realised that the flat was going to be let.

7.2.10.3 Mitigation

Finally, there is the question of the amount of the claim. Did Mr and Mrs Roberts act reasonably in trying to keep their losses down? It is always necessary to apply general questions such as this to the facts of the case. So, the question can be re-worded by asking whether it took Mr and Mrs Roberts an unreasonably long time to find a new tenant. Did they act as reasonable claimants would act in such a situation by appointing an agent? Did they supervise the agent appropriately? Should they have appointed more than one agent?

Consider ways in which these questions might be resolved.

7.2.11 The agent's fees

This head of loss must stand or fall with the claim for lost rent, and so it can be dealt with more briefly in your analysis of the case and, of course, in the opinion itself.

7.2.11.1 Causation

If the loss of rent was caused by the breach of contract, it must follow that the costs of trying to find a new tenant will also be recoverable.

7.2.11.2 Remoteness

If the loss of rent was within the contemplation of the parties at the relevant time, the costs of trying to find a replacement tenant must also have been within their contemplation.

7.2.11.3 Mitigation

It seems reasonable to use an agent to try to find a replacement tenant. It is therefore almost certain that the fees (unless excessive) will be recoverable. If Mr Cork were to argue that the agent's fees were unreasonable, what evidence could Mr and Mrs Roberts adduce to rebut this?

7.2.12 Can Mr and Mrs Roberts recover the contract price?

Mr and Mrs Roberts may well wonder whether they can get their money back, as well as receiving compensation for their losses. They might be thinking to themselves, 'He did a dreadful job—why on earth should we pay him a penny for it?'

The usual aim of damages for breach of contract is to put the parties in the (financial) position they would have been in had the contract been performed correctly. This is sometimes known as 'expectation loss' (although this is a term which should not be used in an opinion, as it is too academic).

We have to apply that general test to the facts of the particular case. If the contract in the present case had been performed correctly, what would the financial position have been? Mr and Mrs Roberts would not have incurred the expense of re-decoration and would not have lost their prospective tenant, but they *would* have had to pay Mr Cork the money they had agreed to pay him.

Another way of thinking of it is to use the benefit/burden analysis of contractual relationships. Each side undertakes a burden in order to receive a benefit. So, the customer undertakes the burden of paying the price and receives the benefit of the work being done; the decorator undertakes the burden of doing the work in return for the benefit of the contract price. So, the payment of the contract price (the 'burden' from the point of view of Mr and Mrs Roberts) confers on them the right to have their flat decorated to an appropriate standard (the 'benefit'). They cannot receive the benefit without paying the burden.

We are not told whether Mr Cork was in fact paid for the work he did. You should think about whether this would prevent Mr and Mrs Roberts from suing him at all, or whether he would simply be able to counterclaim for the contract price (which would then be set off against the damages he has to pay to Mr and Mrs Roberts).

It would be legitimate not to mention the question of the recoverability of the contract price in the opinion, unless you have been asked specifically to advise on it. As you have identified the losses that are recoverable, the reader can assume that any losses not specifically mentioned in the instructions to counsel are not recoverable if you have not advised that they are recoverable.

7.2.13 Conclusion

Every opinion must give advice, since that is what the client is paying for. Sometimes it will be possible to give a fairly certain prediction about the outcome of the case (based on the evidence as it currently stands). In other cases, counsel has to ask for more information or evidence in order to be able to give more definite advice as to the likely outcome. The present case falls into the latter category.

It is important to advise on the prospects of success for each issue and for each head of loss or damage. For example, there may be two causes of action but one is stronger than the other; there may be several heads of loss or damage but the prospects of recovering damages for some are better than the prospects of recovering damages for others.

Mr and Mrs Roberts have a good claim against Mr Cork, but only if there is evidence that his workmanship fell below the appropriate standard; whether or not some of the losses are recoverable depends on the state of Mr Cork's knowledge and the reasonableness of what Mr and Mrs Roberts did after the breach of contract by Mr Cork. The conclusion of the opinion in this case will therefore have to reflect the need for further evidence before firm advice can be given.

7.2.14 Next steps

An opinion should also give advice on the 'next steps' to be carried out. In a case such as the present, the next steps to be taken involve the acquisition of the evidence that is needed in order to enable more definite advice to be given. In other cases there may be specific procedural steps to be taken, such as seeking permission to amend a statement of case or to join an additional party to the claim.

The next steps must take full account of the procedural context of the case. We must consider, even at this early stage, which track the case will be allocated to. That allocation will necessarily affect the steps which have to be taken to pursue the claim and the volume of evidence that it is legitimate to gather, remembering always that the costs spent pursuing—or indeed defending—a claim should be proportionate to the amount of money involved in the claim. Expenditure which is not proportionate would not be recoverable from Mr Cork even if Mr and Mrs Roberts were to win the case against him. It follows from this that you should attempt to estimate how much the claimants are likely to recover.

How much do you think Mr and Mrs Roberts are likely to recover? To which track do you think their claim will be allocated? What restrictions does this impose on the expenditure which can be incurred in bringing the claim?

You can find further details of track allocation, and the consequences thereof, in the *Civil Litigation* manual and in *Blackstone's Civil Practice.*

One step that it may be appropriate to consider is the availability of some form of alternative dispute resolution. For example, if the intended defendant is a member of a trade or professional body (a fact that will usually be apparent from their headed notepaper or invoices), it may well be that the body offers an arbitration scheme. Care should be taken before agreeing to participate in such a scheme as appeals from the decision of the arbitrator may be very limited and use of the scheme may preclude subsequent litigation. The extent of the scheme should be examined carefully—does it, for example, cover all the losses that your client has suffered and could potentially claim in court proceedings?

7.3 Writing the opinion

Detailed guidance on writing the opinion itself may be found in **Chapter 5** of this manual. Remember that you should have adopted a structured approach to the task of case analysis prior to the writing of the opinion and that you should adopt a similarly structured approach when writing the opinion itself. Using checklists such as those in **Chapter 5** of this manual will assist you in this task.

The structure in the present case will be along these lines:

- What is the cause of action?

- How will breach of contract be proved?
  - Give specific advice on the evidence that is needed to prove that Mr Cork's work was sufficiently far below the acceptable standard to amount to a breach of contract (which will involve thinking about how the standard itself will be proved).
- Identify the losses suffered by the claimants.
- Is there any reason why some or all of the losses may not be recoverable?
- What evidence is needed to prove those losses?
- What evidence is needed to resolve the question of recoverability of losses?

By convention, most opinions begin with a summary of the facts of the case. This is not an invitation to regurgitate the entire story contained in the brief. Rather, it requires you to explain *concisely* the really important facts of the problem. The ability to set out the salient facts is an important aspect of case analysis, as it shows your ability to identify the most crucial facts of the case. You should not attempt to include every fact which you intend to discuss at some point in the opinion: rather, the summary should be a concise description of the facts so that the reader can understand the nature of the case about to be considered in detail in the body of the opinion.

Another convention is that the opinion should summarise what counsel has been asked to do. This paragraph (which usually appears after the paragraph summarising the facts) often begins, 'I am asked to advise ... '. Again, this is important. If your instructing solicitor has asked you to advise on specific matters, you must ensure that you do so. Noting any specific requests for advice in an introductory paragraph in the opinion helps to ensure that you do not neglect to deal with these specific matters.

Some barristers also have a further paragraph at the start of the opinion setting out their conclusions (which should normally include advice about the client's prospects of success in making or defending the claim, or recovering each of the heads of damage, as the case may be). Although not all barristers set out their conclusion at the start of the opinion, it is an extremely good discipline. It is essential that, before you start to write out your opinion, you know exactly what advice you are going to give. Otherwise, the opinion is likely to be rambling and discursive. In essence, you should set out your conclusions and then, in the main body of the opinion, show how you have reached those conclusions (and what further steps need to be taken). If you do not set out your conclusions at the beginning of the opinion, you must set them out at the end. Think about how you would express your conclusions in the case of Mr and Mrs Cork.

Note that your reasoning will generally be confined to the body of the opinion and will not also appear in your list of conclusions.

Your opinion will normally contain a section on 'Next Steps', in which you give advice on how to proceed with the case. This is, of course, one of the major differences between academic essay-writing and practical opinion writing. In some cases there is very little to say, but usually there is much advice that you can give on procedural matters. You may also wish to include advice about how to deal with the problem outside the courts; this is sometimes described as 'problem-solving'. Sometimes you may wish to comment on matters which may affect the lay client's decisions on how to proceed, such as their present or future relations with the 'other side'. Unless there is so little advice to give that it can conveniently be included at the end of your conclusion (if you give it at the start of the opinion), this section conventionally and logically comes at the end of the opinion.

There is a further section that may appear at the end of your opinion. Because you are writing a practical document, you will have been considering evidence throughout the body of your opinion. Many opinion writers add a summary of all the evidence or further information mentioned in the body of the opinion. This can be very helpful to the instructing solicitor, particularly if the opinion is a long one. It should go without saying that if you do add such a section it should match exactly the evidence/further information sought in the body of the opinion.

Remember that this chapter has focused on the analytical process which must precede the writing of an opinion. Much of the material produced in the analysis can safely be discarded when you come to write the opinion itself.

Make sure that you read through your opinion once you have written it. When you read through your opinion, you should ensure that:

- you proofread it carefully (correcting any errors of spelling, grammar or punctuation, and re-writing any parts that are not expressed clearly);
- you have covered all the matters that should be covered (including any matters upon which you were specifically asked to advise and any matters on which your advice is sought implicitly);
- your conclusions on the client's prospects of success on each issue are set out clearly and prominently and that those conclusions are consistent with your reasoning;
- you have given advice on what steps should be taken next (eg, procedural steps or the gathering of further information or evidence).

You should now have a go at writing out an opinion in the case of Mr and Mrs Roberts.

This chapter has been written about a brief in the form you might receive it from instructing solicitors. Note that under the 'Bar Direct' scheme barristers are increasingly likely to receive instructions directly from the lay client.

In Appendix D there is a sample opinion in the case of Mr and Mrs Roberts. It should be borne in mind that each barrister has their own personal style of opinion writing, and so you should avoid the temptation to use this sample as any sort of precedent. Rather it is intended to set out the matters that ought to be covered in the advice to those particular clients (remember that every case is different!) and to illustrate one way in which a barrister might express that advice.

8

An illustration of the opinion writing process

This chapter endeavours to set out the process of moving from a more realistic set of instructions than those found in **Chapter 7** to the writing of an opinion, looking both at the mental process and the preparatory work required. As in much skills work, this guide is not intended to be mandatory, but to provide a suggested basis on which you can build good working practices. This chapter picks up and illustrates many of the points made in **Chapters 5, 6 and 7**.

8.1 Instructions to counsel

<u>JACKIE RUSSELL</u>

<u>v</u>

<u>WATCHDOGS LIMITED</u>

Counsel is instructed on behalf of Mrs Jackie Russell, who is the owner of Falstaff Farm, Gadshill, Kent where she breeds and trains racing greyhounds.

At night the greyhounds are locked into the kennel compound, which consists of two kennels, each housing about ten dogs, in a courtyard enclosed by a high wall with a single iron gate. Outside the courtyard is an exercise area entirely surrounded by a wire-mesh fence. To keep watch, Mrs Russell hires a security company, Watchdogs Ltd ('Watchdogs'). By a contract made in January 2003 Watchdogs agreed, for a fixed charge (at the material time £250.00 per week), to provide a night patrol service whereby a patrolman would visit and check the kennel enclosure four times a night between the hours of 9.00 pm and 7.00 am. The contract contained the following clause:

> Under no circumstances shall the company be held responsible for any loss suffered by the customer through burglary, theft, fire, criminal damage or any other cause, except insofar as such loss is attributable to the negligence of the employees of the company acting within the course of their employment.

Throughout the period of the contract the regular patrolman has been Mr Harry Prince, whom Mrs Russell and her family have got to know quite well. However, on occasions (eg, when prowlers have been seen, or the night before a major race meeting) Mrs Russell has felt that additional security is necessary and has telephoned Watchdogs which has provided an all-night watchman at a fixed fee of £300.00 per night. There is no mention of this service in the contract.

On 18 April 2007 Mr Prince reported to Mrs Russell that on two occasions the previous night he had seen prowlers near the perimeter fence who had run off when challenged. Mrs Russell asked him to be particularly vigilant the next night and immediately telephoned Watchdogs to ask for an all-night patrol that night, which was agreed. No payment in advance was requested and indeed nothing was said about money.

That night, Mrs Russell's daughter, Elizabeth, was in the Boar's Head Inn, which is 100 yards away from Falstaff Farm, and saw Harry Prince drinking with a companion. He was there at 9.00 pm when she arrived and was still there at 11.30 pm when she left. Believing an all-night patrol had been arranged, she thought nothing of it. In fact it seems no all-night patrolman arrived.

The next morning, 19 April, Mrs Russell found that raiders had broken into the kennels. Two greyhounds, Pistol and Poins, were missing and a third, Peto, was dead. A veterinary surgeon found that he had been strangled and put the time of death at around midnight. The police found evidence that two men had cut a hole in the wire fence, sawn through the padlock on the iron gate and picked the lock on the kennel door. All had been left open. The police estimate that it would have taken the raiders about one hour to get in.

Pistol has never been found and it appears that he was the raiders' target. Poins apparently escaped through the open fence and roamed the countryside for two days. He was shot dead by a local farmer when he attacked the farmer's sheep.

Pistol had just retired from racing and was now at stud. He was expected to earn around £15,000 a year over the next five years in stud fees. Poins and Peto were both successful dogs each of whom was expected to win races worth £7,500 in all in 2007 and again in 2008. They would then have retired. Poins would have gone to stud. The estimated value of the three dogs is: Pistol £30,000; Poins £24,000; Peto £10,000. Mrs Russell was deeply distressed at the loss of her three favourite dogs and suffered from depression for several months.

Instructing Solicitors have received the following letter from Watchdogs:

Dear Sirs,

We must inform you that we have no record of any telephone conversation with your client on 18 April 2007 and we deny that any agreement to provide an all-night watchman service on that night was entered into. Mr Prince's log for that night shows that he made four visits, at 12.30, 2.30, 4.30 and 6.30 am. Your client's loss is plainly not attributable to any negligence on the part of our employees and we must accordingly deny any liability.

Yours etc

Mrs Russell on 3 July 2007 received a bill from Watchdogs containing the following items:

	£
Night patrol service 1 April to 30 June 2007 12 weeks at £250.00	3,000.00
All-night watchman service 3 nights at £300.00	900.00
	3,900.00

Mrs Russell says she arranged for an all-night watchman on three occasions in the period covered by the bill: on 2 and 18 April and 31 May.

Counsel is requested to advise Mrs Russell as to liability and quantum.

8.2 Preparing to write an opinion

8.2.1 Read the brief thoroughly

Your first step is to read the instructions in *Jackie Russell v Watchdogs Ltd* slowly and carefully. This brief consists only of instructions with no enclosures, so this is quite straightforward. There is no need to order papers before you start to read.

Be careful of forming strong views about the case on first reading, or you may prejudice the depth and width of your analysis in the following stages. In reading this brief the point is not to label the case 'breach of contract' as soon as possible, but on initial reading only to absorb as much of the factual background as possible. At this stage your mind should be asking questions about what caused the dogs to be lost, which is clearly the client's central problem, rather than starting to take decisions. The brief should provide counsel with all essential information or the solicitor may be found to be in gross dereliction of duty (*Locke v Camberwell Health Authority* The Times, 11 December 1989), but for reasons of time and cost it will rarely be very comprehensive.

8.2.2 Clarify your objectives

What do your instructions ask you to do? The instructions will never ask you to write all you know that is vaguely legally relevant, but will set you specific tasks, which are normally set out at the start or the end of the instructions. Here you are asked to advise on liability and quantum—whether the client can sue and if so how much she will get.

Having read the brief once and clarified your objectives, it is useful to read it again and annotate it. Annotating on first reading can be dangerous as what you are being asked to do may not be clear in your mind, especially in this case where your tasks are only set out at the end of the instructions. In annotating you should underline or highlight those points which are most relevant to whether there is a cause of action and to what has been lost, perhaps using a separate coloured pen for different aspects of the case, such as cause of action and damages.

8.2.3 Analyse the facts

Before you form views on the appropriate legal solution you will need to carry out a thorough fact management exercise. The legal argument must be based on the facts, not twisted to fit your preconceived legal theory.

Methods of fact management are dealt with in the fact management chapters of *Case Preparation*. Written notes of facts will be part of preparing to write any opinion. The following is a very basic analysis of the *Russell* case.

People	Mrs Russell. Client. Claimant.
	Watchdogs Ltd. Employed to keep watch on premises. Potential Defendant?
	Mr Prince. Employee of Watchdogs Ltd. Regular patrolman. Witness? Potential Defendant?
	Elizabeth Russell. Daughter of client. Witness?
	Police. Report on break-in.
	Vet. Report on death of dog.
	Those who broke in. Seems they cannot be traced.
Places	Mrs Russell's kennels. A plan would be useful.
Dates	January 2003. Contract for patrol service made.
	18 April 2007. Prowlers suspected.
	Mrs Russell calls to book all-night service.
	9.00–11.30 pm. Mr Prince in the pub.
	12.00 am. Break-in.
	12.30, 2.30, 4.30, 6.30 am. Mr Prince visits.
	19 April 2007. Loss discovered.
	July 2007. Quarterly bill for April–June sent.
Figures	Cost of patrol service. £250.00 per week.
	Cost of all-night watchman. £300.00.
	Loss of dogs. Capital value of Pistol, Peto and Poins £64,000.
	Income. Loss of stud fees for Pistol £15,000 per year 5 years.
	Loss of winnings for Poins and Peto £7,500 per year 2 years each.

Having analysed the basic facts, three further stages of factual analysis are important in preparing to write an opinion, because they are all closely related to exercising your judgment on the chances of the case succeeding.

(a) *Identify any gaps in the facts*   Almost certainly your instructions will not give you all the facts, as it would be very expensive and time consuming for instructing solicitors to collect everything before sending a case to a barrister. Your opinion will have to be based on the facts that are available. Gaps in the facts are important first because they may prove a weakness in developing a legal case, and secondly because in your opinion you will need to indicate to instructing solicitors what extra information should be sought. The main gaps in the facts in this case are:

(i) limited information about the agreement for an all-night watchman on 18 April;

(ii) limited information about the actions of Mr Prince that night;

(iii) limited information about the break-in;

(iv) limited information about the ability of the dogs to win races.

(b) *Identify which facts are probably agreed, and which are probably in dispute*   The point is that a case can be most firmly founded on facts that are agreed. Where facts are in dispute, your case is open to challenge and is less strong. Again this will be directly relevant to exercising your judgment on the case. In this case the facts which are probably agreed are:

(i) the existence of the original contract;

(ii) that the dogs were lost.

The main facts which are likely to be in dispute are:
(i) whether there was an agreement for an all-night watchman to come on 18 April;
(ii) what Mr Prince did on the night of 18 April;
(iii) precisely when the break-in occurred;
(iv) loss and damage.

(c) *Identify which facts you have evidence of* This is especially important in relation to facts in issue—if you have a fact in issue on which you have little or no evidence your case is very weak! Again this will be important when you come on to exercise your judgment. Also, your opinion should indicate to instructing solicitors where evidence is required.

In this case, the evidence which we have is:
(i) the original contract;
(ii) Mrs Russell's evidence;
(iii) Elizabeth's evidence;
(iv) Mr Prince's evidence (but query if he would appear as a witness for our client or for Watchdogs, and how useful his evidence would be if he is still employed by Watchdogs):
(v) the police report about the break-in;
(vi) the quarterly bill (which is not very clear as it does not give dates for the all-night service);
(vii) veterinary evidence on the death of Peto;
(viii) the farmer's evidence on the death of Poins.

(d) *Identify which facts you need evidence for* The further evidence we will need is:
(i) all possible evidence about the making of the contract for an all-night watchman on 18 April;
(ii) evidence about what Mr Prince did on the night of 18 April;
(iii) evidence of the capital value of the dogs (you cannot simply assume the figures in the brief are correct);
(iv) evidence of the income the dogs would have earned, which may be pure conjecture.

There is an important point about analysing the facts in the brief. When students start learning to write opinions it is very common for them to say that they feel they cannot proceed until they know all the facts. Such an attitude shows a failure to appreciate what the role of the barrister is and how cases must be put together in real life. Of course it is right that in practice one can telephone a solicitor to get further information, or even have a conference with a client, but this is not a reason for failing to write an opinion at an early stage, for several reasons:

(a) It is unrealistic to think that you will ever have all the facts about a situation. Some information is lost or destroyed, and other things are simply never recorded in any form.
(b) Some information is just not available to a client or his representatives as it is known only to the other side or to someone else.
(c) Only limited information will be available at an early stage in a case when initial advice must be given.

(d) Information takes time to collect, and it may well be that a client wants a general opinion without waiting.

(e) Information costs money. Costs should only be incurred gathering information when it is clear that this is necessary.

(f) Solicitors will normally not wish to spend time and money gathering substantial factual information before sending a case to counsel. They will wait for counsel's directions as to what is really required.

Therefore you must get used to dealing with gaps in factual knowledge in a positive way. Do identify precisely what information is needed and why and also build up confidence in using professional judgment.

8.2.4 Analyse the legal issues

Once the facts are fully analysed it is safe to start analysing the legal issues. This is where the professional ability of the barrister begins to come into play, deciding what legal possibilities there are, and which is strongest. The first question here is whether there is a cause of action, and it is best to try to consider every possibility, even if some are then dropped.

(a) *Breach of contract* The fact that there is a contract makes this an obvious possibility, but you must define precisely the contract and the breach. The contract in this case might be either the written contract signed in 2003, or a separate contract for an overnight watchman made orally on 18 April 2007.

As for the breach, start first by considering the express terms and how they might have been broken. There may be a breach of an express term, if it could be proved that Mr Prince never visited the premises at all on the night in question, or if there was a contract for an all-night watchman, and no all-night watchman came.

Go on to consider possible implied terms, remembering that you need to find terms that the court would be prepared to imply, and which you can show have been breached, leading to your client's loss. This needs clear thinking. It is not easy in this case as a number of terms that might be implied would not give rise to a claim, because the theft of the dogs would still not have been prevented. In other words, breach of the term would not have caused the loss.

(b) *Negligence* The fact that there is a contract should not lead you to think that only a contractual action is possible. This is the sort of error that results from taking quick decisions when reading instructions. The claim here may be based on breach of an implied term that the contractual services would be carried out with reasonable care and skill. In such cases there is almost certainly also a duty of care at common law, so that the claim may be brought concurrently in negligence. Liability is primarily contractual, but if there is also liability in tort it is usual to plead negligence, since the claim is founded on the identical facts. If, in this case, you decide there is a possible claim based on the failure of Mr Prince to carry out his duties properly, you will need to consider parallel tortious liability.

(c) *Other tort actions* As the central problem is the loss of the dogs, suing those who killed or took the dogs for conversion or trespass is an option. The difficulty here is obviously that these people cannot be traced. It is important to think widely in this way in planning an opinion, even if the option is dropped immediately as not being feasible.

Having looked for the range of possible causes of action, there is also the need to consider who should be sued. As has already been said, suing those who broke in is impossible here. The suggested defendant is Watchdogs Ltd, and this appears to be justified as the contract is with them. There is also the possibility of suing Mr Prince for negligence, but the case against him personally might be difficult to prove, and he is unlikely to be able to pay a substantial amount of damages. Professional judgment would therefore suggest simply relying on the vicarious liability of the employer.

8.2.5 Analyse the case against you

The case against you needs to be analysed in factual terms and in legal terms. Factual points were dealt with in **8.2.3** above, with the need to identify gaps in facts, facts in issue, and evidential difficulties. All of these are directly relevant to deciding whether the case will succeed.

In legal terms it is necessary to consider possible defences. Here the most likely defence is that Watchdogs will simply contend that there was no contract to provide an overnight watchman, which means that factual and evidential difficulties on this are particularly important. The second possible defence is that Watchdogs will dispute any implied terms on which you rely, and deny breach of them. You will need to prepare good legal arguments on this point. The third line of defence is to rely on the exclusion clause, the effect of which will therefore require full consideration.

8.2.6 Carry out any necessary research

It is important to take careful decisions as to what areas to research, or you will waste a substantial amount of time. **Do not start any research until you have fully analysed the facts and the law and can therefore draw up an appropriate research plan.** This cannot be over-emphasised. It is all too easy when first learning to write an opinion to do far too much legal research, for reasons that are not hard to see:

- academic study of law does require looking at the law in great detail, and it can be difficult to get away from this approach;
- if your knowledge of a particular area of law is limited or a little rusty it is very tempting to seek to re-learn the entire area;
- it is easy to be lured into feeling that reading a lot on an area may reveal a small point that will make a lot of difference to a case.

However, excessive legal research simply reveals a lack of good analytical powers and a lack of professional ability to work efficiently. This is not to say that detailed legal research of appropriate areas is not important, but it should be limited to what you have identified as being important for the case. The client does not want to know fine legal details but wants a result, and it is not reasonable to expect a brief fee to cover many hours of research that are not really necessary.

In this case you should not need to carry out any substantial research into contract law, as much of the law is basic principle. The legal analysis outlined in **8.2.5** might suggest that you would wish to research two areas:

- The circumstances in which a court will imply a term into a contract and what sort of term it might imply.
- The validity and effect of exclusion clauses.

8.2.7 Use your professional judgment

Now the professional ability really comes into play! You have a number of factual and legal pieces to fit together in a way that gives the client and the solicitor clear guidance. There is no easy way to explain how to do this—the proper exercise of professional ability can only come with practice—but what you are trying to do is to unite all the areas that have already been outlined:

- to assess all the legal possibilities;
- in the light of the facts; and
- in the light of the evidence; and
- in the light of what you know of the case for the other side;
- to weigh up which course is best;
- to meet the client's objectives.

Learning to use professional judgment is not easy. It is almost a chicken and egg situation. You cannot use judgment without professional experience, and you will not have the experience until you have had plenty of practice on cases. Thus to some extent a leap in the dark is required. However, confidence is an essential quality in a barrister, so you must have the confidence to start experimenting with using judgment to fill in gaps in a case and take decisions.

The first task in this case is to advise on a cause of action. From the points outlined above it would seem that the correct decision is that an action should be brought for breach of the all-night watchman contract. It is less clear whether a claim would succeed for breach of in implied terms of the night patrol contract and/or in negligence. You will need to consider this very thoroughly, choose your possible implied terms with care, and examine accurately whether it will be possible to establish breach of them. Then you must find arguments to avoid the operation of the exclusion clause.

The second task is to advise what the client can recover. This requires drawing up a comprehensive list of the heads of loss, looking at the arguments on each from the legal and practical point of view. The heads of loss are:

- The capital value of the three dogs.
- The lost prize money of all three.
- The lost stud fees.
- Mrs Russell's depression.
- The damage to the premises.

The difficulties are:

- Whether all loss is foreseeable.
- Whether all the loss can be proved.
- Whether there is any element of double recovery in claiming lost income and lost capital.

Figures for each head, collected together in analysing the facts, should be fully analysed here, with any appropriate calculation carried out.

8.2.8 Decide how to express your opinion

This is a professional skill that may require substantial practice and may well only come with experience. The difficulty is that you need to satisfy various requirements in expressing your opinion:

- Your opinion must be absolutely clear.
- If there are any options, they must be clear.
- Your opinion needs to weigh up and express the chances of success.
- Your opinion should avoid being too dogmatic or authoritarian. Give guidance on the law, but decisions on the case must finally be those of the client.

Combining these requirements is not easy, as they in some ways conflict. Guidance on expressing your opinion and giving your reasons is provided in previous chapters. Do practise trying to find appropriate words and expressions.

8.2.9 Draw up a skeleton opinion

Before writing your opinion, you should draw up a framework of all the elements to be included. This should ensure that everything is covered, and that a clear structure is followed. It is a false economy to start by going straight into writing an opinion without drawing up a skeleton, as you will often find that you miss something out or get confused and have to start again. *You should never have to waste time writing an opinion out twice. The properly planned opinion will be right first time.*

In drawing up the framework, you should be synthesising, summarising and choosing from all the preparatory work you have done. *A good opinion is a summary of all the work you have done on the facts and the law; it should never include details of fact management or legal research.* Thus much of the analysis carried out in this section would never appear in the finished opinion.

The following suggested framework amalgamates the points discussed above in a way that forms the basis for the opinion that follows in **8.3**.

OPINION

1   Introduction

    (a) Summarise briefly main facts of contract and loss.

    (b) Summarise conclusion.
        (i)   Action for breach of contract to provide all-night watchman.
        (ii) Action for breach of implied term of reasonable care and skill.
        (iii) Will get damages for loss of dogs, but problems with causation and foreseeability, and with distress.

2   Causes of action

    (a) Discuss whether one contract or two, one for regular service and one for all-night watchman on 18 April. Conclude better to allege two for clarity and to help avoid problems with exclusion clause.

    (b) Express terms and breaches:
        (i) That there would be an all-night watchman. Provided prove contract for all-night watchman, which may be difficult, clear breach.

(c) Implied terms and breaches:
  (i) That visits would be regular and/or sufficient for security. Implied to give contract business efficacy. Can probably show visits not sufficient for security, though note other side argues four visits made.
  (ii) That watchman would act with reasonable care and skill. Can rely on Supply of Goods and Services Act 1982, s 13. Can probably show breach of this, not only in that break-in, but in that should have discovered it quickly (they claim Prince visited at 12.30).

3 Defences

(a) Other side may argue that no contract for overnight watchman/no implied terms. Importance of evidence on the former, and legal argument and detailed wording on the latter.

(b) Other side may seek to rely on exclusion clause. We should refute this by arguing:
  (i) not part of contract for all-night watchman;
  (ii) on proper construction does not apply, *Photo Production Ltd v Securicor* [1980] AC 827;
  (iii) there was negligence so liable anyway.

Can't get rid of clause under Unfair Contract Terms Act 1977 since not dealing as consumer.

4 Quantum of damages

(a) Capital value of dogs. Will need proof of value. May be causation and foreseeability problems with Peto and Poins.
£30,000 + £24,000 + £10,000 = £64,000

(b) Loss of winnings. Can get damages for loss of a chance, *Chaplin v Hicks* [1911] 2 KB 786. Need evidence of ability. Also problem of double recovery, as capital value partly based on ability to win. Also deduct cost of keeping dogs.
£7,500 × 2 years × 2 dogs = £30,000

(c) Loss of stud fees. Similar arguments.
Pistol £15,000 × 5 = £75,000
Poins the same? = £75,000

(d) Depression. Can't normally get this for contract action, but see *Jackson v Horizon Holidays* [1975] 1 WLR 1468. Just a chance if argue security of mind part of contract, *Hayes v Dodd* [1990] 2 All ER 815.

(e) Damage to premises. Should be able to get damages for this. Need to establish figure.

5 Conclusion

Enclose draft. Offer further advice if appropriate.

                                                   Signed

Address

Date

8.3 Sample opinion

JACKIE RUSSELL

v

WATCHDOGS LIMITED

OPINION

1 I am asked to advise Mrs Russell with regard to the loss of three dogs from her kennels at Falstaff Farm, Gadshill, Kent, where she breeds and trains racing greyhounds. This loss was suffered on the night of 18/19 April 2007, when following a break-in, one dog was taken, one escaped and one was killed. I am asked to advise whether Watchdogs Limited, a security company, can be held responsible for this loss for failing to keep adequate surveillance on her premises, and if so, what sum may be recovered by way of damages.

CONCLUSIONS

2 In summary, I would advise that Mrs Russell can sue Watchdogs Limited, alleging breach of the agreement to provide an all-night watchman, and breach of implied terms that the watchman would be present for sufficient periods to provide security, and would carry out his job with reasonable care and skill. There is a good chance that this action would succeed, and that Watchdogs would not be able to rely on the exclusion clause in the contract.

3 I would anticipate recovering a substantial figure in damages, based primarily on the capital value of the lost dogs (£64,000), though there may be some difficulty with causation as regards Poins. Arguments of foreseeability, double recovery and mitigation will almost certainly prevent full recovery of figures for lost winnings and stud fees (£180,000). I have some doubt whether a claim for distress suffered by Mrs Russell will succeed. Subject to the strength of evidence on the capital and income values of the dogs and the circumstances in which they met their deaths, damages recovered might be below £70,000.

THE CONTRACT(S)

4 The first issue is the precise contractual basis on which Watchdogs were employed. While I am sure that Instructing Solicitors have brought to my attention all the relevant terms of the written contract that Mrs Russell made with Watchdogs in January 2003, I would be grateful for a full copy of it. It is not clear whether the service on the night of 18/19 was provided under this contract and/or under an oral agreement made by telephone on 18 April.

5 It appears to have been the understanding of the parties that all services were provided under one contract. There appears to have been no separate negotiation of terms beyond the mentioning of a price when an all-night watchman was provided previously, and the fact that Watchdogs appear to have understood all services to be provided under one contract is evidenced by their sending a single invoice for all. Perhaps Instructing Solicitors could check with Mrs Russell if this was her understanding.

6 However, the possibility that there was a separate contract for the all-night watchman is supported by the basic contractual principle that once a contract is reduced to

writing it will normally be taken to include all the terms agreed between the parties. I am told that there was no provision at all for the all-night service in the written contract, and it seems that Mrs Russell did not even know that such a service was available until after she signed the contract. There is clearly a separate fee for the all-night service. Although it makes relatively little difference whether there was one contract or two, I would advise arguing that there were two contracts, both for the sake of clarity, and so that it can be argued that the terms of the written contract, in particular the exclusion clause, do not apply to the oral contract.

THE BREACHES OF CONTRACT

(a) The agreement for an all-night patrol

7 The obligation under the oral agreement was to provide an all-night watchman for the evening in question. If we can establish this, there is a clear breach as it is admitted that no such watchman was supplied. The difficulty is to establish the agreement, as it was purely oral and has now been denied by Watchdogs. The evidence of Mrs Russell herself will be vital—could Instructing Solicitors please ascertain details of the telephone call she made. When did she make the call? Who did she speak to? What did she say? What was the reply? Can Instructing Solicitors also ascertain from Mrs Russell for what hours such a watchman would normally remain on the premises.

8 Evidence to support the making of an agreement for an overnight watchman on the night of the 18/19 would be very valuable. The difficulty here is of course that anyone who simply overheard the telephone conversation or was merely told about it will almost certainly only be able to provide hearsay evidence. It appears that the all-night watchman was sought following a conversation with Mr Prince. His evidence of this conversation might assist, but it is not clear whether we could or should lead his evidence. If Mr Prince is still employed by Watchdogs, he may well be called as a witness by them, and he may in any event not prove to be a useful witness for us due to a possible fear of losing his job. Even if he is not still employed by Watchdogs, our allegations cast doubt on his ability to do his job properly.

9 It may be possible to use the bill sent by Watchdogs as evidence of the agreement for the all-night watchman, though it does not specify the dates for which the charge is made. To define the issues between the parties at an early stage we should seek clarification from Watchdogs now as to the dates to which they allege the bill refers. Hopefully this will lead to a concession that there was an agreement to provide an all-night watchman for 18/19 April. There may be other evidence of this agreement in the records that Watchdogs disclose on exchange of evidence.

(b) The written contract to provide a night patrol service

10 The obligation under the written contract was to provide a regular night patrolman, his duty being to visit the kennel enclosure four times during the night between the hours of 9.00 pm and 7.00 am, and I understand that the regular patrolman making such calls was Mr Harry Prince. I assume he would not be the person to act as an all-night watchman when one was requested. As Watchdogs claim that Mr Prince did visit four times on the night in question there would seem to be no breach of any express term (but can Instructing Solicitors check with Mrs Russell whether she has any knowledge whether he did visit at the times alleged).

(i) Breach of implied term to spread visits over whole night

11 The first possibility is to imply a term that the patrolman should visit regularly, or at least spread his visits so as to provide reasonable security. It could be argued that there is a breach in spreading visits over only six hours rather than over the full ten hours from 9.00 p.m to 7.00 am. I would advise that such an implied term be alleged on the basis that it would give business efficacy to the contract, though I have some doubt whether we would succeed in establishing it, not least because it would undermine the purpose of security if the watchman always came at the same time as a result of spreading his visits evenly. It may be that we will need to get evidence of the business practice of security firms if this issue proceeds to trial.

(ii) Breach of implied term to act with reasonable care and skill

12 The alternative is to allege that there is an implied term that the watchman should do his work with reasonable care and skill. Such a term is implied by the Supply of Goods and Services Act 1982, s 13, and it will be easier to establish breaches of it, not least in that Mrs Russell had asked for particular vigilance on the night of the break-in. Watchdogs have admitted in their letter that Mr Prince was the regular patrolman for the evening in question, so a breach would arise when he spent at least two and a half hours drinking before doing his night's work—thus undermining his ability to do his job properly. Could Instructing Solicitors please get a full statement from Elizabeth Russell to establish the details of this. What was Mr Prince drinking? How many drinks did he have?

13 A further breach would arise in that Mr Prince totally failed to realise that the premises had been broken into although he apparently called four times after the break-in occurred! As there is only one gate he can hardly have been doing his job properly. Although I am grateful for the description of the premises provided by the Instructing Solicitors, I would like to have a detailed plan of the premises, with measurements. A statement from the vet as to time of death of Peto will be required to prove the time of the break-in.

THE EXCLUSION CLAUSE

14 Instructing Solicitors rightly draw my attention to the exclusion clause in the contract. While on the face of it this clause presents difficulties, as Watchdogs will certainly seek to rely on it, I feel that there are three ways of arguing that the clause should not apply. I do not think it can be argued that the clause should not apply as being unreasonable under the Unfair Contract Terms Act 1977, s 3, since it seems unlikely that Mrs Russell was dealing as a consumer.

15 First, if it is argued that the oral contract is separate from the written contract, it can be argued that the written term does not apply to the agreement for the all-night watchman. However, Watchdogs might argue that the clause does apply as a result of the course of dealing between the parties. Alternatively, it can be argued that on a proper construction the clause simply does not apply at all: *Photo Production Ltd v Securicor Ltd* [1980] AC 827. Such an argument would be based on the exact circumstances of what happened, and on the reasonableness of the term: *George Mitchell (Chesterhall) Ltd v Finney Lock Seeds* [1983] AC 803. Finally, it can be argued that even if the exclusion clause does apply it does not prevent recovery, as on its own wording there is no restriction of liability where loss is caused by the negligence of an employee of

Watchdogs. Clearly Mr Prince was negligent if he failed to notice the break-in during one of his four admitted visits, and if whoever took the phone call booking the all-night watchman failed to properly record it, they were negligent.

MEASURE OF DAMAGES

16 In general terms, if it is established that there was an agreement for an all-night watchman, then the failure to provide one can be said to have caused all the loss suffered by Mrs Russell. If an all-night watchman had been present there would presumably have been no break-in at all. If only breaches of implied terms are established, however, causation may present more difficulties, as it may be difficult to show that proper performance of duties would have prevented the break-in. However, it may be argued that at least the break-in would have been detected soon after it occurred, when it might have been possible to pursue the raiders and recover at least two of the dogs.

(a) The capital value of the dogs

17 The capital value of all three dogs should be claimed, but in addition to causation there may be arguments on the foreseeability of the loss of all three dogs. It seems that Pistol (£30,000) was taken by the burglars, but Poins (£24,000) merely escaped and was later shot by a farmer. I anticipate that we can successfully argue that it is foreseeable that a dog may escape following a break-in, may get hungry and attack animals, and may therefore properly be shot by a farmer, but we must be prepared for some difficulty. As regards Peto (£10,000), it appears that the dog was strangled, but it is not clear why. I can only presume that the dog barked or tried to bite one of the burglars, and it should be possible to argue that it is foreseeable he might be killed as a result.

(b) Winnings and stud fees

18 I anticipate difficulty in recovering the full sums lost under these heads. As regards the potential winnings of the dogs, £15,000 each for Poins and Peto, it will be necessary to provide expert evidence on the potential of each dog. There must be some doubt over how often each dog would have won, so while damages for loss of a chance are recoverable (*Chaplin v Hicks* [1911] 2 KB 786), it is highly unlikely that the full figure will be awarded for each dog. In *Chaplin v Hicks* the claimant was only awarded damages of 25% of the prize she might have won. The potential earnings at stud (£75,000 Pistol and a similar figure for Poins) are affected by similar arguments. Again expert evidence of the potential stud earnings will be required, and as it is possible that either dog might have failed to realise its full potential, a substantial reduction is likely to be made. Damages for the loss of both stud fees and winnings would also have to be reduced to take into account the cost of keeping the dogs.

19 There is a further problem with the figures for prizes and stud fees—they involve a strong element of double recovery in that the capital value of the dogs is presumably high simply because their potential winnings and earnings were good. At first glance it may seem better to go for loss of income (potentially £180,000) rather than capital values (£64,000), but the court is most unlikely to award anything like the full amount of income loss for the reasons already given. I would therefore advise that it is preferable to go for the loss of the capital value of each dog which can be more easily proved and is recoverable in full. However, the client must be consulted about this.

(c) Mrs Russell's depression

20   As for Mrs Russell's depression at the loss of her dogs, I am of course sympathetic, but as Instructing Solicitors will appreciate, the recovery of damages for distress is by no means an easy matter in a contractual action. Damages may be awarded (*Jackson v Horizon Holidays* [1975] 1 WLR 1468) but generally only when personal enjoyment is an element of the contract. In *Saunders v Edwards* [1987] 1 WLR 1116 damages for disappointment were awarded in a case where it was represented that a flat had a roof terrace when in fact it had not. However, in *Hayes v James Charles Dodd* [1990] 2 All ER 815 the claimant got no damages for distress when his garage did not have the rear access that had been represented to him as the court held that a commercial contract was involved. It might be possible to argue that Mrs Russell was buying peace of mind with the contract, but as the contract is really a business contract I am no more than 20% confident of success. It would be necessary to get medical evidence of Mrs Russell's depression, and she may well feel that she does not wish to go through with this with a low chance of success.

(d)   Damage to the property

21   Some damage was caused to the kennel enclosure by the burglars, and damages may be claimed for this. Figures should be sought for the cost of repairing the enclosure.

(e)   Taxation and insurance

22   Mrs Russell should be made aware that since the damages awarded compensate her for a loss in her trade of breeding greyhounds, any income damages awarded will need to be entered into her trading accounts, and will be liable to income tax. This might be an additional reason for seeking the capital value of the dogs, though then the possibility of liability to capital gains tax may arise, unless the money is used to purchase other dogs.

23   My instructions do not make it clear whether Mrs Russell was insured against the loss of her dogs. Perhaps Instructing Solicitors could investigate. While insurance would not affect the basis of this action, it might mean that Mrs Russell could recover from her insurers any sums she cannot recover from the defendants.

NEXT STEPS

24   I would advise that a letter before action setting out the key elements of this claim is sent to the other side forthwith. If a satisfactory response is not forthcoming then I would be happy to draft Particulars of Claim. Instructing Solicitors will be aware that the potential damages claim could justify commencing proceedings in the High Court, but as the case is not very complex the county court would be preferable, not least as regards to keeping costs down.

25   Hopefully this case will settle, and I would be happy to advise on terms of settlement or a Part 36 offer if so instructed. It would be helpful if such Instructions could include further evidence on the following if available:

(a) The response of Watchdogs as regards the dates covered by the bill (paragraph 9).
(b) Any further evidence from a veterinary surgeon or anyone who witnessed the event as to the manner of death of Poins and Peto (paragraph 17).

(c) Evidence from an expert as to the potential earnings of the dogs, and the likelihood that they would achieve those earnings (paragraphs 18–19).

(d) Medical evidence as to Mrs Russell's depression (paragraph 20).

ANN O'NIMOUS

3 Stone Court
Temple EC4

8th September 2007

8.4 Feedback on sample opinion

The above opinion is in many ways quite good. It is practical and realistic, it addresses the facts rather than the law, but uses the law where appropriate to substantiate the reasoning. It also gives thought as to how the case can be proved, and advises on further evidence required. Were it to have been written by a student, it would most probably be graded very competent.

However, there are some weaknesses and errors, which might be validly criticised. If you did not notice any when you were reading it, go back and read it again with a view to identifying where it could be improved. Then read the following points of criticism.

(a) The overall length is excessive. The complexity of the case does not justify an opinion of this length. There are various reasons why it has turned out to be so long. There are some matters that are really rather peripheral and could be left out. There are some issues which are dealt with in unnecessary depth. The writer shows a general desire to be somewhat over-thorough in reasoning and explanation.

(b) Paragraph 1 is not a good introductory paragraph. It does little to tell the story or set the scene. It presumes that the reader already has full knowledge of the facts. Although this may be true, it is still good practice to set the facts out more fully, so as to introduce the case to someone unfamiliar with them.

(c) Paragraphs 2 and 3 are probably trying to set out too many conclusions. What Mrs Russell and the instructing solicitor want to know at this point is simply whether liability could be established and whether Mrs Russell would recover in full for the loss of the dogs. The various bases of liability, the various heads of loss and the complications with regard to quantum could be dealt with later. A summary of conclusions at the end could be as detailed as this; an overall conclusion at the beginning need not be.

(d) The section on 'The contract' (paragraphs 4–6) is long-winded and to a considerable extent unnecessary. Since the conclusion at the end of paragraph 6 is that 'it makes relatively little difference whether there was one contract or two' and advises treating them as two, the preceding paragraphs are largely redundant. One could simply say that there is some doubt, but it doesn't much matter and leave it at that.

(e) Paragraphs 7–9 deal with the issue of whether it can be established that there was an agreement for an all-night patrol. Since this is so central, the writer is right to deal with it fairly fully. But this section lacks the most important ingredient:

a conclusion as to whether this can be established, or at least an assessment of the chances. The issue has been left undetermined, and so not properly advised upon.

(f) The statement in paragraph 8 that anyone who overheard the telephone conversation will only be able to provide hearsay evidence is misleading. If someone overheard Mrs Russell asking for an all-night watchman, this will be perfectly admissible direct evidence that she did so. It will only be hearsay as to whether Watchdogs agreed to provide an all-night watchman.

(g) In paragraph 11 the writer advises that we should allege an implied term that 'the patrolman should visit regularly, or at least spread his visits so as to provide reasonable security'. This advice is inconsistent with the advice in paragraph 2 that the implied term to be alleged should be that 'the watchman would be present for sufficient periods to provide security'. It is not just a matter of saying the same thing in different words. In paragraph 2 it is suggested that the term should relate to the duration of the visits, whereas in paragraph 11 the writer seems to have changed her mind and be thinking of an implied term which relates to the spacing of the visits. It does not look good to offer contradictory advice in this way.

(h) Also in paragraph 11 the writer advises that it might be argued that the term can be implied to give business efficacy to the contract, without explaining what the argument might be. If there is no argument, it might be better to go straight to the conclusion which follows, namely that there is not much chance of such a term being implied.

(i) The statement in paragraph 12 that Mr Prince would put Watchdogs in breach of contract simply because he spent two and a half hours drinking before doing his night's work is too sweeping and incautious. Of course he would be negligent if he were too drunk to do his job properly, but we would need more evidence of this. Elizabeth does not say *what* or *how much* he was drinking. Even if it was alcohol, it does not follow that drinking in moderation would make him unable to perform his duties with reasonable care and skill.

(j) In paragraph 13 the writer deals with the possibility that Mr Prince was negligent in failing to notice a gaping hole in the fence. As dealt with at this point, the advice seems to be that this might be a sound basis for liability. Only in paragraph 16 does the writer point out that there is a problem with causation. It seems perverse to separate breach and causation so misleadingly in this way. The issue clearly needs to be dealt with as one.

(k) When considering breach of an implied term in paragraphs 12 and 13 the writer should also have dealt with breach of a duty of care at common law, giving rise to concurrent liability in negligence. Although there is little to be said about this, since the claims are entirely co-extensive, it should be mentioned.

(l) The exclusion clause is dealt with in paragraphs 14 and 15. The same fault appears as in the section on the all-night contract: there is no conclusion on the issue of whether the exclusion clause could or could not be relied upon by Watchdogs. Only the arguments are rehearsed—there is no advice.

(m) The subheading 'Measure of damages' above paragraph 16 is wholly inappropriate: the paragraph is dealing with the issue of causation.

(n) The point in the last sentence of paragraph 16, that if the break-in had been discovered early there would perhaps have been a greater chance of recovering the dogs, is a valid one. But it will be very difficult to produce evidence to show

84　An illustration of the opinion writing process

this. The writer treats it as a matter of argument rather than evidence, which is misleading and speculative.

(o) Paragraph 18 deals with the recoverability of the lost winnings, and although it rightly points out the evidential difficulties, seems to express the view that these losses are recoverable. But then in paragraph 19 the writer seems immediately to contradict this opinion by pointing out, again correctly, the problem of double recovery and in the end advising that the claim is in reality for the value of the dogs. It would surely be better to raise the double recovery point at the outset, and then reach the same conclusion. This will save time.

(p) The advice in paragraph 20 is muddled. The writer has confused distress and depression. It is correct to conclude, for the reasons given, that Mrs Russell is unlikely to recover damages for distress. But the instructions refer to depression, which is in many cases a medical condition. If Mrs Russell suffered from clinical depression, then this was a personal injury, and damages would in principle be recoverable, if not too remote. Further instructions are needed.

8.5　An alternative opinion

<u>JACKIE RUSSELL</u>

v

<u>WATCHDOGS LIMITED</u>

<u>OPINION</u>

1　On the night of 18/19 April 2007, thieves broke in to the kennel compound at Falstaff Farm, Gadshill, Kent, where Mrs Jackie Russell breeds and trains racing greyhounds. Three of Mrs Russell's favourite dogs were lost: Pistol was stolen, Poins was allowed to escape, and was later shot by a farmer, and Peto was strangled. Mrs Russell was distressed and suffered from depression for several months.

2　Security was supposed to be provided at the compound by Watchdogs Limited ('Watchdogs') at two levels and under two separate agreements. There was a written agreement to provide a regular night patrol service, under which a patrolman (Mr Harry Prince) was to make four visits a night between the hours of 9.00 pm and 7.00 am. Mrs Russell says that there was also an oral agreement, made by telephone on 18 April, to provide an all-night watchman for just that one night. But Mr Prince seems not to have made any of his four visits until after the thieves had departed; and the all-night watchman never turned up.

3　I am asked to advise Mrs Russell as to liability and quantum in any claim that might be made against Watchdogs for the loss of the dogs.

CONCLUSION

4　In my opinion there is a good chance that liability can be established against Watchdogs for breach of the all-night watchman agreement (though not the night patrol agreement) and that Mrs Russell will recover damages representing the value of the three dogs, about £64,000, plus incidental expenses. It may be possible to recover a larger sum representing the lost earnings of the dogs, but this is not likely and will be hard to prove. My reasons are set out below.

LIABILITY

The all-night watchman agreement

5   Watchdogs are denying that they agreed to provide an all-night watchman on the night of 18/19 April 2007. They claim they have no written record of the telephone call made by Mrs Russell on 18 April. However, they sent a bill charging Mrs Russell for an all-night watchman on three occasions between 1 April and 30 June, and Mrs Russell says that those three occasions include the night of 18 April. Unless Mrs Russell has forgotten some other occasion when she used the service in this period, this bill should provide good evidence of the existence of the agreement. I advise that a copy should be sent to Watchdogs, or their solicitors, inviting them to say on what dates they allege the all-night service was provided, and to admit that one of the dates referred to is 18 April. It would also be useful to find out if any member of Mrs Russell's family (Elizabeth perhaps?) overheard her asking for an all-night watchman on the telephone. Unless any evidence to the contrary appears, I think it likely that the existence of the all-night watchman agreement can be established.

6   Once it has been shown that Watchdogs agreed to provide an all-night watchman, liability should be established without difficulty. Watchdogs admit that no such service was provided on that night. I think a court would have little difficulty in concluding that if it had been, the break-in would probably not have occurred. Both breach and causation can therefore be made out.

7   Watchdogs' only possible defence would be to rely on the exclusion clause referred to by Instructing Solicitors. They would have to show that the clause was incorporated into the oral agreement. On the face of it, this is unlikely. The night patrol contract makes no reference to the all-night watchman service, and it is difficult to see how it could be argued that this service was provided under the written contract. It would have to be argued that the exclusion clause was incorporated into the oral agreement by implication. There are two ways in which this could be the case:

(a) If the implication is based on the previous dealings between the parties; for example if they had on other occasions expressly agreed to incorporate it. I would ask Instructing Solicitors to find out from Mrs Russell if anything along these lines has ever been discussed.

(b) If the exclusion clause is contained in a separate document comprising standard terms and conditions which is merely referred to in the night patrol agreement. If so, it might be argued that the standard terms affect all agreements made between the parties. I would like to see a copy of the relevant documents, in order to see if this might be the case.

Neither of these possibilities seems likely. If, as I am instructed, arrangements for an all-night watchman have always been made by telephone, and Mrs Russell has no memory of the exclusion clause or standard terms being mentioned, then it probably was not.

8   But even if the clause is incorporated into the oral agreement, I do not think Watchdogs will be able to rely on it. Applying the principle of *Photo Production Ltd v Securicor Transport Ltd* [1980] AC 827, it cannot have been the parties' intention, on a true construction of the contract, that the exclusion clause should protect Watchdogs in the event of their failing to perform the contract altogether.

9   In my opinion, therefore, the chances of establishing liability for breach of the all-night watchman agreement are good.

The night patrol agreement

10   I think it is unlikely that liability could be established for any breach of the night patrol agreement. There is no evidence to suggest that Mr Prince did not make the four visits he was supposed to make, except perhaps the surprising fact that he apparently never noticed the hole in the fence. But I do not think this alone would prove his failure to patrol, and there is no more. The times of his visits did not apparently coincide with the probable time of the raid. Therefore there is no breach of the express terms of the agreement. It could be argued that there must be an implied term in the agreement that there would be a reasonable space between the patrol visits—all four visits in the space of an hour between 6.00 am and 7.00 am, for example, would surely defeat the purpose of the agreement. But I do not think Mr Prince's pattern of attendance that night (as alleged by Watchdogs) could be said to be unreasonable, given the need not to be too consistent, and the very low cost (about £36 per night) of the service.

11   There is of course also an implied term in the agreement to the effect that Mr Prince would patrol with reasonable care and skill (Supply of Goods and Services Act 1982, s 13) and Watchdogs would owe the same duty at common law. It might be shown that Mr Prince was negligent either in having consumed too much alcohol or in failing to notice the hole in the fence, or both (the two might be connected). But no causation would flow from such a breach. If the raid occurred before midnight, no amount of vigilance on Mr Prince's part could have prevented it. The only faint possibility of establishing liability on this basis rests on being able to show that if Mr Prince had noticed the break-in at 12.30 am and raised the alarm, Pistol and Poins would have been saved. But it is hard to see where evidence to support this could come from, and I do not think a court would find it inherently probable.

12   I do not therefore think there is much chance of establishing any liability for breach of the night patrol contract. Even if the problems I have mentioned could be surmounted, I think Watchdogs probably would in this instance be able to rely on their exclusion clause (unless liability was based on Mr Prince's negligence). It is not in my opinion an unreasonable exclusion given the very limited amount of security Watchdogs were supposed to provide and the low cost of the service.

QUANTUM

The loss of the dogs

13   Mrs Russell would in my opinion be able to recover damages for the loss of all three dogs. I do not think there is any problem of remoteness in respect of Pistol or Peto, but it might be argued that the death of Poins was too remote. However, I think this argument would not succeed. It was plainly within the contemplation of the parties that if there was no security provided at the compound, a dog could be stolen or harmed or escape. It was foreseeable that a dog that escaped might come to harm. It does not matter if the precise manner in which Poins met his death was not within the parties' contemplation providing the type of harm was contemplated (*Parsons (H) (Livestock) Ltd v Uttley Ingham & Co Ltd* [1978] QB 791).

14   The question arises whether Mrs Russell can recover damages based on the value of the dogs, their likely earnings, or both. On the assumption that their market value

reflects their profit-earning potential, it will not be possible to recover the lost earnings in addition to their value, as that would amount to double recovery. There is no doubt that Mrs Russell will be entitled to the market value of the dogs; that is the normal basis of assessment for the loss of goods (even such treasured goods as Pistol, Poins and Peto). But where the goods are profit earning, it is sometimes possible to recover instead the loss of profit.

15 On the face of it, that seems to be a significantly larger sum—up to £180,000 or more as against £64,000. But the figures I have for likely earnings are presumably gross, and must be reduced to take account of the costs of keeping, training, guarding and insuring the dogs. Doubtless this would bring the loss of earnings down substantially. There would also be the difficulty of proof. Mrs Russell would have to produce evidence as to the likely earnings of the dogs over the rest of their lives, which may not be easy, and would require some speculation. I think it likely that the court would prefer expert evidence of value, taking account of earning potential, in any event. I therefore advise Mrs Russell to claim on the basis of value, unless she is able to put forward strong evidence to show a probable level of net profit significantly greater than these sums.

Distress and depression

16 I do not think Mrs Russell can recover damages to compensate her for her grief or distress. Such damages may be recoverable in contract where the contract is one to provide peace of mind, or personal enjoyment, as in the spoilt holiday cases. They may be recoverable where that is only part of the purpose of the contract: *Farley v Skinner* [2001] 4 All ER 345. But however much she loved her dogs, Mrs Russell is essentially running a business, and I think the court would treat this as a commercial contract, in which case damages for distress are almost certainly irrecoverable: see for example *Hayes v James Charles Dodd* [1990] 2 All ER 815.

17 On the other hand if Mrs Russell's depression was a depressive illness requiring medical treatment, then she has a potential claim for personal injury. If Instructing Solicitors could arrange for a medical report to be obtained substantiating this, then I advise that such a claim can be made. However, I do not have great confidence in its success. The difficulty would be remoteness. I think Watchdogs might well argue successfully that personal injury of this kind was not a foreseeable consequence of their failure to provide an all-night patrolman.

Damage to property

18 In addition, Mrs Russell should be able to recover damages for the cost of repairing the fence and replacing the padlock, any veterinary bills in connection with Poins' and Peto's deaths and any other incidental expenses resulting from the break-in.

EVIDENCE

19 It may help Instructing Solicitors if I recap on the further steps to be taken and evidence that might be sought. I advise the following:

(a) Send a copy of the bill received on 3 July 2007 to Watchdogs or their solicitors, inviting them to admit that one of the nights referred to is 18/19 April 2007.

(b) Ask Mrs Russell whether anyone (Elizabeth possibly) overheard her telephone conversation with Watchdogs on 18 April 2007. If so, seek evidence from that person as to what they heard Mrs Russell say, in particular whether they heard her ask for an all-night patrolman that night, and whether it sounded as though Watchdogs were agreeing to that request.

(c) Obtain all documents relating to agreements between Mrs Russell and Watchdogs, especially any documents containing standard terms and conditions and documents referring to the all-night watchman service.

(d) Ask Mrs Russell whether all previous requests for an all-night watchman have been made by telephone, and, whether in any of those phone calls, reference has been made to standard terms and conditions or exclusion clauses.

(e) Obtain expert evidence on the value of Pistol, Poins and Peto immediately prior to their deaths, taking account of their earning potential.

(f) Consider whether it is reasonably practicable to obtain evidence of the likely earnings of Pistol, Poins and Peto over the remainder of their natural lives, both in winnings and stud fees, together with an estimate of the costs of keeping, training, guarding and insuring those dogs over the same period. Only go ahead with obtaining such evidence if it is reasonably practicable to do so, and likely to result in a larger claim than £64,000.

(g) Enquire whether Mrs Russell has been diagnosed as suffering from a recognised depressive illness, and if so obtain a medical report relating to this illness, its consequences, treatment and prognosis.

(h) Collate bills and receipts relating to the cost of repairing the fence and the padlock, veterinary expenses in relation to Poins's and Peto's deaths, and any other incidental expenses caused by the break-in.

Conclusion

20 I advise accordingly that a claim should be pursued against Watchdogs for their breach of contract in failing to provide an all-night watchman and that it has good prospects of success. The claim should provisionally be for the market value of the three dogs, plus incidental expenses and possibly also for Mrs Russell's depression, but this last may not be recovered. I would be happy to advise further and draft Particulars of Claim if so requested.

JOSEPH BLOGGS

4 Gray's Inn Place
8th September 2007

9

Examples of barristers' opinions

The five opinions in this chapter are all real opinions or advices written by barristers in real cases. Only names, places and dates have been changed. They will serve to give you some idea of differences in style, and how opinions can be tailored for different circumstances.

9.1 Liability and damages—personal injury

This first opinion is a fairly typical practical example of an opinion on liability and damage in a personal injury case. Note the emphasis not just on liability, but how it can be established. This opinion is also an example of a case where not everything is straightforward or in the claimant's favour when it comes to damages.

DAVID GATTON Claimant

and

JOHN DONALDSON Defendant

OPINION

Introduction

1 I am asked to advise Mr Gatton as to his prospects of successfully recovering damages for personal injuries sustained in a road traffic accident that occurred on 13th September 2005. To assist me in considering both liability and quantum, Instructing Solicitors have provided to me a bundle of documents, including a statement from the client and a medical report dated 28th February 2006 prepared by Mr Woodhead, a Consultant Orthopaedic Surgeon who was jointly instructed by the parties.

Background

2 According to Mr Gatton, he was (together with two friends) in the process of crossing the road at the junction of Boggle Road and Boggle Hill, Nuthatch, Kent. There is no central refuge on this part of Boggle Road, and Mr Gatton and his friends were crossing at the point at which the footpath on either side of Boggle Road is lowered. As he did so, the Defendant (who was driving along Boggle Road in an easterly direction towards the Nuthatch town centre) drove through a red light controlling traffic travelling east on Boggle Road and, as a result, struck Mr Gatton. His friends were

fortunate enough to be able to run to the other side of the road. It may well have been that, faced with the apparently sudden approach of the Defendant's vehicle, Mr Gatton was affected by a moment of indecision as to whether to continue or retreat, though this, it must be said, is presently unclear.

Liability

3   I note that the Defendant's insurers have rejected Mr Gatton's claim and that this is on the basis that it was he that was responsible for causing this accident. The Defendant's response to the Letter of Claim was to allege that he had lawfully travelled through the traffic signal, which was green in his favour, when Mr Gatton drunkenly wandered into the path of his vehicle. It seems to be common ground that Mr Gatton had consumed some alcohol. There is, however, some apparent discrepancy between his own account to Instructing Solicitors (having had one drink) and the statement attributed to him by the police that he 'had had several drinks', though in each case he maintained that he was not drunk. In addition, Mr Gatton's account, given to police, was that the vehicle was not in view when he began to cross the road, and that he was already in the middle of the road when it arrived. However, according to his companions, the car was in view as it was stationary at the traffic lights. To the extent that this might amount to a discrepancy in the eyewitness accounts, it may be explained by the fact that Mr Gatton said that he had little recollection of the events immediately before he was struck. This potential gap in Mr Gatton's recollection may very well be accounted for as a consequence of his injuries but no doubt the Defendant may want to assert that it is due to the effects of alcohol.

4   There appears to be one additional witness, the driver of a Ford Focus, who it appears might be the only independent eyewitness. This witness had, on the facts presently before me, been travelling in the opposite direction to the Defendant and had arrived at and was stationary at the traffic signals. He was therefore on the same side of the road from which Mr Gatton and his friends were crossing. It seems from the correspondence that it is being suggested that this potential witness may provide favourable evidence on the Defendant's behalf though his insurers have been curiously reluctant to provide Instructing Solicitors with any specific details about the witness and any information that he has provided to them about the circumstances of the accident. Of course, such an independent witness may prove to be highly significant and the Defendant's insurers may consider that the information that he is able to give will be set out in due course in a witness statement. If that is the approach that is being adopted it is of course not just regrettable but would be somewhat inconsistent with the pre-action protocol which requires the parties to cooperate and to facilitate the early exchange of information. Those instructing may wish to write again to the Defendant's insurers reminding them of these obligations and also of the likely cost consequences for failing to cooperate.

5   There is a conflict of evidence between Mr Gatton and the Defendant on a number of key issues that the court will need to consider. First, of course, is the question of whether the traffic signals were red against the Defendant. It is important to note that the driver of the Ford Focus had brought his vehicle to a halt at the traffic signal. That fact is clearly not consistent with what the Defendant asserts, and may explain the reluctance of the insurers to provide any further details about the witness. A second issue may be that, in crossing the road from what would be the Defendant's right to left, the Defendant would have had ample time to see the group. Mr Gatton and his

friends had got to a point in the road (at least in the centre if not beyond) where they would have been visible directly ahead of the Defendant as he approached on Boggle Road. Mr Gatton then proceeded to cross the junction. If the court were to find that the Defendant failed to see Mr Gatton in the middle of the road or to slow his vehicle and drove on regardless, then it is likely that the issue of primary liability would be decided in Mr Gatton's favour. Given the likely conflict of evidence about what the Defendant did and how Mr Gatton came to be in the road, there will clearly need to be very full statements obtained from each of Mr Gatton's friends. It is also important for a detailed sketch plan of the location to be prepared, and this should be supported by photographic evidence of views of the junction and the east and west approaches to the traffic signal on Boggle Road.

General Damages

6 Mr Gatton, who was aged 22 at the time, was taken to the accident and emergency department of the Nuthatch Hospital where he was examined but was not detained overnight. He was a student at the time of the accident coming to the end of a three-year course in pottery. He had played soccer for his college team and in fact had started coaching a local under-nines mini-soccer team. Since the accident and the injury to his legs he has been unable to play football and has also had to give up his interest in coaching the mini-soccer team.

7 To assist me in considering general damages, I have been greatly assisted by the report prepared by Mr Woodhead. When examined, Mr Gatton was found to have suffered a number of injuries including muscular ligamentous injuries to both knees, soft tissue injuries and bruising to the right foot, right thigh, hip, right shoulder and elbow, and bruising and tenderness over the right temple. Mr Gatton was clearly very badly shaken up and was clearly in very significant pain. The notes record that there was some suggestion that he was suffering pre-accident amnesia. He was discharged home and remained in substantial pain from his injuries, and was unable to bear weight on his right foot, which became swollen over the following days. As a result, a week after the accident, he consulted his general practitioner who again referred him to the Nuthatch Hospital. On this occasion an x-ray was taken which showed a comminuted fracture of the right foot with swelling and tenderness along the left calf.

8 Curiously, that fracture to the right foot and calf was either not detected or not noted at the time of the initial examination at the hospital. Whilst the failure to diagnose those injuries would not alter my assessment, which attributes primary liability to the Defendant, I am concerned that it may be relevant as either having caused or contributed to the deep vein thrombosis that appears to be the cause of the majority of Mr Gatton's present problems. That condition is happily rare in individuals of Mr Gatton's age, but if its occurrence is connected with the failure to detect and treat appropriately the injuries to the right leg, then consideration may need to be given as to whether a claim ought to be made against the local area's NHS Trust. Of course, were it to be concluded that there was evidence sufficient to indicate that there had been clinical negligence on the part of the NHS Trust, there would arise a need to give notice as required by the Pre-Action Protocol for the Resolution of Clinical Disputes.

9 Over 12 months have elapsed since Mr Woodhead's report was prepared. The initial assessment was that Mr Gatton would make a full but staged recovery from his injuries over a period of about six to 12 months. That assessment addressed mainly the orthopaedic injuries that Mr Gatton had suffered. There was neither detailed

consideration of the effect of the injury to his head, nor the onset of the deep vein thrombosis. Moreover, it is clear from the statement that has been provided to me that there are ongoing problems associated with the client's right leg and his shoulders, and there may be some continuing amnesia. I understand that the parties consider that it is appropriate that a supplementary report should be obtained to deal with these and the issue in the last paragraph, and also to provide a detailed prognosis dealing with Mr Gatton's capability to undertake the work that he had trained to do. I respectfully agree with that approach and hope that arrangements can be made promptly between the parties for Mr Woodhead to examine Mr Gatton again. Mr Gatton appears to have suffered some amnesia and it would be prudent to also consider whether the head trauma he suffered (the blow to the right temple) could have caused that condition. The extent of Mr Gatton's amnesia and the effect upon him should also be considered. In these circumstances it seems to me that a concluded view as to the likely level of general damages cannot be provided at this stage, and ought properly to await the outcome of the examinations and any additional medical reports that are obtained.

Special Damages

10   I turn then to consider special damages. The most significant element under this head would appear to be a claim for loss of earnings but, in addition, there are claims connected with various out-of-pocket expenses such as travel and medical expenses, that ought to be recoverable by Mr Gatton.

11   So far as loss of earnings is concerned, at the time of the accident Mr Gatton was still a student, but had already applied for a job with Fragile Pottery Company, which was a business run by a Mr M Smith. There seems to have been some competition for the job, but Mr Gatton was accepted one week after the accident. Mr Smith states that the job was permanent though subject to one month's trial period. Mr Gatton was unable to operate the manual-operated pottery wheel, which required him to activate the wheel by depressing a lever with his left or right foot whilst stabilising himself in a seated position with his other foot. He could not put weight on his right foot and therefore was unable to do the work. Mr Smith was unable to keep the position open and the employment was thus lost. Mr Gatton is of the view that he could ultimately have become a partner with Mr Smith or may have gone on to start his own business. Whilst the question of Mr Gatton's progress into partnership, or his ability to set up his own business, might call for some speculation, he appears to have lost the opportunity of working beyond the initial trial period as he had planned and was agreed with Mr Smith.

12   Mr Gatton appears to be unable to work, so there is, *prima facie*, an ongoing claim for loss of earnings. As to that and any future loss of earnings (or alternatively any *Smith v Manchester* type claim for loss of earning capacity), there may well be an issue as to whether the inability to work is due to the injury caused by the accident, or whether Mr Gatton is now prevented from working by the effects of the deep vein thrombosis that is referred to in Mr Woodhead's report. The theoretical level of the loss of earnings can, of course, be ascertained by obtaining from Mr Smith information about the progress of the person that was employed in Mr Gatton's place. However, as with general damages, no concluded view can be expressed about quantum that might reasonably be expected to be recovered as it remains unclear whether and to what extent the injuries sustained in the accident prevent Mr Gatton from working.

13 I was asked to consider too the prospects of Mr Gatton recovering damages for the loss of his business, or alternatively for his ability now to commence a new business. Mr Gatton was able to set up his business but soon after it failed. In my view, there is no evidence that the failure of the business was due to the effects of the accident as opposed to ordinary commercial pressures. As presently instructed, I am inclined to the view that it is less than likely that such a claim would succeed, and there are very considerable grounds for concluding that the court would find such a claim too remote.

Conclusion

14 It follows from the views expressed above that, on the evidence presently before me, the court may find that the Defendant is primarily liable for the accident. The fact that Mr Gatton had consumed alcohol, and that he had come out into the road, may lead the court to attribute some contribution for the accident. However, in my view, any finding is unlikely to exceed about 25 per cent.

15 I regret that I am not at this stage able to provide a more certain view on the level of damages but I shall, of course, make myself available to deal with those matters as soon as the additional medical reports and additional information from the independent witness have been obtained.

CHARLES BELL

8 Grosvenor Buildings
Temple
London EC4
19th March 2007

9.2 Liability—insufficient information

The writer of this opinion finds it impossible to reach a conclusion on the basis of the information provided. Note, however, that the opinion still advises as far as it can on the basis of the information to hand, and gives a clear indication of what further information is required and how it could affect liability.

RE: JOHN EDWARDS

ADVICE ON LIABILITY

1 On the 8th March 2006 Mr Edwards suffered personal injury when he collided with the corner of an open window. He was in the process of leaving his place of work by taking a route to the car park along a pathway. The pathway bordered the offices of a company called Reality Publishing Limited who appear to be lessees and occupiers of the premises where the relevant window is located. It seems that a window was open to the maximum extent and neither Mr Edwards, nor a colleague to whom he was talking as they walked, observed the danger in time. I am now asked to advise on liability.

2 The accident occurred at about 4.45 in the afternoon. Mr Edwards states that although it was not quite dusk, the light was beginning to fade and the weather was overcast. The window was open to its maximum extent and encroached some two feet

into the path which was five foot wide. I have photographs which show the scene of the accident though obviously they were taken in much better light than at the time of the accident.

3 I am instructed that Mr Edwards is a partner in a firm of Chartered Accountants who have their offices at 35/37 Coral Street London NW4. The offices of Reality Publishing Ltd are at the same address. I gather that the two organisations use different parts of the one building, perhaps in conjunction with a number of other organisations. Therefore the windows used in the two sets of offices were almost certainly the same despite the fact that Mr Edwards states he has not personally opened windows in his office that overlook any path or walkway, Mr Edwards is likely to have been familiar with the windows and the manner in which they opened, at least from the inside. I do not know how long Mr Edwards's firm had been at the address. The photographs indicate that the building is relatively modern and it may be that no substantial period had elapsed between the time when his firm moved in and the date of the accident. However, even if this were correct it would appear that emphasis would have to be laid on the degree that this particular window was opened rather than surprise that there was a window which could be opened at all.

4 At first sight this would seem to be a case involving consideration of the Occupiers' Liability Acts. However it may be that liability will rest under the principle of common law negligence. I doubt that Mr Edwards could be construed as a visitor to premises occupied by Reality Publishing Limited. It would surprise me if any lease that the company held gave control over the path or walkway which ran past the windows of the offices. Assuming that all occupants of the building had a right to use the path in question control over the path may rest with the freeholders and, in my view, it would be difficult to argue that the 'owners' or occupiers of the path were responsible for what happened. It is more probable that the potential liability of Reality Publishing Limited should be considered on the basis of opening a window so that it protruded over someone else's land, which would be beyond the scope of the Occupiers' Liability Acts.

5 Unfortunately I am unable to advise on the basis of the information that I have at present. There are a number of aspects about which I would require further instructions. I need to know:

(a) Whether there are other ways of proceeding to the car park from where Mr Edwards's office is and if so how much longer a route they represent. A plan of the whole building and its car park area would be very helpful.

(b) Which window Mr Edwards collided with. It may be important to know how far along the path Mr Edwards had gone before the injury happened. The distance of travel, at the very least, affects the length of opportunity to observe the protruding window edge.

(c) How many people could be expected to use the particular path during the course of the day and at what times.

(d) Lighting up time for the date of the accident.

(e) Whether the lamps that are situated above a number of the windows depicted in the photographs were illuminated at the relevant time and if not why not. I would also like some idea as to the type and quality of light that these lamps produce.

(f) How many times Mr Edwards had made the journey to the car park via the path before and whether he had noticed windows open to a full or maximum extent during such journeys.

6 It would be advisable to have the benefit of a statement from Mr Edwards' colleague, Mr Morris, at the earliest opportunity. His corroboration as to the quality of light at the material point and the difficulty he had of seeing the window edge may be helpful for the purposes of negotiation as well as for the purposes of my advice.

7 I should mention that I am a little puzzled why a window of this size should be open to its maximum extent at 4.45 pm at the beginning of March. One would have expected the temperature outdoors to be too low to contemplate such a course of action. Has Mr Edwards any information or explanation? I am thinking either of a breakdown of the heating thermostat in the building so that the temperature indoors was much too hot, or a very unseasonal outside temperature on that particular day, or perhaps that cleaners were in the office and were engaged in cleaning the windows.

8 On receipt of the above information I will be able to advise properly on the question of liability and if appropriate contributory negligence. I do note, however, at this stage, that simple steps such as advocated by the local authority of fixing stays together with coloured corners to the windows would have prevented this injury. I am at a loss to know why the windows were not designed with those safeguards from the outset. However, it seems to me that a potential claim against the designers would be more costly, more time consuming and less likely to succeed than one aimed at those responsible for opening the window in question. I would advise therefore that liability against the latter be examined exhaustively before any decisions are made as to the former.

9 Finally, I would remind those instructing me of the requirement under para 3.1 of the Pre-Action Protocol to send to the proposed defendant two copies of a Letter of Claim **immediately** sufficient information is available to substantiate a realistic claim and before issues of quantum are addressed in detail. I shall be happy to settle such a letter if required.

10 I hope that assists and I shall be happy to assist further in due course.

MARIA COLES

Lincoln House Chambers
17th August 2007

9.3 Quantum—personal injury

This is an opinion solely on quantum in a personal injury case. Read it in conjunction with **Chapter 11** of the *Remedies* manual. There is no one right way to set out the reasoning, but it is important to make reference to the comparable cases which the writer has looked at, and to deal in hard and fast figures, adjusted for inflation.

Re: MR. FREDERICK JOHN ACTON

OPINION

Introduction

1   I am asked to advise Mr Acton as to the quantum damages that he can expect to be awarded by the Court in respect of personal injuries unfortunately suffered in a road traffic accident that occurred on 12th July 2005. I am obliged to Instructing Solicitors for enclosing the medical report that has been prepared by Mr Dalston FRCS dated 7th March 2006.

The Facts

2   There appears to be no dispute about how the accident occurred. Mr Acton was riding his Yamaha motorcycle along East Pelham High Street. In fact his was one of three motorcycles travelling along that road when a motor vehicle emerged from a side road, Ripple Way, without stopping at the stop line and give-way sign at the junction. As a result, Mr Acton was unable to avoid colliding with the front near side of the vehicle and he was thrown headlong over the bonnet and landed very heavily on the road.

Liability

3   I note, from the correspondence passing between the insurers of the driver of the motor vehicle and those instructing, that liability has been admitted in that correspondence. That early admission is important, but of course, given the facts outlined above, it is difficult to see any sustainable ground on which there could be a defence to this claim.

The Injuries and Their Effects

4   In essence, Mr Dalston identifies the following injuries. Mr Acton suffered bruising on the inner side of his left arm and left thigh and lower leg, all of which resolved in a period of about two months. By far the most serious injury, however, was a partial dislocation of the joint between the collar bone and the left shoulder blade. As a result, he was unable to return to his work as a garage owner/mechanic for three months, and even today, 18 months after the accident, experiences pain around the left shoulder when lifting anything heavy overhead. He also suffers regular aching, and is unable to lean comfortably on his left arm, or lie comfortably on his left side for long periods. It is doubtful if this will improve substantially in the future and there is a real, although less than 50 per cent, prospect that he will require a minor operation in the future. There is an almost certain prospect of osteoarthritis with the passage of time. I am unaware whether Mr Acton is right or left handed, but I shall presume the former.

5   This type of injury falls, in my opinion, within the definition of 'serious' shoulder injuries set out in The Judicial Study Board Guidelines of the Assessment of General Damages in Personal Injury Cases. There, the guideline bracket set out in paragraph 6 is between £7,375 and £11,200, a level of compensation that relates to:

'Dislocation of the shoulder and damage to the lower part of the brachial plexus causing pain in shoulder and neck, aching in elbow, sensory symptoms in the forearm and hand, and weakness of grip.'

6 In addition to the Guidelines, I have also been assisted by the following cases in which there are injuries that, though not identical in each case, offer useful comparisons:

(a) *James v Victoria Palace Theatre Ltd (24 March 1999, unreported)* The Plaintiff, a self-employed carpenter, slipped on the newly glazed stage of a theatre. He fell on to his (dominant) right side. He sustained an injury to his right shoulder and sprained two fingers on the right hand. The sprain was slow to resolve and the fingers suffered swelling for about 18 months. He continued to suffer some reduced grip. The rotator cuff of the right shoulder was the site of pre-existing degenerative changes, which had been symptomatic 14 years earlier but had then resolved. He was left with intermittent pain and stiffness in the shoulder. Raising his arm caused significant pain. The agreed medical evidence was that the effect of the accident had been to accelerate the onset of symptoms in the shoulder by between one and two years. General damages of £5,000 were awarded. This award would be worth about £5,800 at today's rates.

(b) *Roberts v Chapman (18 June 2003)* The claimant was involved in a road traffic accident in which he suffered injuries to his neck and non-dominant left elbow and shoulder, together with psychological sequelae. The neck injury consisted of a minor sprain, the symptoms of which gradually improved over the weeks following the accident. By five months post-accident, these symptoms were low grade only. The injury to the elbow was left tennis elbow, caused when the claimant jarred his hands against the steering wheel during the accident. The symptoms continued to trouble him quite markedly at five months post-accident, but had resolved by 22 months post-accident. The most serious injury was to the left shoulder. The initial injury was either a strain of the rotator cuff or a sprain of the acromio-clavicular joint. This initial injury led to an impingent syndrome in the shoulder. The medical expert stated that shoulder symptoms were severe and disabling during the 12 months following the accident. General damages of £5,000 were awarded. This award would be worth around £5,200 at today's rates.

(c) *Johnson v Berry (24 November 2005, unreported)* The claimant was involved in a road traffic accident in which he sustained a minor displaced fracture of the distal end of his left collarbone and a soft tissue injury to his neck. He experienced immediate pain in the left shoulder area. His neck symptoms developed over the days which followed the accident. He was treated at hospital where his non-dominant left arm was put in a sling which he had to wear for about two months. He also took painkillers and underwent two months of physiotherapy. He experienced acute symptoms of pain, discomfort and disability for two to three months. He took two months off work, was unable to drive for two months, and for three to four months he could not muck out his horses so that friends and family had to do that for him. The accident was responsible only for the first 18 months of neck symptoms. The claimant was also experiencing occasional aching in his left shoulder which was attributable to the collarbone fracture. A prognosis was made for full recovery from all shoulder symptoms within five years of the accident. General damages of £5,200 were awarded.

(d) *Harrison v Throop & Spiers (18 September 2001)* The claimant, an engineering technician, was injured when a steel platform fell on him, trapping him against a lorry. His left arm was grazed and, while his wounds recovered within two weeks, he was left with modest scarring. His chest was bruised and remained so for eight weeks. The most significant injury was to his right shoulder. There was a small fracture to the clavicle, which resolved leaving a minor physical deformity. He wore a sling for nine weeks. All his injuries left him bedridden for four weeks and he did not work for six months. He suffered significant pain in the shoulder, which gradually improved, but discomfort remained. After seven months, he complained of pain and aching on exertion and that was likely to be permanent. There was no risk of arthritis. General damages of £6,000 were awarded. This award would be worth about £6,500 at today's rates.

(e) *Knott v Brown (22 October 2001)* The claimant sustained a dislocation of the left shoulder and minor grazing/bruising injuries after a road traffic accident. Damage was caused to the acromio-clavicular joint and the coraco-clavicular ligaments. His left (dominant) arm was placed in a sling which he wore for four weeks post-accident and he returned to work as a telecommunications engineer after only one day and a weekend recovery period. The claimant suffered constant pain for two weeks and thereafter acute symptoms remained for about three months. He used Ibuprofen on a daily basis for 18 months post-accident and thereafter on an occasional basis. His sleep was disturbed on a regular basis for approximately two years post-accident but thereafter this was reduced to approximately a twice-monthly occurrence. The effect of the injury to his dominant arm did not cause any loss of range but there was initially difficulty in performing domestic tasks and personal grooming. The risk of degenerative arthritis was slightly increased. General damages of £7,500 were awarded. This award would be worth about £8,100 at today's rates.

(f) *Hutchinson v Cunningham (11 May 2000, unreported)* The claimant, when cycling, was involved in a road traffic accident when a vehicle cut across his path and sent him careering onto the pavement. He fell heavily on his left side and hit a lamp post. He was an exceptionally fit man before the accident and would run and cycle long distances, training up to five times a week. He would go fell running and hill walking. He suffered bruising and abrasions to his groin, left shoulder, left hand, left knee and otherwise down the left hand side of his body. These injuries healed within a few weeks. He suffered a serious injury to his right dominant shoulder. His right arm was in a sling for three weeks. He suffered some deformation around the outer side of the clavicle. Mobility in his shoulder was limited and would be permanent. Abduction without pain was only possible to 120 degrees. Pain would move up his shoulder and into his neck. Flexion was limited permanently to 130 degrees and external rotation to 20 degrees. He could not easily use his right arm for heavy tasks. His shoulder ached from time to time and kept him awake at night. An associated soft tissue injury to the cervical spine recovered within one year of the accident. This led to a post-traumatic anxiety condition, which left him depressed, anxious, tearful and angry. The psychiatric injury was characterised as moderate in nature due to the limited duration of severe effects. General damages of £14,500 were awarded. This award would be worth about £16,100 at today's rates.

In this latter case the primary injury to the shoulder was similar to that suffered by Mr Acton. However, the impact was more serious and there was severe adverse psychological and psychiatric damage. This is reflected in the level of the award in this case which in my view is somewhat higher than the client might reasonably expect to recover.

7   Bearing all of these matters in mind, in my opinion the likely award that provides reasonable compensation for the pain and suffering that Mr Acton has suffered falls in a band between £8,500 and £9,500. Of course, much will depend upon the degree to which the Court considers that future degeneration is likely, and/or whether there will be a need for remedial surgical intervention.

Special Damages

8   Mr Acton is entitled to recover all non-remote expense that has been caused as a result of the accident. I have before me an engineer's report dated 25th August 2005 prepared by Mr Davidson whose conclusion was that the motorcycle was beyond economic repair. It seems to me unarguable that the client is entitled to recover the value of the motorcycle, which Mr Davidson assesses as being worth approximately £1,750 on the open market prior to the accident. Having lost the use of the motorcycle and being unable to easily use public transport, Mr Acton has been using taxis. It is unclear whether the cost exceeds those that he would otherwise have incurred but clearly, if it does, he is entitled to recover the excess.

9   Additionally, however, Mr Acton considers that his business has suffered as a result of his being unable to play as full a role in it as he would otherwise. This will be difficult to prove, and expert evidence will be required. This will necessitate an examination of the accounts, of the jobs performed by Mr Acton (both presently and in the future), and an assessment of the extent if any to which any decline in profits can be reasonably attributable to the injury rather than market or other forces. I regret that I cannot advise any further on this point until such evidence is available.

I can suggest the names of suitable experts if that would assist. I would remind those instructing me of the need to obtain the services of a jointly instructed expert if possible, and of the procedure for instructing experts set out in paragraphs 3.14–3.20 of the Pre-Action Protocol for Personal Injury Claims. Please also bear in mind the requirement to send two copies of a detailed Letter of Claim immediately upon having sufficient information to substantiate a realistic claim. I shall be happy to assist in the drafting of a suitable letter if required.

10   In the meantime I hope that Mr Acton continues to make progress, and I will naturally be pleased to advise further if required.

CHARLES BELL

8 Grosvenor Buildings
Temple
London EC4
19th March 2007

9.4 Opinion based on the law

This short opinion, though not complex, raises almost no issues of fact. The answer to the question asked by the clients is to be found almost entirely in the law. This opinion is therefore an example of how to make use of legal reasoning to give the required advice.

RE PASTORS COTTAGE, BRIGHTON, EAST SUSSEX

OPINION

1 I am asked to advise Mr and Mrs Lemmon in respect of their occupation of Pastors Cottage, Brighton in East Sussex, where they have lived since they moved in immediately after they were married in July 1979.

2 Initially, Mr and Mrs Lemmon did not pay rent on the property as Mr Lemmon worked on the adjoining farm, the owner of which, a Mr Spinster, also owned the cottage. Unfortunately however, Mr Lemmon was made redundant in May 1982 and it appears that although Mr Spinster requested him to vacate the property for an 'incoming tenant', Mr and Mrs Lemmon were, in the event, allowed to remain in the property upon payment of rent. The sum required was £2.50 per week which was increased to £5 per week on or about 19 December 1983, this date being the first entry in Mr and Mrs Lemmon's rent book.

3 Mr Spinster unfortunately died sometime in 1984, and the Lemmons then paid their rent to his personal representatives until, on 1st November 1985, they were served with a Notice to Quit as the property was apparently going to be sold. Notwithstanding that, it appears that the Lemmons did not vacate the property even though there seem to have been some discussions about leaving between Mr Lemmon and solicitors for the subsequent landlords.

4 The property changed hands again in about September 1986 and Mr Lemmon paid the rent to the new landlords until 23rd May 1987, when he was informed that the cottage had been sold and the new owners would be taking over the following week. He was not told the identity of the new owners. Since that time he has continued to occupy and look after the cottage with Mrs Lemmon but there has been no request for rent and they have not paid any. They did attempt to ascertain the identity of the owners but such efforts have been unsuccessful.

5 Mr and Mrs Lemmon have therefore occupied the property on a rent-free basis for about 20 years. Section 15(1) of the Limitation Act 1980 provides that no action can be brought to recover land after the expiry of 12 years from the date on which the right of action accrued, and section 17 provides that the title of the owners is extinguished upon the expiry of that period.

6 In *Treloar v Nute* [1976] 1 WLR 1295 Sir John Pennycuick, having reviewed what are now sections 15(1) and 17 of the 1980 Act, stated (at p 1300):

> *The law, as we understand it, is that if a squatter takes possession of land belonging to another and remains in possession for 12 years to the exclusion of the owner, that represents adverse possession and accordingly at the end of the 12 years the owner's title is extinguished.*

What is necessary, for the extinction of the owner's title therefore, is for there to have been uninterrupted adverse possession of the property for a period of 12 years from the date that the owners were entitled to its recovery.

7 The date from which the 12 years is to run is governed by Schedule 1 to the 1980 Act and depends, *inter alia*, upon the nature of the lease under which the Lemmons occupied the cottage. There does not appear to be any written agreement to rent the cottage (the existence of a rent book being insufficient to create a lease in writing: *Moses v Lovegrove* [1952] 2 QB 533) and accordingly the tenancy has, in my view, been an oral weekly tenancy.

8   As such, by virtue of Schedule 1, paragraph 5 of the 1980 Act, the tenancy is deemed, for the purposes of the Act, to be determined at the expiration of the first week and the right of action of the owner to recover possession of the property accrues at the date of that deemed determination. However, paragraph 5(2) goes on to provide that if rent is received after such determination (which, of course, in this case it was) the right of action is deemed to have accrued on the date of the <u>last</u> receipt of rent. That date in this case was 23rd May 1987 and accordingly the period of limitation seems to have expired.

9   There seems little or no dispute that the Lemmons have been in possession for that period without interruption. What seems to concern the Portsmouth District Land Registry is their suggestion that time has not run against the owners because the Lemmons have not been in *adverse* possession as required by Schedule 1 paragraph 8(1) of the 1980 Act. In my opinion this concern does not take into account the fact that the tenancy is deemed to be determined by the operation of Schedule 1 paragraph 5(2).

10   The letter from the Land Registry of 3rd November 2005, setting out their concern about the Lemmons' application to be registered, referred those instructing me to a passage in *Ruoff and Roper on Registered Conveyancing* which states that mere non-payment of rent cannot amount to adverse possession for the purposes of the Act. This assertion is, in my view, accurate in respect of tenancies for a term of years, as the tenancy continues to operate notwithstanding the tenant's default, and in such circumstances it is the tenant who occupies the property, and he is therefore estopped from denying the landlord's title (*Industrial Properties (Barton Hill) Ltd v Associated Electrical Industries* [1977] QB 580). Accordingly his possession cannot be adverse to the landlord's title.

11   In my view the position is different in the case of a periodic tenancy, as this is deemed to be determined under Schedule 1, paragraph 5(2). In *Moses v Lovegrove* [1952] 2 QB 533 the defendant in an action for the recovery of a property was a weekly tenant until 1938 after which time he had not paid any rent. The county court judge held that the owner's title had been extinguished by virtue of the Limitation Act. The Court of Appeal upheld that finding, Romer LJ stating (at p 543):

> *The point is that after the expiration of one week from the date of the last payment of rent, the defendant is deemed to have had no contractual right to possess and therefore to have been a trespasser or squatter.*

Further examples can be found in the cases of *Hayward v Chaloner* [1968] 1 QB 107 and *Jessamine Investment v Schwartz* [1978] 1 QB 264. See also *JA Pye (Oxford) Ltd v Graham* [2002] 3 All ER 865.

12   Thus, in respect of a periodic tenancy, the non-payment of rent is, in my opinion, sufficient to constitute adverse possession because the tenancy is determined as a result and the occupier becomes a trespasser or squatter. Accordingly it is my view that for a period of 18 years Mr and Mrs Lemmon have had possession of the property which has been, and continues to be, adverse to the owner and in such circumstances are entitled to be registered as proprietors of the cottage under section 75 of the Land Registration Act 1925.

13   As a result, I suggest that a further application to the Portsmouth District Land Registry should be made setting out the position in respect of the periodic tenancy under which Mr and Mrs Lemmon occupied the cottage until it was determined by

operation of the Act, and hopefully the position will be reconsidered, and they will be invested with the title. I will naturally be pleased to advise further if required.

CHARLES BELL

8 Grosvenor Buildings
Temple EC4
7th June 2007

9.5 Opinion following legal research

Not only does this opinion contain a great deal of law, but the writer has clearly had to do a significant amount of legal research in order to find that law. Note how the opinion nevertheless addresses the issues rather than the law, and applies the law to the facts, thereby avoiding an academic approach. It sets out the fruits of the research, not the research itself.

IN THE MATTER OF THE CASTERBRIDGE SHOPPING COMPLEX

OPINION

1   I am asked to advise Tess Ltd ('Tess') in this matter. Tess are the tenants of the above premises ('the Complex') and hold under a lease ('the Lease') dated 25th May 2007 from D'Urberville Ltd ('D'Urberville'). Tess contend that D'Urberville are in breach of covenant in that they are not managing the Complex properly, so that vandalism is becoming rampant. This is reducing Tess's profits substantially, despite the heavy service charges which include a large amount supposedly for security. The vandalism creates a climate of fear. Many traders have left giving as their reason lack of security. Shoppers too stay away. One problem is that D'Urberville seem not to be exerting themselves overmuch to try and resolve these problems. Another is lack of evidence to prosecute offenders. I am asked to advise Tess whether there has been a breach of covenant and whether they can have the Lease determined. I am not at present asked to advise on remedies.

A breach of covenant?

2   Tess contend that D'Urberville are in breach of Clause 6 of the Lease. This reads as follows:

   6   To administer the Complex according to principles of good estate management.

Clause 6

3   Tess must prove that D'Urberville's failure to take any or any effective steps to prevent the losses which Tess are presently suffering through vandalism contravenes the 'principles of good estate management'.

4   I have scoured the practice books and cannot find any authority on the meaning of 'good estate management'. That being so, in my opinion it must be a question of fact to be determined by expert evidence. This means that we need a suitably qualified expert to give an opinion on whether taking steps to avoid this type of trouble falls within the ambit of good estate management. We need a firm of surveyors who specialise in

estate management. If Tess can obtain a report from such a firm, I shall be happy to advise further.

The covenant for quiet enjoyment

5 The Lease contains (Clause 9) an express covenant for quiet enjoyment, which is in fairly standard form. Tess contend that this has been broken.

6 The express covenant, even though it is followed by the words 'or by any other person or persons whomsoever' (which is not so in the instant case), does not extend to the unlawful acts of third parties having no title: eg *King v Liverpool City Council* [1986] 1 WLR 890 (CA) (damage by vandals). Where the covenant is general against everyone, the alleged breach must show an interruption or disturbance by some person having *lawful* title: *Lucy v Leviston* (1673) Freem 103. Here the covenant is expressly limited to 'any *lawful* interruption or disturbance from or by the Lessor or any person or persons *lawfully* claiming under or in trust for it'. (My italics.)

7 In my opinion therefore, Tess cannot sue for breach of the covenant for quiet enjoyment here.

Rescinding the lease

8 Ideally Tess would like to rescind the Lease. This I can quite understand after what they have suffered. One can rescind a lease for mistake or misrepresentation: *Solle v Butcher* [1950] 1 KB 671 (mistake); and *Sowler v Potter* [1940] KB 271 (where a tenant with a previous material conviction took a lease under a different name from that under which she had been convicted. The lease was held void for mistake). I should perhaps point out that these older cases must now be read in the light of section 1 of the Misrepresentation Act 1967, which permits rescission even after the contract has been completed (here by the granting of the Lease). This, however, does not apply to a breach of condition, only to a precontractual misrepresentation made to induce the contract in the first place.

9 In my opinion there is no evidence here of any misrepresentation or mistake at the time the contract was entered into. The question then becomes, can one rescind a lease for a breach of a condition? If so, the question becomes, is the trouble here sufficient to constitute a breach of condition, or is it only enough to create a breach of warranty?

10 I have found two cases on this topic, neither of which is directly in point on the facts of the instant case. In *Johnstone v Milling* (1886) 16 QBD 460 a lease for 21 years was determinable by the tenant after the first four years on six months' notice. The landlord covenanted to rebuild the premises after the first four years on six months' notice from the tenant requiring him to do so. Within the first four years the landlord often told the tenant that he could not procure the money to rebuild. The tenant therefore gave the requisite notice determining the lease. The tenant remained in possession hoping the landlord would rebuild, but when this did not happen the tenant claimed damages. It was held as follows: (1) The covenant to rebuild was never actually broken, because the lease had ended before the time for its performance arrived. (2) Therefore the tenant could not recover damages unless there had been an anticipatory breach by the landlord within *Hochster v De la Tour* (1853) 2 E & B 678. (3) In the circumstances of this case, the landlord's acts did not amount to repudiation, because he did not indicate that he would not rebuild *whether or not* he had the money (*per* Lord Esher MR at p 468). (4) Even if he did, there was no breach of contract unless the tenant

elected to treat those acts as ending the contract. (5) Here the tenant had not so elected. *Quaere* whether *Hochster v De la Tour* applies to a lease or a contract containing various stipulations, where the whole contract cannot be treated as ended on the wrongful repudiation of one stipulation by the promisor.

11   In *Surplice v Farnsworth* (1844) 7M & G 576 the Defendants were yearly tenants to the Plaintiff of certain malt-offices at £25 payable half yearly. They took possession at Michaelmas 1838 and quit in March 1843, because the premises were not in a fit state of repair for malting. It was held (*per* Tindal CJ; Coltman and Cresswell JJ agreeing) that where the landlord covenants to do repairs under a lease, there is no implied condition that the tenant can quit if the repairs are not done.

12   *Prima facie* these two cases are directly against us. Here Tess wishes to rescind the Lease for the breach of two covenants contained in the Lease neither of which goes to the whole consideration. Equally there is no express term in the Lease allowing them to do so. Can these two cases be distinguished? In my opinion the only way we might achieve this without an express stipulation in our favour in the Lease would be to show that it was expressly contemplated by Tess and D'Urberville, when the Lease was granted, that the problems Tess are now facing would not happen. It might be possible to argue that certain dicta of Lord Esher MR and Cotton LJ in *Johnstone v Milling*, though they clearly state that one cannot rescind a lease for breach of covenant, leave the way open for an action for rescission for breach of condition. They also appear to contemplate that a lease *could* be rescinded for breach of condition (if, but only if, the breach were sufficiently serious) on the basis that it is a contract. The difficulties which I see with this argument are first that the actual decision in *Johnstone v Milling* went the other way, secondly that *Surplice v Farnsworth* is even more strongly against us. In particular it says that one cannot rescind a lease for breach of covenant unless there is an express term allowing one to do so. Thirdly I have been unable to find any authority in which a lease was actually rescinded in circumstances which were akin to the instant case. Indeed even if I were able to devise a stronger argument for distinguishing these cases, I would still have to advise Tess that they would probably have to fight a test case right up to the House of Lords in order to establish this point, with all the uncertainties and risks as to costs which that would entail.

13   I must therefore advise Tess that in my opinion they cannot rescind the Lease on the present facts.

Frustration

14   Another way in which Tess could rid themselves of the Lease would be if they could argue successfully that it has been frustrated by the actions of the vandals. The doctrine of frustration can apply to an executed lease, but in practice it will rarely occur: *National Carriers v Panalpina (Northern) Ltd* [1981] 2 WLR 45 (HL). In this case the only access road to the demised premises was closed by the local authority for an expected period of about 20 months while a Victorian warehouse in a dangerous condition was demolished. Lords Hailsham, Simon and Roskill said: Frustration occurs when the nature of the outstanding rights and obligations is so significantly changed by some supervening event from what the parties could reasonably have contemplated at the time of its execution that it would be unjust to hold them to its performance. Here there was no triable issue as to frustration, having regard to the likely length of the lease after the interruption in relation to the original term.

15   In my opinion there are two insurmountable hurdles if trying to argue frustration in the instant case. First, in my opinion the instant case is a less serious contender on its facts for the application of the doctrine than the *Panalpina* case. Secondly, and in the light of that, there is the comment by the House of Lords that in practice it will rarely apply to leases.

Final points

16   I should perhaps just mention two things. First, Tess may be able to obtain specific performance or damages from D'Urberville. Secondly, the legislation makes provision for challenging service charges which are excessive. If Tess wish to consider either of these possibilities, I shall be happy to advise further.

Conclusion

17   My conclusions are as follows:

(a) To prove a breach of Clause 6, we require expert evidence from a surveyor specialising in the field of estate management, that D'Urberville are not adhering to the principles of 'good estate management'. On receipt of such a report I shall be happy to advise further.

(b) In my opinion Tess cannot sue under the covenant for quiet enjoyment, because the trouble is not being caused by the landlord or someone claiming *lawfully* under or through them.

(c) In my opinion, Tess cannot rescind the Lease on the present facts.

(d) In my opinion Tess cannot extricate themselves from the Lease by invoking the doctrine of frustration.

(e) Therefore any remedy lies in damages, specific performance or challenging the service charges.

CHARLES BELL

8 Grosvenor Buildings
Temple EC4
3rd September 2007

10

Advising for the purposes of public funding in civil cases

10.1 Introduction

10.1.1 Legal aid—a brief history

In post-World War 2 Britain, the introduction of legal aid in 1949 was but one of the social reforms to assist those of lesser means. The post-war government wanted the state to provide health care, welfare, housing and the opportunity for all to have access to justice. However, none of the architects of the legal aid system could have dreamed how demand would spiral in successive decades. The cost of the system led to a process of reform of the structure, workings and availability of legal aid to limit this growing public expense. These reforms took effect in the year 2000. The overall cost of both civil and criminal cases to UK taxpayers was, for 2005–6, £2.13 billion.

The Access to Justice Act 1999 came into force on 1 April 2000. The legislation represented a significant overhaul of the way in which civil litigation is funded within the jurisdiction. This chapter will deal with the civil context only. Since the Access to Justice Act 1999, more experienced practitioners have had to familiarise themselves with changes to the structure and terminology of what was formerly called 'legal aid'. All legal aid is now referred to as *public funding*. In addition, the Legal Aid Board is now the *Legal Services Commission*, a central body which controls the provision of public funding, both civil and criminal. In 2005/6 the Legal Services Commission assisted more than 2 million people.

10.1.2 Public funding—the current scheme

As stated above, public funding is the new name for legal aid and the Legal Aid Board is called the Legal Services Commission. However, the changes to the system are more than just changes to the nomenclature.

Public funding is now limited to authorised providers called *franchise holders*. These are firms of solicitors, and voluntary organisations such as Law Centres, Citizen's Advice Bureaux and independent advice agencies. Solicitors who do not have a franchise are no longer permitted to offer publicly funded work. This is why there has, since 2000, been a large reduction in the number of solicitors' practices who carry out publicly funded work. There are currently 7,000 franchise holders.

All public funding providers are part of what is known as the *Community Legal Service*. In addition there are Community Legal Service Partnerships: local networks of agencies including firms of solicitors, Citizen's Advice Bureaux, Law Centres, local authority advisory services, etc. These partnerships have referral procedures between each other, meaning more directed services with better continuity for clients than existed before the partnerships.

There are seven levels of public funding: *legal help* (covers advice only), *help at court* (where there is one-off representation for the purpose of a particular hearing), *general family help, legal representation* (funding of litigation services and advocacy services for those who are contemplating legal proceedings or are a party to legal proceedings), *help with mediation, family mediation* and *specific directions* (where specific order or direction is made by the Lord Chancellor). This chapter does not propose to deal with all of these levels and will only deal with legal representation.

There are a number of *excluded* categories of cases. Generally, *no public funding* is available in the following cases:

- allegations of negligently caused injury ('personal injury' claims), death or damage to property, apart from allegations relating to clinical negligence;
- defamation and malicious falsehood;
- company or partnership disputes or other matters arising out of the carrying on of a business;
- trust cases (other than those involving joint ownership or occupation of domestic property);
- the making of wills, although a small amount of legal help for advice can be available in special circumstances (see paragraph 3G013 of the Funding Code guidance);
- conveyancing, unless necessary to previous funded proceedings or to give effect to an agreement in a family case reached under public funding;
- boundary disputes;
- attending an interview conducted on behalf of the Secretary of State with a view to reaching a decision on an asylum claim.

There are exceptional circumstances where the Legal Services Commission has authority to grant public funding in excluded cases, and further guidance is available in the Funding Code if required. Generally, the Commission may fund excluded cases if the proceedings have a significant wider public interest, or where there is a hearing where the liberty of the client is in issue. This means that the types of cases above will be funded by other means such as private means, conditional fee agreements and insurance contracts. Please note, public funding does not cover representation in every type of court; for example the Employment Tribunal and small claims track of the County Court are both excluded from public funding for representation.

The cases which may now obtain public funding can be any matter of law in England and Wales not within the restricted categories above. However, the cases generally covered by public funding do tend to be family cases and social welfare law cases (housing, social security, immigration, education, public law, etc).

Public funding operates so that the work authorised is closely controlled. There are limits as to the amount of work done both in terms of cost and scope. The merits and value (to the client) of a case will justify the continuance of funding (subject to the 'Funding Code' which will be explained below). As a result, you may be frequently instructed to advise as to whether public funding should be extended or allowed to continue in a certain case.

Do remember that even where a case is not funded by public funding, giving your advice involves careful and explicit *risk analysis*. You will need to consider the costs of the case and the financial implications for the client of those costs. When considering your advice, it is often useful to have regard to the public funding guidelines discussed below as they are a good checklist of relevant considerations as to merits and means.

When advising in a conditional fee case, no reference is made in the opinion as to the fact or details of the conditional fee agreement. The agreement is reduced to writing separately.

10.2 Advising for the purposes of public funding

10.2.1 Public funding under Legal Services Certificates

Public Funding is granted to clients under Legal Services Certificates. These certificates invariably contain restrictions. These are restrictions on the *scope* (the nature of the work that can be done under them) and the amount of costs which may be incurred before a further extension—the *financial limit*. The scope is expressed to indicate the steps which your instructing solicitor may take before a further extension is required. To illustrate how scope is noted on a certificate, here are two examples: 'limited to the obtaining of counsel's opinion on the merits and quantum and thereafter the settling of the relevant statement of case' or 'limited to all steps up to and including exchange of witness statements and thereafter obtaining counsel's opinion'. The financial limit is expressed in money terms.

You should always check the Legal Services Certificate before you advise the client. Your instructing solicitors should provide it with your instructions—and if not, they should at least indicate in your instructions the certificate number, scope and costs limitations. You should state in your opinion the level of service (as set out in **10.1.2** above) under which the opinion you are writing is being given, and which of the Legal Services Commission's case categories the matter falls under. You need this information so that you can ensure that the work you are asked to do is within the scope and the financial limitations, and in addition, so you can ensure you are paid. Instructing solicitors are required to keep up-to-date totals as to the amount of money spent per file, so they should be able to inform you where the file stands in relation to the costs limit.

Please note that if any work is done beyond the limits of the Legal Services Certificate neither counsel nor instructing solicitors will be paid for the work concerned. The effect on the client is that the client will have no costs protection in respect of the unauthorised work.

It is important to remember that public funding, if granted, can be withdrawn or revoked. Funding can be withdrawn due to 'unreasonableness', because funding is not in the interests of the Community Legal Service fund, change in eligibility financially and on the merits, and for any failure by the client to provide documents, or information on contributions.

10.2.2 Professional conduct and public funding

Publicly funded work, like any work carried out by a barrister, has to be conducted ethically. All of the normal principles of professional conduct relating to opinion writing apply to publicly funded work. However, there are additional considerations of which you will need to be aware. Paragraphs 303 and 304 of the Code of Conduct of the

Bar of England and Wales impose a duty on Barristers to comply with the obligations set out in the Access to Justice Act 1999 and any regulations or codes in effect under the Act. Further, Annex E of the Code of Conduct, Guidelines on Opinions Under the Funding Code also apply.

All barristers and solicitors conducting publicly funded work have an overriding duty to the Legal Services Commission. This was formerly known as the duty to the legal aid fund. The duty is such that you are obliged to inform the Legal Services Commission of circumstances which should or may affect the continuation of a public funding certificate *even where these circumstances are adverse to your client*. This includes (but is not limited to) advising the Legal Services Commission of any offer made by the other side to settle the claim, and any circumstances which adversely affect your client's prospects of success. However, if an offer of settlement is made which is below your estimation of the likely quantum, you are entitled to say so, and indicate your estimated level of damages.

If you believe a case has no prospect of success following the discovery of new facts (for example after a conference with the client), you are bound by your duty to the Legal Services Commission. In practice, you would initially inform your instructing solicitors that they ought to apply to the Commission for termination or discharge of the public funding certificate due to the adverse circumstances, and only if they refuse to do so should you inform the Legal Services Commission yourself. The Commission can take a few weeks to terminate or discharge the certificate. Please note that the Commission must be informed well in advance if there are any future hearings in the case!

If you consider that your client has obtained public funding improperly, you have a clear obligation under the Code of Conduct. Initially you should try to ensure that the issue is discussed with your lay client and/or professional client (your instructing solicitors). It may well be that they agree to inform the Legal Services Commission of the difficulty. If the lay client does not agree to correct the information given to the Commission, you should cease to act. However, whatever the position of your lay client or instructing solicitors, you are required under Rule C44 of the Funding Code Procedures to inform the Regional Director of the Commission if it appears that the lay client may have given defective information, or new circumstances which affect the terms or continuation of the Certificate come to light. You should ensure you are familiar with rule C43 'Duties of the Solicitor' and C44 'Duties of Legal Representatives' before advising in any case. Barristers are required to comply with rule C43. It is correct that you are entitled (under paragraph 22 of Annex E Guidelines on Opinions Under the Funding Code) to inform your instructing solicitors of any difficulty and request that they pass on the information to the Commission. However, if you consider that this may not happen, you should inform the Commission directly. If you have a suspicion but fail to report it to the Commission, you may have to explain your reasons why later.

10.2.3 Introducing the Funding Code

Generally speaking, the format and structure of an advice for the purposes of public funding should not differ from an 'ordinary' advice on merits or on evidence. The special requirements of advising a publicly funded client involve the consideration of the Funding Code.

What is the Funding Code? It is:
'a code setting out criteria according to which [the Legal Services Commission] is to decide whether to fund (or continue to fund) services as part of the Community Legal Service for an individual for they may be so funded and, if so, what services are to be funded for him' (s 8(1) Access to Justice Act 1999).

The Funding Code can be found in the *Legal Services Commission Manual*. The manual is a five-volume looseleaf text published by The Stationery Office (TSO), and the relevant volume is Volume 3, The Funding Code. Each updated version of the Funding Code must be approved by Parliament (as required by s 9 of the Access to Justice Act 1999). You will find the volumes on the statutory framework and the Funding Code the most useful. Another useful source of the Funding Code is the Legal Services Commission's website:www.legalservices.gov.uk.

The Funding Code is the central source of information for the guidelines for when public funding will be granted. It covers the two aspects necessary for the grant of public funding: first, *financial eligibility* and secondly, sufficient *merit* to the case.

10.2.4 Financial eligibility under the Funding Code

Public funding is only available to those least able to fund their own legal matters, and as a result there are strict limits on financial eligibility. The Legal Services Commission requires applicants to disclose their means for assessment, upon which eligibility is assessed. Whilst it is correct that your instructing solicitors will calculate eligibility and ensure that the client submits means information to the Legal Services Commission, it is very important that all barristers conducting public funding work are aware of the eligibility limits and method of calculation. The means test involves both income and capital. Income is calculated on a monthly basis. Capital is assessed on a disposable capital basis, with special rules for pensioners. If the client's means change, then any change should be immediately reported to the Legal Services Commission.

Those who receive Income Support or Income-based Jobseekers Allowance qualify for funding *automatically*. Those who receive other benefits or are employed have their means assessed and if their income or capital is above a certain threshold, may be required to pay a contribution to their public funding. A contribution is a sum of money paid monthly by the client to the Legal Services Commission directly, and is calculated on a 'sliding scale'. Failure to pay results in the withdrawal of public funding. The amount of any contribution can be very relevant to barristers advising a publicly funded client as it can have an impact on whether the client should accept offers of settlement.

The financial eligibility rates change from time to time (often annually) so it is vital to ensure you are dealing with the right rates. These can be checked on the Legal Services Commission's website, and the journal *Legal Action* often produces an annual eligibility limit summary (a good tip is to keep a copy stuck inside your diary).

It is important to note that, even if a client is financially eligible, if alternative sources of funding litigation are available (either through insurance or other means), public funding is unlikely to be available.

Please note that there is no means test for obtaining legal representation in cases before the Mental Health Review Tribunal. In addition, the financial eligibility limits are lower for legal representation before the Immigration Adjudicator or Immigration Appeal Tribunal (the financial eligibility being the same as for Legal Help).

10.2.5 Eligibility on the merits under the Funding Code

Please note that the part of the Funding Code dealing with the merits of a case is split into sections. One part of it is the General Funding Code applicable to the majority of cases; however, there are specialist sections. The Standard Criteria (Section 4 of the Funding Code) applies to all cases, general and specialist. The specialist sections have different requirements to be met for the granting of public funding. The categories of cases which have these special requirements are:

- very expensive cases (referred to the Special Cases Unit of the Legal Services Commission);
- judicial review matters;
- claims against public authorities;
- clinical negligence cases;
- housing cases;
- family cases;
- mental health matters;
- immigration cases.

These specialist cases will not be dealt with further in this chapter. If you need to find out more about these types of case, you should consult the Funding Code for more details.

At the time of writing the most current Funding Code on the criteria for grant of public funding was the December 2005 version, which is in Release 03 of the Legal Services Commission Manual. This has been subject to a number of amendments, which must be read alongside the 2005 Code. Section 5 is the General Funding Code, which states that where alternative funding (but not a conditional fee agreement) is available, or there are complaint systems, ombudsman schemes or alternative dispute resolution or another of the levels of public funding would be more appropriate, public funding may be refused. The small claims track is specifically excluded. If none of these issues apply, then the grant of public funds will depend on the prospects of success and the cost/benefit ratio.

For publicly funded cases, the prospects of achieving a successful outcome should be estimated in percentage terms. Giving an indication of 'very strong prospects of success' is not enough. The Legal Services Commission gives categories for the prospects of success and your advice should indicate into which category a particular case falls:

- Very good (80% or more).
- Good (60–80%).
- Moderate (50–60%).
- Borderline (not poor, but because of difficult disputes of fact, law or expert evidence, it is not possible to say that the prospects of success are better than 50%).
- Poor (clearly less than 50% so that the claim is likely to fail).
- Unclear (the case cannot be put into any of the above categories because further investigation is needed).

Should a case in your opinion fall into the categories of borderline or poor, you will need to set out full reasons for the continuation of public funding if you believe such funding should continue. Your reasons and explanation will have to be set out very persuasively to ensure further public funding is granted. You will need to make out a case for exceptional circumstances to obtain any public funding. Under the Funding Code, significant wider public interest or 'overwhelming importance to the client' may be exceptional circumstances justifying public funding. The definition of overwhelming importance under the Funding Code is that the case has 'exceptional importance to the client' which is 'beyond the monetary value' because the case 'concerns the life, liberty or physical safety of the client or his/her family or a roof over their heads'.

If the client is able to fund the litigation by an alternative method to public funding, then public funding will be refused. Therefore if funding is possible under a conditional fee agreement, public funding will be refused.

Here are some useful extracts from the General Funding Code to show how the cost/benefit ratio can decide whether your client will obtain public funding:

5.7.3 Cost Benefit—Quantifiable Claims
If the claim is primarily a claim for damages by the client and does not have a significant wider public interest, Full Representation will be refused unless the following cost benefit criteria are satisfied:

(i) If prospects of success are very good (80% or more), likely damages must exceed likely costs;
(ii) If prospects of success are good (60%–80%), likely damages must exceed likely costs by a ratio of 2:1;
(iii) If prospects of success are moderate (50%–60%), likely damages must exceed likely costs by a ratio of 4:1.

5.7.4 Cost Benefit—Unquantifiable Claims
If the claim is not primarily a claim for damages (including any application by a defendant or a case which has overwhelming importance to the client), but does not have a significant wider public interest, Full Representation will be refused unless the likely benefits to be gained from the proceedings justify the likely costs, such that a reasonable private paying client would be prepared to litigate, having regard to the prospects of success and all other circumstances.

Please note that some of the 'Specialist Areas' have their own definitions of acceptable cost/benefit ratios.

(See **10.2.7** for commentary.)

10.2.6 Contents of a barrister's opinion on the merits

Before advising for the purposes of public funding, you should familiarise yourself with your professional obligations arising from Annex E of the Code of Conduct of the Bar of England and Wales, 'Guidelines on Opinions under the funding code'. An up-to-date version can be found on the Bar Council's website www.barcouncil.org.uk.

Your written opinion on the merits should:

(a) State the level of service under which your opinion is given and which case category the matter falls under.

(b) State your decision as to whether a conference with the client is necessary to assess either his/her reliability or credibility.

(c) Show that the legal merits tests are met, referring specifically to the relevant parts of the Funding Code. Apply the Funding Code directly to the case.

(d) Set out any conflict as to facts concisely to enable the Legal Services Commission to assess the relative strengths of rival factual versions.

(e) Express a clear opinion as to whether the applicant's version is likely to be accepted by the court and why.

(f) Summarise any issues of law sufficiently to enable the Legal Services Commission to come to a view about them without going outside the opinion. Remember to use plain English for clarity.

(g) Express a clear view as to whether the legal case has a reasonable prospect of being accepted by the court and why.

(h) Draw attention to any lack of material or other matters which could now or in the future materially affect your assessment of the outcome of the case and consider the need for a conference.

(i) Quantify at least the bracket within which damages are likely to be awarded (where damages are claimed). You should take into account any contributory negligence and whether the opponent may be unable to pay.

(j) Confirm that you are of the view that the proceedings are cost-effective—ie, that the costs are likely to be justified by the potential benefit to the applicant (bearing in mind the statutory charge). The opinion must address whether the specific cost/benefit ratio for the type of case has been satisfied.

(k) If the case concerns a benefit to the client other than damages (for example the client is seeking to uphold rights or defending possession proceedings), that benefit must be made clear. The benefit will need to be justified given the expense to the public purse.

(l) Suggest any limitation or condition that should be placed on the certificate (subject to any further advice), in order to protect the interests of the Legal Services Commission.

(m) If there is a wider public interest, identify such interest by person, group of people (giving numbers), legal issue and type of benefit.

10.2.7 Unquantifiable claims and the 'privately paying client' test

As stated above, where the claim is unquantifiable (it concerns a right or non-monetary benefit) no public funding will be granted 'unless the likely benefits to be gained from the proceedings justify the likely costs, such that a reasonable private paying client would be prepared to litigate'. The question which must be asked here is: assuming that the client had the means to pay the likely costs, would he or she be advised to take or defend the proceedings at their own expense?

You should assume that the client would have moderate but not excessive means. Such a client should therefore be taken as being able to meet the likely costs in a privately paid action, albeit with some difficulty, or as something of a sacrifice.

10.2.8 The statutory charge

The statutory charge is such that public funding is provided as a 'loan' rather than a 'grant'. It is a charge over 'any money or property recovered or preserved as a result of the proceedings'. Therefore, if a recipient of public funding obtains damages (either from the court or by means of a settlement), the *Legal Services Commission are entitled to recoup their money from those damages*. The statutory charge applies, regardless of the client's means. The charge can also be attached as a charge to registered land.

However, the statutory charge can be satisfied in full if the whole of the costs of a case are recouped from the opponent and the solicitor decides to forgo any additional publicly funded costs. In practice, this usually only happens where the costs are agreed by both sides. If the costs are assessed, there is usually a shortfall between the costs paid by the opponent and the total costs (which would then be subject to the statutory charge).

When considering the settlement of a case, you should check whether costs are included in the proposed settlement and if not, the effect upon the client. A barrister must be able to advise the client on the true implications of a settlement: how much will the client get after the statutory charge has been paid?

10.3 Sample opinion—advice for the purpose of public funding

RE: GERALD GALTIERI

OPINION ON THE EXTENSION OF PUBLIC FUNDING

1   I am asked to advise Mr Galtieri on a proposed claim for damages for professional negligence against his former solicitors, Grant and Runciman. My Instructing Solicitors have obtained Public Funding under Level 4 'Legal Representation' which is limited to Solicitor's investigations and Counsel's opinion on the prospects of success. Those instructing me have obtained a copy of Grant and Runciman's client file on Mr Galtieri's case. They have also taken a statement from the Estate Agent involved. I also have a statement from Mr Galtieri and an expert report from a structural surveyor. This advice is sought to specifically address whether Public Funding should be extended to Full Representation. I advise that it should and that an appropriate scope limitation at this time would be to include issue and service and all steps up to disclosure. We will then know whether negligence is admitted and be better able to estimate the costs of a trial on quantum only. At this stage I do not consider a conference with the client to be necessary, given the clear merit apparent in Mr Galtieri's claim as stated below.

2   The background facts are that in 1999 Mr Galtieri became interested in buying a 3 bedroomed house at 7, The Vale, Hendon. He wanted to add the property to his small accommodation portfolio which he then let out and which formed his main source of income. Sadly, for reasons unconnected with this case, he no longer owns any property other than his own modest home, and is unemployed. I am instructed that Mr Galtieri is currently in financial difficulties, owing multiple debts under a number of credit cards, and that he is in mortgage arrears. In addition he is currently paying off some of his debts following creditors obtaining County Court Judgements against Mr Galtieri. He is therefore financially eligible for Public Funding.

3   Mr Galtieri made an offer of £203,000, against an asking price of £220,000, which offer was accepted, per the Estate Agent's statement, which I have had the benefit of reading, because the vendors wanted a quick sale. Mr Galtieri then contracted with Greenboyce and Co, a firm of chartered surveyors, for a survey of the property. Mr Galtieri says that he met with Sidney Boyce, a partner in the firm of surveyors in June 1999 and that he specifically explained that he intended to let out the property for profit and that he wanted the survey done as soon as possible so that the deal could be completed and tenants installed at the earliest opportunity. Since the property has a basement kitchen, and Mr Galtieri has some experience of such buildings, he says he wanted particular attention paid to the question of whether the basement benefited from an adequate damp proof course and was damp free.

4   I have seen the survey, which gives the property effectively a clean bill of health. It addresses the decorative condition of the kitchen but makes no comment specifically on the question of damp/damp proof course. Mr Galtieri, in reliance on the survey, purchased the property and installed tenants at a rent of £700 per calendar month in August 1999.

5   In October 1999, Mr Galtieri says that a fitted wardrobe fell off the wall in an upstairs bedroom, revealing a 2 and a half to 3 inch crack to the exterior wall. Further inspection revealed that the property was extensively affected by subsidence. The tenants moved

out in December 1999, after the Council's Environmental Health Officer served notice on Mr Galtieri to remedy the defects but not before dampness in the kitchen had risen to about 2 feet from the floor and caused losses to the tenants that they alleged to amount to £1,500. The Environmental Health Officer threatened to serve a closing order to prevent the property being re-let without repair. Unfortunately Mr Galtieri had not purchased buildings insurance, there being no compulsion on him to do so because he did not need a mortgage to buy the property.

6   Mr Galtieri could not afford to repair the property and in January 2000 was forced to sell the property to a developer for £150,000, a loss of some £53,000 on the purchase price.

7   In February 2000, Mr Galtieri consulted Grant and Runciman who advised him to institute proceedings against Greenboyce and Co for negligent valuation. For reasons that are not entirely obvious, Grant and Runciman failed to issue proceedings before July 2005. By then the action was statute barred. Greenboyce succeeded in their pleaded limitation defence and in October 2005, Mr Galtieri's case was struck out. In September 2006, Mr Galtieri was advised by a friend that he might have a case to sue Grant and Runciman for negligence. At that time he visited those now instructing me and they have spent 6 months investigating the case and complying with the pre-action protocol.

8   I have no hesitation in recommending that Public Funding be extended to issue and service of proceedings. Grant and Runciman were clearly negligent in failing to issue within the limitation period. We do not know what they may attempt to say in their defence but it is a failing that cannot be excused. The only circumstances I can think of where a Solicitor would be entitled not to issue would be where they were not in sufficient funds from the client, and even then the client would have to be clearly warned of the consequences. Mr Galtieri deals with this in paragraph 10 of his statement where he responded promptly to all requests for funds and all correspondence from Grant and Runciman and far from failing to cooperate with his Solicitors, has evidence from his phone bills of the time of at least 15 calls to Grant and Runciman in December and January 2005, all of which he says were not returned save a couple of calls from a secretary saying the person concerned was ill and away from the office and someone would get back to him.

9   There seems little doubt that Grant and Runciman's failure to issue caused Mr Galtieri to lose the chance to recover damages from Greenboyce for negligent valuation. The question is what Mr Galtieri can now recover from them. In Solicitor's negligence cases, damages are assessed by calculating the recoverable damages in the primary action (in this case *Galtieri v Greenboyce*) first. The trial judge will then make a finding of what the prospect of success would have been in Mr Galtieri succeeding in his case against Greenboyce. The recoverable damage figure is then multiplied by the percentage prospect of success to give the loss of chance damage figure recoverable against Grant and Runciman.

10   We have the benefit of an expert survey report stating that Greenboyce were in breach of their standard of care and negligent in that they:

(a) failed to undertake an adequate inspection to reveal faults (structural subsidence) that any reasonably competent surveyor would have made clear; and

(b) failed to respond to the specific instruction to check for damp proof course and dampness in the kitchen.

It is right that Grant and Runciman will be allowed their own expert evidence in the proceedings but on the evidence before me I advise that:

1. Mr Galtieri has an excellent prospect of establishing liability against Grant and Runciman. I put this at 85–90%.
2. He has a good, though not excellent, prospect of establishing that he would have succeeded on liability against Greenboyce and Co. I would say 60–75%.

His measure of damage against Greenboyce would have been diminution in value (*Watts v Morrow* [1991] 1 WLR 1421). This equates to the price he paid less the true value of the house at the time of purchase, were the defects known. We will need expert valuation evidence on this point since, at present, we only know the difference between the price he paid and the price he sold for approximately six months later. This is £53,000 and I will take that figure for now as the closest we can estimate without a valuation report.

11   Added to this will be Mr Galtieri's loss of income from the lack of tenants and he must give my Instructing Solicitors a breakdown of this and some supporting evidence. If he can prove payment of the £1,500 compensation to the tenants, he can also claim that together with any incidental costs such as advertising the vacancy or other business expenses which have not been offset against tax.

12   That gives damages of a minimum of £54,500. This multiplied by his minimum prospect of success against Greenboyce (60%) amounts to damages of £32,700. There is no apparent difficulty for Mr Galtieri to recover damages in full since Grant and Runciman should (as a firm of Solicitors regulated by the Law Society) be covered by professional indemnity insurance to the full value of Mr Galtieri's property transaction at the very least. As a result, there is no need to discount Mr Galtieri's damages any further.

13   My Instructing Solicitors tell me they estimate the costs of the case to be £12,500. This is a case with a good prospects of success. The Legal Services Commission requires damages in this category to exceed costs by a ratio of 2:1. This test is clearly satisfied.

14   I am aware that it is theoretically possible for Mr Galtieri's case to be funded by means of a conditional fee agreement (CFA). However, it would be unjust and impractical to expect Mr Galtieri to fund his case in such a way. The CFA would not cover my Instructing Solicitor's disbursements in this matter, and given the need for expert evidence and insurance in case Mr Galtieri is unsuccessful, these are likely to be considerable. Mr Galtieri is, as I have indicated earlier in this opinion, in a poor financial position. He is unable to afford these disbursements to the extent that his lack of means would deny him a remedy to which he is entitled. This is therefore a case suitable for Public Funding.

15   I advise that Public Funding be extended to a Full Representation Public Funding Certificate to allow my Instructing Solicitors to obtain the valuation evidence I have advised and to cover the issue and service of proceedings and all steps up to exchange of evidence. I would then be pleased to advise further. My Instructing Solicitors are in a better position than I am to recommend appropriate costs limitation.

22 February 2007   Napoleon Incendiary
                                                                                        1 Middle Temple Stroll
                                                                                                Temple EC4

11

Advice on evidence in a civil case

11.1 An approach to writing a civil advice on evidence

11.1.1 What is the purpose of a civil advice on evidence?

The purpose of the advice on evidence in a civil case is to tell the solicitor what further things need to be done in order to ensure that the case is in proper order for the trial.

11.1.2 What should an advice on evidence contain?

A good advice on evidence should tell the instructing solicitor, clearly and succinctly, precisely what needs to be done in order to prepare the case for trial. It will provide the solicitor with a plan of campaign, both for dealing with all outstanding preliminary matters and for assembling and presenting the evidence which counsel will tender to the court on the client's behalf at trial.

The contents of an advice on evidence will vary from case to case. There are no rules which govern what must and what must not be said. What is required is a practical advice, suited to the particular case and to the particular solicitor to whom it is addressed.

However, almost every advice on evidence will contain at least the following:

(a) A list of the matters in issue in the claim, stating on whom the burden of proving each issue lies. The purpose of this is to help the solicitor in the preparation of the case, by identifying the relevance of the items of evidence which must be produced. It also serves to identify the matters upon which it is *essential* that evidence is tendered on the client's behalf in order to make out his or her case. Even in apparently simple cases, claims may be lost for want of some certificate or other formal piece of proof.

(b) A list of the things which need to be done to get the case ready for trial. The preparation of this list will usually involve:

  (i) a review of the statements of case that have been served and of the disclosure that has been given;

  (ii) a review of the case management directions that the court has made and of the requirements of the CPR applicable to the case, and a consideration of what has been done so far and what needs to be done in the future, to comply or to compel compliance with those directions and requirements;

  (iii) a consideration of what other steps might be taken (such as requesting further information or specific disclosure, putting written questions to the other side's expert, making or responding to a Part 36 offer, etc) or other directions might be sought (for example, in relation to expert evidence, or for a split trial or a trial of preliminary issues, etc) to advance, one's own case or to attack one's opponent's case prior to trial;

(iv) a consideration of what further practical steps (such as making further enquiries, searching for additional documents, taking further witness statements, asking your side's witnesses to comment on what is in the other side's witness statements, commissioning reports by experts, etc) should be taken to obtain evidence for the trial.

(c) Details of the evidence to be tendered at trial, giving the names of the witnesses who will be required to attend court to give evidence, a list of the documents which need to be included in the trial bundles, etc.

(d) Advice on the things that need to be done in order that evidence may be tendered to the court at the right time and in the proper manner (eg, exchanging witness statements, serving any necessary notices under the Civil Evidence Act, advice on the expert evidence, advice on the form and content of the trial bundles, etc).

11.1.3 Structure

A barrister's advice on evidence is almost always set out in the following way:

(a) The advice is headed with the names of the parties.
(b) Underneath that, the words 'Advice on Evidence' appear in block capitals between tramlines.
(c) The advice itself is written in short numbered paragraphs, in clear grammatical English.
(d) At the end, the advice is signed by the barrister in the bottom right-hand corner (usually above his or her typed name) and the barrister's chambers address and the date of the advice are stated in the bottom left-hand corner.

11.1.4 How should I set about writing an advice on evidence?

Every barrister has his or her own way of approaching this task, which is one of the most important parts of the work of a junior barrister.

Just as success at trial so much depends upon the care with which the case is got up beforehand, the writing of a successful advice on evidence depends upon careful analysis and preparation. As with all of a barrister's written work, the golden rule is: think before you write. Once the thinking and analysis have been done, the actual writing will be straightforward.

An important part of this analysis is the barrister's ability, using his or her experience and knowledge of the rules of civil procedure and evidence, to run the case through in the mind, from the very first words of the case to the last. The barrister must imagine what is likely to happen at each stage during the trial, anticipate what may go wrong, fill in any blanks and ensure that everything that needs to be done to be prepared for each point in the trial is noted and put in hand.

11.1.5 When should the barrister be asked to write an advice on evidence?

In cases of any substance, counsel may well have been involved from a very early stage. Under the Civil Procedure Rules 1998, parties are expected to carry out thorough investigations and, where possible, to attempt to resolve their disputes by negotiation before starting proceedings. Litigation is intended to be a last resort: see the Practice Direction—Protocols, paras 1.4 and 4.1, and the various Pre-Action Protocols made under that Practice Direction.

The structure of the Civil Procedure Rules therefore assumes that each party will know its case from the outset, and so will be able to assist the court in its active management of the claim at each stage. Counsel may therefore be asked to advise on matters of procedure and evidence at any point. In particular, counsel's advice may be sought before the action is started, at the allocation questionnaire stage (CPR, r 26.3), at the case management conference stage on the multi-track (CPR, rr 29.3 and 29.4), and at the stage of listing (CPR, rr 28.5 and 29.6–29.8).

In cases allocated to the fast track or the multi-track, the ideal time for counsel to be asked to write a formal advice on evidence will usually be after disclosure but before the service of witness statements. However, the appropriate time will vary from case to case.

In reality, the point at which counsel is asked to advise on evidence is entirely in the hands of the instructing solicitor: and it is a part of a barrister's practical skill to be able to tailor the advice given accordingly. For example, if counsel is asked to advise only days before the date fixed for trial to begin, there is little point in advising lengthy further investigations unless (which is unlikely) it is practical to obtain an adjournment of the trial date.

11.1.6 A step-by-step approach

In order to ensure that they do not leave out any important matters, many barristers adopt a step-by-step approach to writing their advices on evidence. By following the same scheme as a checklist on each occasion they can ensure that they have considered all of the relevant points.

One such step-by-step approach goes like this:

11.1.6.1 Step 1: read the brief

(a) *Ensure that you have been sent the materials that you need to write your advice*
The first step in writing any advice is to read your instructions: and the first stage in reading your instructions is to look at the list of contents with which your instructions will usually begin and to check that you have, in fact, got all the enclosures which the solicitor says have been sent down to you.

The second stage is to ensure that the solicitor has sent down to you all of the things that you need in order to be able to write your advice. You should normally expect to have been sent:

(i) copies of all statements of case and requests and responses to requests for further information (including those in any additional claims brought under Part 20) that have been served;

(ii) copies of all completed allocation questionnaires and pre-trial checklists that have been filed, together with copies of any accompanying costs estimates and/or case summaries;

(iii) copies of all interim orders giving case management directions that have been made;

(iv) copies of all other interim orders that have been made, and of any witness statements used on any interim applications that have been made;

(v) copies of any pending applications for any interim orders, and of any witness statements served in support of or opposition to such applications;

(vi) copies of any Part 36 offers that have been made;

(vii) copies of the lists of documents that have been exchanged and of the documents referred to in those lists;

(viii) copies of any witness statements that have been exchanged; or, if you are advising prior to the exchange of witness statements, draft witness statements from at least the principal potential witnesses on your side;

(ix) copies of any experts' reports that have already been obtained or disclosed.

It is often helpful for you also to see the material parts of the correspondence between your instructing solicitor and your client and of the correspondence between your instructing solicitor and the solicitor on the other side.

If any of these items are missing, you should telephone your solicitors and ask them to send you the missing items. It is important that you read your instructions as soon as possible after you receive them, so that no time is wasted in getting together the materials that you need in order to be able to write your advice.

(b) *Extract the relevant information from the materials you have been sent*
Before you can start your analysis, you must master the contents of your instructions and ensure that you have an overall 'feel' of the case.

Each barrister must work out his or her own system for 'gutting' a set of papers, flagging important documents and highlighting relevant passages. If you have not already done so, now may be a good time to make a chronology and a list of the *dramatis personae* in the case.

A useful tip is also to make a list, as you read through your papers, of any obvious points, inconsistencies, omissions, etc that you notice as you go along. By writing these down as you first think of them, you save yourself from forgetting them when it comes to writing your advice.

11.1.6.2 Step 2: examine the statements of case

(a) *Check your own statements of case* You should examine your own statements of case in the light of the witness statements and documents that you have been sent, to see whether they actually put forward the case which you will wish to, and be able to, put forward at the trial.

Statements of case are important. Although the court will usually grant permission to amend where any injustice to the other side can be compensated by a suitable award of costs, there are some cases which are won and lost on points arising from problems with the way statements of case are formulated: see, eg, *Furini v Bajwa* [2004] EWCA Civ 412; [2004] 1 WLR 1971. In any event, the statements of case are usually the first documents which the judge considers. It is desirable that they should present your case as well and convincingly as possible.

Also, you will use the statements of case in the next step in the preparation of your advice on evidence to find out what the issues in the case are. If some material allegation is missing from your statements of case, it will also be missing from the list of issues.

The purpose of this check is to satisfy yourself that your statements of case are *sufficient in law and accurate in fact.*

(i) *The law* If you did not settle the statement of case, you will want to ensure that the view of the law taken by whoever drafted the document is the view which you consider ought to be put forward on your client's behalf at trial.

Even if the statements of case are your own drafts, you should reconsider them at this stage. The law may have changed or been clarified by decisions of the courts, or your own view of the law may have changed since you prepared your drafts.

(ii) *The facts* You are likely to have more factual information about your case than was available when the statements of case were settled. You will have seen the other side's statement of case. If there have been any interim applications (eg, for summary judgment) there may be witness statements or other written evidence telling the story from different points of view. Disclosure will have made available the other side's documents. You may have additional written evidence and further documents from your own side. Depending upon the stage in the case at which you are advising, you may even have your own and the other side's witness statements before you, so that you can see what the evidence-in-chief at trial is likely to be.

You should check that your case as set out in your statements of case is (1) the best case that your evidence will support, but (2) is also one that can properly be verified by a statement of truth, and (3) is one that can be established by the evidence that is likely to be available to you at trial.

(Note the provisions of the *Code of Conduct*, para 704, and of the *Written Standards for the Conduct of Professional Work*, para 5.8 on exercising personal judgement and not devising facts.)

(iii) *Amendment* If you want to change the way that your case is put—for example, because you can tell at this stage that there is likely to be a discrepancy between what is said in your statements of case and the evidence that you are going to call at trial—now is the opportunity to seek to amend.

But remember: any change in the way that you put your case on the facts may undermine the credibility of your evidence, and all amendments have costs consequences, some more serious than others. *Necessary* amendments have to be made, but the possible advantages of merely *desirable* amendments should be weighed against their possible disadvantages. You must use your judgement.

If you consider it is necessary or desirable to seek permission for your statements of case to be amended, then settle draft amendments and make a note to advise your solicitor that these amendments need to be made, and how to go about getting permission. Make a note to warn the solicitor of any serious risks and of the costs consequences involved in the course which you propose.

(b) *Look at the other side's statements of case* The purpose of this examination is threefold. First of all, to find out what the other side's case is going to be. Secondly, to see whether the other side's case is sufficient in law and accurate in fact, so as to identify any strengths or weaknesses. Thirdly, to see whether the other side's statements of case tell you enough about their version of events.

If the other side's statements of case do not provide sufficient details, or allow them too much latitude at trial, draft a request for any further information to which you consider that you are entitled and make a note to advise your solicitor to administer that request, and how to get the further information in the event that the other side does not supply it voluntarily.

11.1.6.3 Step 3: list the issues

Once you are satisfied that the statements of case are adequate, then use them to prepare a list of issues.

By following each allegation in the Particulars of Claim through the Defence and the reply, and each allegation in a Counterclaim through the Defence to Counterclaim, etc, you should be able to isolate from the statements of case what matters are in issue in the Claim.

This gives you a list of the matters to which evidence will have to be directed at trial. By analysing on which side the burden of proof on each of these issues lies, you will be able to tell the issues upon which your side *must* adduce evidence if it is to make out its case.

Many barristers prepare their list of issues in the form of a table. The left-hand column gives a reference number, the next column states the issue, the next columns (one each for Particulars of Claim, Defence, Reply, etc) identify the paragraphs in the statements of case which give rise to that issue, and the column after that states on whom the burden of proof on that issue is placed.

Other columns in the same table can be used later on in preparing to write your advice on evidence to identify the issues upon which particular witnesses are able to give, or might be able to give, useful evidence, to list the documentary evidence available on each issue, etc.

11.1.6.4 Step 4: consider what evidence is available to you on each issue

Your consideration of the evidence should be a two-stage process: (a) What is available? and (b) What should we tender? At each stage, it is often useful to run through the various types of evidence, taking each separately, in order to reach your decision.

There are some things which one need not prove. For example, there are some matters of which the courts will be prepared to take judicial notice. Also, some issues may have had a special direction made under CPR Parts 32 to 34 as to the mode of proof. It is useful to note these issues on your table of issues.

(a) *Oral evidence* Go through the witness statements (or draft statements) that are with your papers. Mark on your table (perhaps with a tick) the issues upon which each witness can give useful evidence. Where it seems possible from the circumstances that the witness would be able to give useful evidence on an issue, but their statement does not deal with it, mark that (perhaps with a question mark) on your table as well.

When you have completed this exercise, your table will be able to show you how many witnesses can give evidence on each issue. It will show up any issues upon which you have no (or not enough) oral evidence available. It will also highlight the issues on which you should ask your solicitor to take further statements from the witnesses you intend to call, so that you know the outline of *all* of the evidence that they will give at trial.

It is also useful at this stage to mark on the table any special considerations affecting the witnesses, for example, that it may be difficult to get them to trial (eg, because they are ill or old, overseas or likely to prove reluctant, etc). In this way you can identify whether any special steps need to be taken to ensure that their evidence is available to the court if, at the next stage, you decide it would be desirable for their evidence to be tendered.

(b) *Expert evidence* You should consider on what issues it is necessary or would be helpful for you to be able to tender expert evidence.

One of the objectives of the Civil Procedure Rules 1998 is to limit the use of expert evidence to that which is reasonably required. Where possible, matters requiring expert evidence should be dealt with by a single expert. Expert evidence must, wherever possible, be given by written report. Permission of the court is always required to call an expert or put an expert's report in evidence.

You should therefore always consider first what directions (if any) the court has already given with regard to expert evidence, and what expert evidence has already been obtained and/or disclosed.

If the court has given directions under CPR, r 35.7 for a single joint expert, and that expert has not yet reported, you may need to consider what instructions have been and/or need to be given to that expert on behalf of your side. If that expert has already reported, you may need to consider whether you wish to put further written questions. In either case, you should draft whatever is necessary and make a note to advise your instructing solicitor of the necessary procedure.

If directions in relation to expert evidence have not been given, you should consider what directions would best assist your client. Would a single joint expert be appropriate, or are there good reasons for each party to instruct its own expert?

If your side already has an expert, you need to consider whether that expert has the right expertise. Does your expert understand his or her duty to the court? Does the report comply with the requirements of CPR, r 35.10 and PD 35? Does it deal with the right issues? Is it necessary (or would it be helpful) to obtain further information from the other side under CPR, r 35.9 for your expert to comment on? Do you (as a last resort) need to suggest finding another, more helpful, expert?

If experts' reports have already been disclosed, you also need to consider the contents of the other side's expert's report. Does their report comply with the requirements of CPR, r 35.10 and PD 35? Does it deal with the right issues? Is it necessary (or would it be helpful) to put written questions to the other side's expert under CPR, r 35.6? Would it be helpful to seek a direction directing a discussion (or a further discussion) between experts under CPR, r 35.12?

(c) *Documentary evidence* Consider the disclosure given by your client and that of your opponents.

Has your client disclosed all the documents which ought to have been disclosed? If there is a possibility that documents have not been disclosed, make a note to advise your instructing solicitor to ensure that your client gives that further disclosure.

Have the other side given full disclosure of documents? If not, then consider whether you should make an application for specific disclosure. If so, make a note to advise how this should be done. If necessary, draft the application and supporting written evidence.

Consider whether you wish to challenge the authenticity of any document included in the other side's list of documents. If so, make a note to advise your solicitors (i) to give notice under CPR, r 32.19 (if they have not already done so), and (ii) of the evidence, for example from a professional examiner of questioned documents, which will be needed to make or support that challenge. Add this issue to your list of issues.

Finally, consider which of the documents before you are relevant to which issues, so that you know the strength of the documentary evidence available on each of these issues.

(d) *Hearsay evidence* This category overlaps with the previous category. Consider whether there is hearsay evidence available to you which is relevant to any of the issues, and whether a hearsay notice needs to be served under CPR, Part 33.

11.1.6.5 Step 5: selection of evidence

(a) *Oral evidence* Decide who should be called to give oral evidence. Do not omit to call any witness whose evidence is the only evidence that you have on an issue on which the burden of proof is on you. However, do not necessarily call all the witnesses available to you on every point.

Consider whether witness summonses should be served on any of your witnesses. Consider whether any other special step (such as an application for permission for evidence to be given by video conferencing—see Practice Direction 32, Annex 3) needs to be taken to ensure that the evidence of any particular witness is available to the court. This may be particularly important if any of your witnesses is likely to be overseas at the time of the trial. In the last resort, consider applying to move the trial date to allow an important witness (who would otherwise be prevented by urgent surgery or some other unavoidable cause) to attend.

If one of the witnesses whom you wish to call to give oral evidence is elderly or very ill, consider the desirability of ensuring that a signed statement or a deposition is taken from them, so that in the event of their death that statement or deposition can be tendered in evidence.

(b) *Exchange of statements* Having chosen which witnesses you would wish to call to give oral evidence, check that your side are able to comply with the direction for the exchange of witnesses' statements. The order will have been made either in the directions made at the allocation stage or at the case management conference. Consider what more needs to be done in order to convert the draft statements which are with your papers into statements which are suitable for exchange. You may need to settle the witness statements yourself at this stage. Make a note to give the necessary advice to your solicitor.

(Note the provisions of the *Code of Conduct*, para 704, and of the *Written Standards for the Conduct of Professional Work*, para 5.8.) Detailed requirements for witness statements are set out in CPR, PD 32. These include requirements that witness statements must:

(i) be expressed in the first person;

(ii) give the full name and residential/business address of the maker;

(iii) state the occupation of the witness;

(iv) state if the witness is a party to the proceedings or has a connection with any party (eg is an employee/relative);

(v) be divided into consecutively numbered paragraphs;

(vi) generally be in chronological sequence;

(vii) include a statement of truth;

(viii) be signed by the witness;

(ix) be dated.

The CPR, r 32.5(2) provides that unless the court orders otherwise, exchanged witness statements will stand as the witnesses' evidence-in-chief. Rule 32.5(3) and (4) go on to say that witnesses will only be allowed to amplify their statements or to deal with new matters arising since service of witness statements if there is a 'good reason' for doing so. Consequently, you must ensure your witness statements contain all the evidence which your witnesses can be expected to give and which would be asked of them in examination-in-chief. Further, the statements must accord with the oath/affirmation to tell the truth, the whole truth and nothing but the truth.

(c) *Expert evidence* Consider the expert evidence available to you and to the other side, and decide whether expert evidence should be presented to the court and, if so, what evidence should come from your side and how that evidence may most advantageously be deployed. Bear in mind the costs consequences.

Consider how far the expert evidence can be agreed. Consider what directions (if any) have already been given under CPR, Part 35. Decide what further directions (if any) should be applied for. Do you want permission for your expert to give evidence orally? Do you need a direction permitting you to cross-examine the other side's expert? Consider whether (exceptionally) you want to use the other side's expert's report as part of your own evidence, under CPR, r 35.11.

When you have decided these matters, make a note to advise your solicitor accordingly.

(d) *Documentary evidence* Consider what documentary evidence should be put before the court, and the form in which that documentary evidence should be presented.

Decide what advice you need to give on the preparation of the bundles for use at the trial, and make a note accordingly. It is the responsibility of the solicitors for the claimant to prepare the trial bundles, but the solicitors for the other parties will naturally want to have some input into the matter. In any event, PD 39, para 3.9 requires that the contents of the trial bundles should be agreed where possible, and that the parties should also agree where possible (1) that the documents contained in the bundle are authentic, even if not disclosed under CPR, Part 31, and (2) that those documents may be treated as evidence of the facts stated in them, even if no Civil Evidence Act notice has been served. Where it is not possible to agree the contents of the trial bundles, a summary of the points of disagreement must be included with the bundles filed.

The claimant's solicitors must file the trial bundles between three and seven days before the trial. They must also make sufficient copies (a) to supply for the use of their own team, (b) to supply an identical copy to all other parties to the proceedings, and (c) to bring to court for the use of the witnesses.

Consider what advice you need to give on the contents and ordering of these bundles, bearing in mind para 3.2 of PD 39 (which lists what the trial bundle must include) and any relevant specific directions that have been given. Be selective, particularly in deciding what items of correspondence and other documents need to go into the chronological bundle. Do *not* automatically advise that copies of all disclosed documents should be included.

Consider reminding your solicitor of the practical requirements of PD 39, including the requirements that:

(i) The trial bundles must be in ring binders or lever arch files, and each volume must be clearly distinguishable by different colours and/or letters.

In larger cases, it is often helpful to use both colour coding and clear labelling, so that (for example) the claim form, statements of case, requests for further information and responses, and interim orders are in red files labelled A1, A2, etc, the affidavits and witness statements used on interim applications are in green files labelled B1, B2, etc, the witness statements and witness summaries to be relied on are in purple files labelled C1, C2, etc, the experts' reports and responses, etc, are in yellow files labelled D1, D2, etc, the correspondence and other documents are arranged chronologically in black files labelled E1, E2, etc, and the core bundle is in a blue file, labelled F.

(ii) If there are numerous bundles, a core bundle must be prepared containing copies only of the essential documents. It is your job to advise which documents are essential. It is usually better if the documents in the core bundle retain the page numbers given to them in the chronological bundle, and are not given new numbers. In that way, each page has only one reference number, not two.

(iii) Every page of every document in the trial bundle must be fully and easily legible. Each page in each bundle must be numbered consecutively.

Make a note to remind your solicitor that the originals of all documents in the trial bundle must be brought to court for the trial.

(e) *Hearsay evidence* Consider whether any of the evidence which you wish to adduce is hearsay. If so, consider what notices need to be served pursuant to the Civil Evidence Act 1995 and make a note to advise accordingly.

Consider any notices served by the other side, to see whether you should serve a counter notice.

Consider how to deal with any issue raised by any counter notice which has been served by either side.

11.1.6.6 Step 6: final considerations

Bring together in a final note all of the other preparatory matters that you have considered.

Consider how best you can advance your own case or attack your opponent's case. Is there anything more that you need to do to the statements of case, or by way of further information or specific disclosure? Are there any more investigations that need to be made by your instructing solicitor, or an enquiry agent, or accountants, or other experts? Should you apply for security for costs (or additional security)?

Is your case ready for each stage of the proceedings up to and during the trial? Are your witness statements and expert reports ready for exchange? Have all necessary notices been prepared and served? Does your solicitor know what needs to go in the trial bundles? Are your witnesses ready, willing and able to appear at the trial? Should you serve witness summonses on any of the other side's witnesses?

Would it be in your client's interests, even at this late stage, to re-visit the possibility of a negotiated settlement or ADR? If so, how might that best be pursued? Would it be in your client's interest to consider making or increasing a Part 36 offer? Is there an outstanding Part 36 offer from the other side, to which your client needs to respond?

Finally, consider whether your instructions have raised any particular matters for your advice. Are there any specific questions which your solicitor has asked? If so, you should give a specific answer.

11.1.6.7 Step 7: writing

Finally, when all the thinking and analysis have been completed, write your advice. You will already have prepared lists of the things that you will want to say. For example, you will already have notes as to any amendments to the statements of case or further information which need to be requested or given (from step 2). Your list of issues is already ready (from step 3), as is your list of witnesses to give oral evidence (from step 5), etc.

After setting out the title of the claim and the title of the advice, resist the temptation to begin your advice with a long introduction. The most you are likely to need is one or two prefatory sentences, something like:

In this claim my client, Mrs Bloggs, seeks damages against her former employers for personal injuries which she suffered in an accident at work. I am asked to advise on evidence.

Then, list the issues (so that you can refer to each issue by number at later stages in the advice) and set out step by step precisely what you advise your solicitor to do, in accordance with the notes that you have made as you have gone through your analysis.

Divide your advice into short numbered paragraphs.

When you get to the end, remember to sign it and to put the date and your chambers address at the bottom.

11.2 Sample advice on evidence

KENTISH BOOKS LIMITED v SECURITY CAR PARKS PLC

ADVICE ON EVIDENCE

1   The Claimant's claim in this matter that its Peugeot 205 GTI motor car was left in a car park in Darnley Street London WC2 managed by the Defendant on the 10th December 2005. It is suggested that the vehicle was stolen from the car park and that the Defendant's car park attendant on duty was negligent in allowing the thief or thieves to exit with the vehicle from the car park. The time for serving witness statements is fast approaching and I am now asked to advise the Defendant in respect of evidence for the subsequent hearing.

Oral evidence

2   There are a number of aspects on which the Defendant should call oral evidence. I suspect that Mr Enfield who was in charge of the car park at the relevant time would be the appropriate witness on most aspects. He may, however, not be able to deal with them all. My Instructing Solicitors should therefore check with the Defendant. The aspects I have in mind are as follows:

  (1) The system for entry and exiting the car park has to be explained. In essence the procedure averred to in paragraph 1(c) of the Defence has to be confirmed by a relevant witness.

  (2) The presence of notices around and inside the car park setting out the Defendant's standard terms and conditions has to be dealt with. The positioning of the notices or signs is likely to be very important so precise location should be confirmed. Whoever is able to deal with this aspect should also produce a specimen ticket that a motorist is given on entry. I hope that this will confirm something to the effect that entry is subject to the Defendant's standard terms and conditions.

Furthermore I presume that it will illustrate that no details of the particular vehicle for which it is issued appears on the ticket.

(3) Could someone find out whether Kentish Books or Mr Warren, the car driver, held a season or prepaid contract ticket for this particular car park at the relevant time or on any earlier occasion? I suspect it is unlikely but I am seeking to attribute knowledge of the Defendant's standard terms to the Claimant by a history of use of the car park in question.

(4) I understand that this car park or the Defendant in general had only one other alleged car theft from premises it was managing in a seven-year period. This should be adduced at trial.

(5) I have been given details of two ways in which a car theft can be committed that do not involve the absence of a valid ticket when the driver presents himself at the exit barrier. The first is where one car is driven into the car park and the ticket obtained is then used to drive a stolen vehicle away. The other car is collected later without an appropriate ticket but with satisfactory proof of ownership provided. The second involves the use of a prepaid contract ticket which allows entry into and exit from the car park on multiple occasions. It would be helpful if a witness could give evidence of these possibilities. I presume that a third possibility would be if the true owner had obtained a ticket on entry and left it in the vehicle for the thief to use.

(6) I would like to know more about the video recorders that were supposedly in operation. Were they functioning at the time of the alleged theft? Did the police examine the tapes? Where were the cameras positioned?

(7) The witness evidence will have to be put into a form complying with CPR, PD 32 before being exchanged with the other side.

3   Included in my papers is a short report from a security guard employed by Prevention & Detection Holdings Ltd. It records the number and frequency of security inspections of the car park on the relevant day. The requisite notice under the Civil Evidence Act 1995 should be given. Once served the report should be included in the trial bundle. Strictly speaking the Defendant does not need to rely on the truth of the contents of the documents. Evidence that a security firm were employed and that the Defendant was under the impression that regular inspections were being made would suffice, but since the report is even stronger it should be used.

4   There is a suggestion in my papers from enquiry agents that the Claimant may have damaged the car in a road traffic accident. The hypothesis is that there would be a bogus claim that the car had been stolen and that the thieves were responsible for the damage. I feel that this is a very unlikely conclusion. The car seems to have been comprehensively insured subject only to a £100 excess. It also seems fair to assume from the time the police arrived at the scene in answer to a 999 call, as set out in the police report, that the theft must have been reported before that accident occurred. It is possible that the Claimant and the driver at the time of the accident were one and the same but it would greatly surprise me. In the circumstances it seems that to require Bus Inspector Buckley's attendance at court in the hope of identifying the man he saw walking away after the accident would be pointless. However, if my Instructing Solicitors take the view that this avenue should be pursued the Inspector should be requested to come to court or a witness summons must be served. He could then be released if he is unable to give any assistance.

Potential police evidence

5   The onus in this case subject to one *caveat* is on the Claimant to prove that the car was left in the requisite car park, that it was stolen, and that the car park attendant was negligent. I expect the Claimant's employee to give oral evidence in relation to the first two of these aspects. I would be surprised if the witness was able to give oral evidence of the third aspect, primarily because he would not have been present when the alleged theft was committed. The Claimant has pleaded a contract of bailment and if successful in that plea the onus regarding negligence is reversed. A bailee of goods who is unable to return them to the depositor has to show that the loss did not occur due to his or her negligence. Thus it is of special importance to decide whether there was a contract of bailment or simply a licence to occupy a car parking space. In my view the case law favours the Defendant.

6   The Particulars of Negligence in the Particulars of Claim together with the Further Information are quite precise and detailed. The question arises as to who can give oral evidence of such matters. In my view the only relevant person would be the car park attendant or the thief. If the Claimant serves a Civil Evidence Act notice indicating that it plans to use a written statement from the police officer who investigated the allegation of theft, it may be appropriate to seek an order under s3 of the Act for him to attend for cross-examination. Before taking a final decision on this, I would need to see the witness statement which accompanies the notice to see if potential lines of cross-examination are revealed.

Documentary evidence

7   The DVLA search result should be included in the trial bundle together with a copy of the Defendant's standard terms and conditions. I have no doubt that the Claimant's solicitors will wish to include the police report relating to the traffic accident. There is no basis for opposing this, but there is nothing in that document which assists the Defendant. It is true that nothing by way of contents was taken from the car by the driver and his passenger at the time of the accident but items could have been removed earlier in the evening and I understand these personal items are not being pursued against the Defendant any longer in any event. Thus unless the Claimant wishes to include it it can be left out. I suspect also that various invoices disclosed will be sought to be included by the Claimant's solicitors.

8   My Instructing Solicitors have obtained a statement from PC Bull who supervises the property store at the police station where the theft was reported. This confirms that the car parking ticket was not retained by the police. This statement contradicts a handwritten addition to a letter dated the 11th April 2006 from my Instructing Solicitors to enquiry agents. I would like confirmation that the car park ticket was not given to the police. Consequently I advise that the Claimant be served with a notice to admit facts: namely (a) that the Claimant did not surrender possession of the car park ticket to the police and (b) the Claimant did not show the ticket to the investigating police officer. CPR, r 32.18 permits service of such a notice up to 21 days before trial. Consideration of serving a witness summons on PC Bull can be deferred until after the Claimant's response is known.

9   There appears to be no need to utilise the Claimant's accounts. The Claimant operates as a publishing company and its assets are and were at all material times quite extensive. This adds further doubt to the enquiry agent's hypothesis of a fraud on an insurance company.

10   If there are any further matters or further developments that occur as a matter of urgency no doubt my Instructing Solicitors can contact me by telephone.

MARIA COLES

Lincoln House Chambers
8th December 2006

11.3 A more complex advice on evidence

<u>ALPINE SYSTEMS BV v MIDWEST BANK PLC</u>

<u>(1) CHARLES DICKENS AND HENRY JAMES (2) THOMAS HARDY</u>

<u>(3) CHARLES DICKENS</u>

(Part 20 Defendants)

<u>ADVICE ON EVIDENCE</u>

1   The claimant in the main proceedings, Alpine Systems BV ('Alpine'), claims SWF 365,105.70 and interest said to be due from Midwest Bank plc ('the Bank') under the terms of an agreement which Alpine alleges is contained in a letter dated 5th August 2005 which the Bank wrote on behalf of a customer, Paulton Magna Armaments Limited ('PMA'), to Alpine. In the Part 20 claim, the Bank claims an indemnity against Alpine's claim from the three guarantors of PMA's indebtedness (whom I will call the 'Guarantors'). Trial is fixed for 18th May 2008. I am asked by the Bank to advise on evidence. Directions for trial were given by Master Snow at a Case Management Conference on 4th October 2007.

The statements of case

2   I have reconsidered the Bank's Statements of Case in the main proceedings and in the Part 20 claim, in the light of the further documents and information now available. I do not think that any amendments are required.

3   In its answer to the Bank's Request for Further Information under paragraph 3 of the Particulars of Claim, Alpine stated that it could not give further information until after disclosure. Disclosure has now taken place.

4   Similarly, the Guarantors' Further Information under paragraphs 4, 5 (Request 3) and 6 (Request 6) indicates that they cannot give proper information until after they have had access to PMA's records, which were then with the liquidator. Since the liquidation has now been completed, any necessary access could and should by now have taken place.

5   In the circumstances, we should renew our requests for the above information. Drafts of the necessary Requests accompany this Advice.

The issues

6   The real issues in this case can be stated very shortly. Did the Bank, by its letter dated 5th August 2005, take on a liability to Alpine to make payment if it received funds? If so, is the Bank entitled to an indemnity for that liability under the Guarantees, bearing

in mind (a) the purpose for which those guarantees were taken, and (b) the terms of Mr Dickens' letter of 28th October 2005 and of the Bank's replies dated 1st November and 11th November 2005?

7   However, the issues set out in the statements of case are a little more complex. They are:

(a) *On the Claim*:

Issue	PofC	Def
1. Is Alpine a company incorporated in the Netherlands Antilles?	1	1
2. In August 2005:	2	2/3
(a) Did PMA owe Alpine SWF 365,105.70?		
(b) Was Alpine pressing for payment of that sum?		
(c) Was PMA supplying goods to Ruritania and anticipating payment of a substantial sum for those goods later in the year?		
(d) Did the Bank know any of (a)–(c)?		
3. Was any written agreement made between Alpine and the Bank, by the Bank's letter dated 5th August 2005 and Alpine's reply dated 12th August 2005? (Against the background, *inter alia*, of the two similar letters written by the Bank on 7th September 2004, and what happened under those.)	3/4	4/5
4. Did the Bank on behalf of PMA receive sufficient money from Ruritania in October/November 2005 to pay Alpine?	5	6
5. Did PMA subsequently instruct the Bank to pay trade creditors in preference to Alpine? If yes,	5	7
(a) Was the Bank entitled to act on those instructions?		
(b) Did the Bank do so?		
6. Was the Bank's authority/duty to make payments to Alpine ended by the winding up of PMA?	5	7

(b) *In the Part 20 proceedings*:

Issue	Pt20 Def	PT20 Rep
1. What was PMA's business?	2	3
2. Did PMA enter into a contract with the Ruritanian Government in November 2003 for the supply of 10,000 medical kits, and need increased overdraft facilities for that? Did the Bank know of this?	3	3
3. Were the guarantees given specifically to obtain (in October 2003, June 2004 and March 2005) increased facilities for that purpose?	3/5	3/5
4. Did the Bank know of this and 'accept … the purpose and consideration for which the guarantees were given'?	6	1

Issue	Pt20 Def	PT20 Rep
5. Did the Bank on behalf of PMA receive sufficient money from Ruritania in October/November 2005 to extinguish its overdraft?	7	6
6. Did the Bank, *inter alia*, by its letters dated 1st November and 11th November 2005, treat the guarantees as having been discharged (except in the event of a wrongful preference claim)?	8/9	7/8
7. As a result of (3) to (6), is the Bank estopped by convention or representation from asserting that its liability to Alpine is covered by the guarantees?	12	9
8. Did PMA request or authorise the Bank to incur personal liability to Alpine? If not, can the Bank in any event recover from PMA or the Guarantors?	13	10

Two issues not set out in the Part 20 Defence, but which might be raised at trial, are:

9. Were the Bank's letters dated 1st November and 11th November 2005 effective as a release of the guarantees?
10. What was the effect of Mr Dickens' letter dated 28th October 2005 which purported to give notice of discontinuance prior to any demand being made?

Oral evidence

8 Master Snow's Order provided for witness statements to be exchanged by 6 December 2007. The preparation of these statements is therefore now urgent. The Bank's principal witness will be Mr Donne. I should be very grateful if Mr Donne could be sent a full set of the relevant print outs of the Bank's records and documents, statements of case (including further information) and witness statements to refresh his memory of events. Then a full statement should be taken from him, dealing specifically with the contents of each document and with each issue raised in the statements of case.

9 In particular, I am curious to know whether there is any substance whatsoever in the suggestion in the Part 20 Defence that Mr Donne and the Guarantors by common consent treated the guarantees as covering (or assumed that they covered) only the Ruritanian contract indebtedness and no more. His letters dated 1st November and 11th November 2005 give a little support to this allegation. Similarly, I should like to know (a) why, having stated that he had irrevocable instructions to pay Alpine, he did not institute procedures to act on those instructions and did not, in the event, act on them; and (b) what happened to the payments from Indonesia, etc, in respect of which he had previously written similar letters to Alpine. The distinction between Mr Forster's guarantee and the others will also need careful explanation.

10 Apart from Mr Donne, Mr Marvel also seems to have been involved with Mr Dickens' affairs (see, eg Mr Donne's letter dated 29th June 2004 referring to a telephone conversation between Mr Marvel and Mr Dickens). Relevant Bank record entries have the initials STC and WW. Mr Byron and Mr Shelley seem also to have written relevant letters. I should be grateful if statements could be taken from them (after sight of the documents), and from anyone else that they or Mr Donne can identify as having been involved with PMA/Mr Dickens. We can decide whether or not to serve statements from them when we have had the opportunity to consider what they are able to say.

Documentary evidence

11 *Further disclosure* The correspondence with the liquidator is not privileged, is at least arguably relevant to the matters in issue in these proceedings, and ought (as my instructions suggest) to be disclosed in a supplemental list. I cannot see any reference to PMA's bank statements in our List of Documents. Those for 2005 onwards (at least) might be relevant to the issues in this claim, are not privileged, and should also be disclosed.

12 *Bundles for trial* I suggest that the trial bundles should consist of the following:

Bundle (A): Statements of case (together with further information); statements of case in the Part 20 proceedings (together with further information); interim orders; summary judgment witness statements and exhibits.
Bundle (B): The guarantees; the relevant bank statements.
Bundle (C): Correspondence, etc (including the relevant Bank records), in chronological order.

13 I have flagged the pages in sections (8)(9) and (10) in my instructions which I consider should go into Bundle (C) with yellow sticky markers in the top right-hand corners of the pages. Since the Claimant's solicitors will probably be the ones to prepare the bundles, we might tactfully remind them that each page of each bundle must be legible and should be numbered at centre bottom, in accordance with Practice Direction 39. A little nearer the time, it might also be sensible to remind them (again as tactfully as possible) to instruct their advocate to contact me with a view to agreeing a draft trial timetable (which must be filed with the trial bundle (see *The Queen's Bench Guide* para 7.4.1), a list of issues, and a chronology (see *The Queen's Bench Guide* para 7.11.10).

Notices

14 I do not think that it is necessary for us to serve notices on the Claimant or the Guarantors at this stage. If Mr Donne is available to give oral evidence, a *Civil Evidence Act* notice will be unnecessary. The statements of case contain sufficient admissions to make the service of notices to admit unnecessary.

Security for costs

15 My Instructing Solicitor should check that the amount of our present security for costs is sufficient to cover the anticipated costs of a five-day trial. If it is not, we should ask Alpine (and if necessary apply) for more.

Settlement

16 There is no new material in the papers now before me to make me revise my view that the Bank is likely to be held liable to Alpine but entitled to an indemnity from the Guarantors. Three matters, however, suggest that a reasonable commercial settlement might be in the Bank's best interest.

17 First of all, there is the risk that the Bank may be the subject of critical judicial comment. For example, the judge might comment adversely on Mr Donne's actions in stating that he had irrevocable instructions but then not even protesting when those instructions were revoked and/or ignored. The judge might also criticise the Bank for not honouring its word to Alpine if, as I think is likely, he finds that the Bank is liable to them.

18   Secondly, this is a small claim compared with its complexity, even allowing for interest. The costs are likely to be out of proportion to the amount at stake. Thirdly, there is the inevitable litigation risk, that the case will not in the event turn out as we now anticipate.

19   The Bank may be in a good position to 'broke' a without prejudice settlement between the Claimant and the Guarantors. The inevitable discussions about bundles and other preparations for trial may provide a good opportunity to initiate settlement negotiations (or, at least, to suggest that the parties re-visit the possibility of some form of ADR). Of course, the ideal settlement from the Bank's point of view would be for the Guarantors to pay off the Claimant and pay the Bank's costs. However, some discount from this ideal position may have to be made to reflect the risks I have outlined and the irrecoverable costs of fighting this case through to trial.

LEWIS ELLIOT

Gray's Inn Walks
Gray's Inn
London WC1R 5EA

8th November 2007

12

Advice on evidence in a criminal case

12.1 An approach to writing a criminal advice on evidence

'How is this case to be proved?' Answering that question is the prosecutor's first task. If you are defending, it is your first duty to understand the nature and the strength of the case against your lay client, and to consider how it can be met. The advice is written in order to assist your instructing solicitors in their preparation of the case. It is not seen by the other side. You are therefore obliged, and able, to be candid. This is a practical document and clarity is essential. It should demonstrate that you are in command of all the facts and issues.

It should also demonstrate that you are thinking ahead to how the trial will be conducted. Although counsel is immersed in the case, the jury know nothing about it before they come into court. In due course, the Crown will have to present the evidence—and the defence will have to challenge it—in a way that the jurors can follow. How are the pieces to be put together in a coherent way? Can anything be made the subject of section 10 admissions so that the jury is given a chronology and a context which will make it easier for them to concentrate on what is in dispute? The more complex the case, the more necessary it is to put it into a digestible form.

In addition, counsel needs to recognise the situation of those who are instructing them. In an era of franchising and block contracts, solicitors are under pressure when allocating resources to their various cases. The Crown Prosecution Service (CPS) and the police are also restricted by their budgets. This could give rise to professional difficulties, eg, an apparently short, simple case may be decisively defended by the evidence of a handwriting expert or a DNA analysis, but the gravity of the offence may not 'justify' such an expense.

At the same time, the spirit of legal reform (exemplified in the Criminal Procedure Rules) is towards the disposing of cases as quickly as possible and by the narrowing of issues. Because of the requirement of Defence Statements, and of the manner in which judges conduct preliminary hearings, the defence are no longer able to keep all their options open. Defence counsel must draw a distinction between those areas where there is no dispute, and those areas where he or she properly insists that the prosecution prove its case. Prosecution counsel, in turn, must decide which aspects of the evidence need to be given in full, and which matters are more formal and can be summarised.

12.1.1 The charge(s)

The advice should first set out the counts which are on the indictment, and point out their relationship to each other. Are they different ways of looking at the same set of facts? Are they alternatives? Are the particulars sufficiently detailed? Should there be joinder or severance? Prosecution counsel is responsible for the indictment but he or she will often find that the Crown Prosecution Service has already lodged an indictment of their own drafting. That does not release counsel from the obligation to ensure that it is correct and to bring any proposed changes to the attention of the CPS for their agreement before applying to amend. If counsel is asked to draft the indictment, then the analysis of the evidence should include an explanation as to why you have drafted the indictment as you have, and why (if appropriate) you have not followed the charges that were sent for trial.

12.1.2 Summarise the evidence in the light of charges

This should be an analysis, not a mere recitation of the obvious. Concentrate on the narrative, showing how, in their various ways, the witnesses—in terms of oral evidence and of the exhibits which they produce—tell the story and prove the case. Comment on the various strengths and weaknesses and point out any discrepancies. This of course requires extremely careful reading of the entire brief. Have all the documents referred to in the statements been exhibited, and are all the exhibits in your bundle? If something is missing, you must ask for a copy.

12.1.3 Further statements may be necessary

As the prosecutor, you must recognise where there are gaps in your case, and identify who is best suited to fill them: is it an existing witness or a new one? How much further does the case need to expand before the charge can be proved to the extent of the defendant's full criminality? Counsel must indicate which statements are required and must summarise what they should contain, in the sense of setting out the issues that need to be addressed by the witness. This is not an invitation to suggest that the existing witnesses should think better of what they have already said. Having noted discrepancies between witnesses, you must decide what if anything can be done about it. It may be that two people, looking at the same events, have simply remembered things in a different order. Or do discrepancies reveal a more fundamental flaw?

It is important to recall that the defence are entitled to notice of what a witness is going to say. Prosecution counsel cannot use examination-in-chief to rehearse, for the first time, significant evidence against the defendant. If the case is to be fleshed out, then a further statement is required. Counsel must also consider the extent to which matters raised by the defendant after arrest should be dealt with. A defendant might say in interview, 'you can ask X what I was doing that night'. A balance must be struck between 'proving the defendant's case for him' and seeing whether you can undermine it.

You must also consider whether witnesses should be asked to deal with matters which the defendant has raised. Witnesses who are confronted with allegations for the first time when they are in the witness box may not deal with the allegations very well. Where appropriate, they can be asked to make further statements, eg, 'I have been asked by the officer how I could have recognised the suspect. I have seen him in the pub several times before'.

It follows that prosecution counsel should ask himself, 'if I were defending, what would I consider to be the weak point(s)?'

If this is a matter where a Public Interest Immunity application in respect of unused material is appropriate, then that should also be mentioned.

12.1.4 Never expect the defence to admit anything

Despite the defence obligation to provide a Defence Statement, they are not obliged to admit to anything which the Crown cannot prove. The advice should set out each element of the charge and say how the evidence deals with it, bearing in mind that some things can be proved directly and some by inference.

At the same time, if the defence would like to adduce something but cannot, either because a witness is not available or because it would involve the admission of inadmissible evidence, it should be remembered that the prosecution is not obliged to agree to it.

12.1.5 Witnesses are different

In law, the evidence of civilians and of police is of equal weight. In practice, there is an important difference in the way they usually give evidence in court. Any witness may, in the witness box, refresh his or her memory from notes if they were made at a time when the events were still fresh in his or her mind. Police officers habitually make notes, within a few hours, in an Incident Report Book (IRB). Their witness statements are typed up from that. It is common practice for officers who were at the scene together to make their notes together, and to produce a single agreed, common version of events. Because the officers will most likely be entitled to refresh their memory from their original notes when in the witness box, and since the statement is effectively the notebook entry, you can rely on officers, in chief, saying, more or less verbatim, what is in their statement, and, indeed, corroborating what the other officers will also say about those events. However, it is essential to check each police statement against the other to see whether there are discrepancies. They should be noted as with any other discrepancy.

Civilians are less used to making contemporary notes. Their version of events normally is recorded for the first time in a statement which is taken from them by a police officer. If it was taken very shortly after the event, then they, in the witness box, may refresh their memory from it, and it is worth checking to see whether a Crown witness is in that position. More often, though, the statement was taken several hours, days or even weeks later, and the trial may be months after that. The witness is then only entitled to read his or her statement outside court. Once in the witness box, the witness has to recall things as best as he or she can. The result is that the oral evidence may well differ from the written statement in details (eg, the gist of a conversation will be remembered rather than the exact words). Prosecution counsel must anticipate that there will be a certain amount of leeway and take this into account, especially if certain elements of the offence can only be proved if the evidence comes out in a particular way. Reference should also be made to s 120 of the Criminal Justice Act 2003 (which enables some contemporaneous statements to be admitted as evidence).

In respect of all witnesses, it is worth recalling that there may be typographical errors in the statements, and that it may be necessary to check the original.

12.1.6 Admissibility

Consider the admissibility in law of all prosecution evidence against each defendant. This becomes more complicated if there is a co-defendant, especially one who does not stand trial at the same time. Sometimes, the police take very detailed witness statements, which contain conversation and comments which may be inadmissible. Defence counsel in particular should consider these passages: are they the source of cross-examination on consistency? Do you wish them to be heard in any event or excluded? Counsel should point out where editing needs to be done, and every effort should be made to agree this with your opponent. If it is not possible, then you must seek the judge's ruling (usually at the preliminary hearing).

The Police and Criminal Evidence Act 1984 and the Codes of Practice are the basis on which most admissibility arguments are founded. You must be wholly up to date with all the relevant case law. You should not assume that simply because the police officer followed a certain course of action that he or she was correct. Counsel must see whether the rules were in fact adhered to. If there appears to be a breach, then say so. If you are prosecuting then you must warn the CPS that certain matters are likely to be excluded. Both counsel must consider the state of the case on the alternative bases that something is either admitted or not. Where admissibility is likely to be an issue, you should set out the arguments for and against exclusion of the evidence and advise how likely it is that the judge will exclude that evidence.

It is important to make sure that you have a copy of the interview tapes, of the custody record, of any CAD messages (ie radio messages to and from the police control room) and of the CRIS (ie computerised record of reported crimes), subject to any prosecution arguments that it does not undermine their case (see below). The information contained in these may be adduced in evidence by agreement, but you should not assume that your opponent will agree to it. If an entry is important, then you should consider asking the officer who made it to attend the trial. It is not fair to expect police officers to know or to surmise why a colleague made a particular entry.

12.1.7 Submissions of law

The Criminal Procedure and Investigations Act 1996 requires preliminary hearings to take place before all Crown Court trials. The nature of the hearing differs according to whether the trial is likely to be lengthy or complex. However, in both cases, points of law and arguments relating to the admissibility of evidence should be raised at the preliminary hearing.

Where the case is likely to be complex or lengthy, the judge may order a 'preparatory hearing' to take place. The purpose is to identify the issues in the case, to see how the jury can be assisted to understand those issues, to expedite the trial, and to assist the judge's management of the trial (s 29).

Under s 31, the judge can make rulings on the admissibility of evidence or other questions of law likely to arise in the trial. The judge can also order the prosecution to prepare a document setting out the principal facts of the Crown's case, the witnesses who will speak to those facts, and any propositions of law the Crown will rely on. The prosecution can also be ordered to prepare the evidence in a form that is likely to aid comprehension by the jury. Furthermore, the prosecution can be ordered to provide a written notice detailing any documents the truth of which the prosecutor believes the defence should admit. The judge can then order the defence to give written notice of any points of law they will be raising and to state which of the documents referred to in the prosecution notice the defence are prepared to admit; where the defence are not willing to admit the truth of any such documents, they must explain why this is so.

In the case of trials other than those which are likely to be complex or lengthy (in other words, the majority of cases), s 39 of the 1996 Act enables a pre-trial hearing to take place. These hearings are known as 'Plea and Case Management Hearings' (formerly 'Plea and Directions Hearings'). At this hearing, the defendant is asked to enter a plea. Where the defendant pleads 'not guilty', prosecuting and defence counsel are expected to inform the court of matters such as: the issues in the case; the number of witnesses to be called; any points of law likely to arise (including questions on the admissibility of evidence); and whether any technical equipment (such as video equipment) is likely to be needed. It follows that it is very important that by the time of this hearing, the factual and legal issues in the case have been identified.

At this hearing the judge is empowered to make rulings on the admissibility of evidence and on any other questions of law which are relevant to the case. These rulings are binding for the whole of the trial unless there is an application for the ruling to be altered under s 31(11) on the basis that the interests of justice require the judge to vary or discharge it. This is so whether or not the preliminary hearing and the trial are presided over by the same judge.

12.1.8 Plans or photos

On reading the brief, it may seem that the jury would be assisted by seeing a plan of the area (or of a particular building) or photographs. Sometimes the page from the A–Z street directory will do. Photographs are expensive, however, especially as there should always be enough copies to go round. You should also bear in mind that photographs are not an accurate representation of what things look like, in terms of distances, compared actually to being at the scene. A view (that is, a visit to the scene as part of the trial) is an exceptional procedure and requires a good deal of organisation by the court. If you feel it is essential, then the court should be warned ahead of time and the matter should be canvassed with the judge as early as possible in the trial.

12.1.9 Expert evidence

An expert report is admissible as evidence, whether or not the person making it gives oral evidence at the trial. If he or she does not give evidence, then the report is only admissible with the permission of the court. If permission is given, then the report is evidence of any fact or opinion of which the person making it could have given oral evidence (Criminal Justice Act 1988, s 30). A party which wishes to adduce expert evidence must give advance notice to the other side and if this is not done, then the court (whether the trial is summary or on indictment) cannot allow it to be adduced without permission. The report must be provided 'as soon as practicable' and, if the other side request it, they must be provided with a copy of the record of any observation, test, calculation or other procedure on which the finding or opinion is based. See Part 24 of the Criminal Procedure Rules.

The first step is to ask your instructing solicitor to take a statement from the proposed expert. Once the statement has been obtained, the second step is to decide whether or not it advances your case. The defence do not have to serve it on the prosecution if they do not intend to rely on it but they do have to give the name of the expert to the prosecution. Statements of prosecution witnesses who conduct forensic tests which have an inconclusive result or which may support the defence case in some way have to be served on the defence as unused material.

Always have regard to what expertise your witnesses in fact have. For example, the person who can give evidence of the value of goods is someone who is in that type of business. We do not 'all know' the cost of anything. Police officers can be experts in drugs matters, if they have the appropriate experience in the drugs squad. This applies to the value of particular drugs and how they are normally packaged and sold. Such statements are particularly relevant in cases of intent to supply.

12.1.10 Further witnesses for the defence

Although the defendant does not have to prove anything, in practice the defence must also consider the question of further witnesses. Can someone corroborate the defendant's version of events? A patently honest defence witness can persuade a jury that the defendant might well be telling the truth about other matters as well. In the specimen advice in **12.4**, for example, Leahy's defence counsel might consider whether other people have ever borrowed the Mini or whether it was normally kept locked or whether something about the car made it easy for a thief to start it up.

12.1.11 Witnesses to attend court

At the preliminary hearing, it should be agreed which witnesses will be called. The court must be informed if the requirements change. The defence can agree to witness statements being read to the jury (rather than the witness attending to give 'live' evidence). You should not ask for the attendance of witnesses unless they are really needed, ie, witnesses should not be asked to attend on a 'just in case' basis.

12.1.12 Disclosure

An important aspect of the case that has to be monitored is disclosure under the Criminal Procedure and Investigations Act 1996 (as amended by the Criminal Justice Act 2003).

This requires the prosecutor to disclose to the accused any prosecution material which might reasonably be considered capable of undermining the case for the prosecution against the accused or of assisting the case for the accused. The prosecution are under a continuing duty of disclosure, and so the question of disclosure must be kept under regular review.

The defence must (in Crown Court cases) or may (in magistrates' court and youth court cases) serve a defence statement. This has to:

(a) set out the nature of the accused's defence, including any particular defences on which he or she intends to rely;

(b) indicate the matters of fact on which the accused takes issue with the prosecution;

(c) set out, in the case of each such matter, why the accused takes issue with the prosecution; and

(d) indicate any point of law (including any point as to the admissibility of evidence or abuse of process) which the accused wishes to take, and any authority on which he or she intends to rely for that purpose.

Where the accused wishes to rely on an alibi, the defence statement must give full particulars of the alibi and of any witnesses the accused believes are able to give evidence in support of the alibi. The defence must also supply the prosecution with details of any witnesses they propose to call and details of any experts who have been instructed by the defence (whether or not the expert is to be called as a defence witness). The accused is required to serve an updated defence statement prior to trial (or a notice saying that there are no changes to the original).

If the defendant fails to comply with the duties imposed by the Act, adverse inferences may be drawn. This can happen where the accused fails to give an initial defence statement or does so late (where one is mandatory); fails to provide an updated defence statement (or a statement that there are no changes) or does so late; sets out inconsistent defences in the defence statement; at trial, puts forward a defence which was not mentioned in the defence statement, or relies on a matter which was not mentioned in his defence statement when it should have been mentioned, or adduces evidence in support of an alibi without having given particulars of the alibi or of the witnesses to be called in support of the alibi.

Moreover, the defence statement is deemed, unless the contrary is proved, to have been given with the authority of the accused. This means that the accused may be cross-examined on it if he or she departs from it at trial (on the basis that it is a previous inconsistent statement).

These are all matters which have to be considered carefully in any advice on evidence, whether counsel is advising the prosecution or the defence. As well as considering whether there has been full compliance by one's own side, one should also consider whether any point can be taken against the other side on the basis of their non-compliance.

12.1.13 Defence solicitors contacting the prosecution

As well as providing a statement of the defence case under the Criminal Procedure and Investigations Act 1996 (see **12.1.12**) and serving any expert evidence on which the defence intend to rely (see **12.1.9**), defence counsel should ask his or her instructing solicitors to deal with any other matters which involve contacting the prosecution. Some examples are:

(a) Section 9 statements of certain defence witnesses. It may be clear that some matters, eg, medical evidence, are capable of agreement. Statements by such witnesses should be put in proper s 9 form and served in good time.

(b) Discontinuing proceedings. If you feel that the Crown should take a particular view of the matter—eg, having regard to the defendant's mental or physical condition, or to the fact that he or she has just received a custodial sentence and is unlikely to be sentenced to a consecutive term even if he or she is found guilty of the present matter—then counsel should ask that full particulars be sent to the CPS for their consideration. The prosecution cannot be expected to make snap judgments on the day of the hearing. Various parties, including the alleged victim, may need to be consulted.

(c) Offer of a plea to a lesser charge. It may seem from your instructions that the defendant could properly plead guilty to a lesser charge, whether or not that appears on the indictment. If so, advise accordingly and, if the defendant accepts this advice, ask that the offer be put forward to the Crown.

In addition, the defence are obliged to inform the prosecution whether or not they agree the proposed summary of the tape recorded interview. There is often a timetable for this in the directions given at the Plea and Case Management Hearing, which should be adhered to. Having first listened to a copy tape, defence counsel must advise on this. He or she must then ask the solicitors to send a copy of any proposed amendments to the Crown in good time before the hearing, so that prosecution counsel may have the opportunity to consider them. Amendments which are put forward at court may require the CPS to do the editing there and then, with consequent delay to the trial and criticism by the judge. Prosecution counsel should also listen to the copy tape: he or she may find the police summary to be inaccurate or inadequate. Both counsel may, at the end of the day, suggest that the jury listen to the tape itself.

12.1.14 Continuity

Each exhibit in a case must be given a number at the time it is taken into custody. Each witness who deals with it must refer to it by the same number. For example, a police officer should refer to a suspected stolen object as AB/1. If he or she shows it to the real owner, then he or she must also refer to it as AB/1. It is not enough for the loser to say, 'I have been shown a television which I recognise as mine'. The same rules apply to drugs cases, where there must be continuity from the moment the exhibit is found to the time it is re-sealed by the forensic scientist. If there are gaps in continuity, then further statements should be requested.

12.1.15 Summarising

After the body of your advice, summarise in a single paragraph the case against the defendant and give your opinion about its merits. If you want your instructing solicitors to do anything, then summarise your advice by listing all the matters on which action is to be taken. You should make sure that the summary is complete, as those instructing you may well use the summary as a checklist.

12.2 Sample advice on evidence for prosecution

IN THE BARCHESTER CROWN COURT Case No P08–1231

BETWEEN

THE QUEEN

v

PETER SMITH

ADVICE ON THE INDICTMENT AND EVIDENCE

I am instructed to prosecute the above-named Defendant on two counts, one of theft of a car stereo, between 20th September 2006 and 1st October 2006, the other of handling a mountain bike on 25th March 2007. In my opinion the Indictment is defective for the reasons given at section 1 below. Furthermore, the evidence purportedly in support of the count relating to the theft of the radio from the vehicle is not sufficient to secure a reasonable prospect of conviction upon that count for the reasons set out at section 3 below.

1. <u>The Indictment</u>

The Indictment is defective because it clearly offends against Rule 9 of the Indictment Rules 1971 in that the two counts, on any view of the matter, cannot properly be regarded as being either founded on the same facts or as forming part of a series of offences of the same or of a similar character.

The facts on which the theft charge rests are based on the evidence of different prosecution witnesses and there is no nexus between it and the handling matter, which is founded on wholly different facts. The fact that the theft count and handling count are similar offences of dishonesty is not sufficient to justify joinder unless they can be said to form a series of offences and for this criterion to be satisfied there must be a sufficient nexus between the offences in both law and fact. On my analysis of the papers, there is no such nexus on the facts.

The Crown are advised to attend to the course that I propose at section 2 below within the next five days as it seems that the 56-day time limit, with extension, expires on 15th November 2007.

2. The course proposed

This matter was sent to the Crown Court on 20th September 2007. According to Rule 14.2 of the Criminal Procedure Rules, if this Indictment has not yet been preferred then the time limit for preferring the Indictment by the officer of the Crown Court can be extended after 28 days by his own volition for a further 28 days without the necessity of an application by the prosecution: see *R v Stewart* (1990) 91 Cr App R 301.

However, two Indictments ought to be preferred. The first Indictment will contain the handling count and the second Indictment will contain the theft count. This can legitimately be done as the Defendant was sent for trial on both the Theft and Handling charges: see *R v Lombardi* [1989] 1 WLR 73 at p 76, para G.

If this defective Indictment has already been preferred, then I would advise that, at the PCMH, the Crown ought to apply for permission to stay this defective Indictment and prefer two Indictments along the lines suggested. I cannot see any difficulty in obtaining the necessary permission provided the Crown gives the defence appropriate notice of the course that I propose. The course that I suggest was approved in *R v Follett* [1989] QB 338.

3. The lack of evidence in relation to the count of theft from the vehicle

The only evidence that exists in relation to this count is the fingerprints found in the front passenger side of the vehicle on an RAC handbook that was in the glove compartment. When the Defendant was interviewed on tape, he denied being driven in, or driving, a Ford XR2 motor car, and could not provide a satisfactory explanation as to the presence of his prints on the RAC book. In my opinion, the presence of the prints in the car, although they may be consistent with the Defendant having committed an offence of allowing himself to be carried, cannot alone provide sufficient evidence to found a conviction of theft of the radio from the vehicle. In those circumstances I would suggest that a plea by the Defendant to the handling Indictment, upon which there is sufficient evidence, ought to be accepted. Either no evidence should be offered on the theft Indictment or it should be ordered to lie on the file.

However, should the Defendant plead not guilty to both Indictments, then the Defendant should be tried on the 1st Indictment and if convicted the Crown can decide whether to pursue the prosecution of the 2nd Indictment.

Should Instructing Solicitors have any queries in relation to the contents of this advice please do not hesitate to contact the writer.

A D PAUL

Eagle Chambers
Bedford Row
London WC1
2nd November 2007

12.3 Sample advice for defence

IN THE WEST LONDON CROWN COURT

THE QUEEN

v

PETER GRANT

ADVICE ON EVIDENCE

1 Introduction

1.1 Mr Grant is a man of good character who is charged with a single count of theft from his employer. It is alleged that he stole the sum of £60,000 over a two-year period (October 2004–October 2006). In addition he is charged with six counts of false accounting over the same period. He was sent for trial on 19th March 2007 and the PCMH is fixed for 30th April 2007.

1.2 Mr Grant was employed in the accounts department of his employer and it is alleged that he stole £60,000 by drawing money from the company's bank account against bogus invoices prepared by him. It is alleged that he then sought to conceal his activities by altering certain accounting records held on computer.

The prosecution case

1.3 The evidence against him comes from two sources:

    1.3.1   false entries in certain accounts over which he is said to have had sole control; and

    1.3.2   an alleged confession at an internal disciplinary hearing.

The defence case

1.4 Mr Grant denies these offences. His defence (which has already been notified to the prosecution) is as follows:

    1.4.1   he believes another employee, Mrs Eileen Jones, was responsible for the theft;

    1.4.2   in relation to the allegedly false accounting entries, he does not accept that the prosecution's accountant has reached the correct conclusions; and

    1.4.3   he was bullied by his employers into making a confession.

1.5 The lines of defence raised by Mr Grant require further action and I shall deal with each matter in turn.

2 The person responsible for the theft

2.1 Mr Grant has stated in his proof that he believes that Mrs Jones, a prosecution witness, is responsible for the theft. Mrs Jones says in her statement to the police that she was the managing director's secretary and had been with the firm for 25 years. It is apparent from the statements of other prosecution witnesses that she was very popular with the firm as a whole. It is equally apparent that Mr Grant was unpopular with the management of the firm.

2.2 At present, he has not given any instructions as to the basis for his belief that Mrs Jones was the thief or any instructions as to how she may have stolen the money.

2.3 We would have to be satisfied that Mr Grant's allegations were supported by reasonable grounds before we would be entitled to suggest that Mrs Jones was guilty of these offences.

2.4 Assuming Mr Grant can provide such reasonable grounds, he must be aware that accusing Mrs Jones of theft is a high-risk strategy. Unless his suspicions have a substantial evidential basis then such allegations are likely to alienate the jury and rebound on him accordingly. In the event of a conviction, the fact that Mr Grant had sought to blame someone else for the theft would be an aggravating feature in relation to sentence.

2.5 It is necessary for Mr Grant to provide those instructing me with specific instructions on this point. We can then explore it further in conference. Subject to what he says, it may then be necessary to take statements from any potential defence witnesses.

3 The accountancy evidence

3.1 It is apparent from the evidence on which the case was sent to the Crown Court that the allegation in relation to the accounts is complex. The prosecution are relying on the expert evidence of an independent forensic accountant to support their assertions.

3.2 In view of the fact that Mr Grant does not accept her findings, it will be necessary for the defence to instruct an independent accountant to carry out the same exercise. Mr Grant will have to provide detailed instructions on this point in order to assist any accountant instructed by the defence. I advise that it is appropriate to ask the Criminal Defence Service to authorise the expenditure to cover this essential work.

3.3 Once our accountant has completed his work, we will need to discuss his findings in order to see whether they do in fact advance our case. If we decide that they do advance it, then his findings will need to be put into the form of a statement and served on the prosecution (under Part 24 of the Criminal Procedure Rules).

4 The confession

4.1 Mr Grant says that once certain alleged discrepancies came to light, he was hauled in front of the managing director and one of the external auditors. He says he was subjected to shouting and other verbal bullying. He was told that if he said he had taken the money, he could save his job by owning up. As a result, he made a false confession. He says that he was not cautioned and no notes were made of any conversations.

4.2 At trial it will be necessary to challenge the admissibility of this confession under the Police and Criminal Evidence Act ('PACE') 1984, ss 76(2)(a) and (b) and 78.

4.3 Section 67(9) of PACE states that the Codes of Practice apply to 'persons other than police officers who are charged with the duty of investigating offences'. Whether or not persons come within this definition is a question of fact in each case (*R v Bayliss* (1994) 98 Cr App R 235). The Court of Appeal has held that the duty applies to commercial investigators if they are 'charged with the duty of investigating offences' (*R v Twaites and Brown* (1991) 92 Cr App R 106).

4.4 The defence will argue that the managing director and the external auditor come into this category. This issue should be raised at the PCMH. If the judge accepts Mr Grant's version of events regarding the interview I am optimistic that the confession will be excluded.

5 Witness orders

The preliminary hearing is fixed for 30th April 2007. We must inform the court and the prosecution of which witnesses we require at trial by 16th April 2007. This can be discussed and finalised when we meet in conference.

6 Defence Statement

It appears that the prosecution has made disclosure, pursuant to s 3 of the Criminal Procedure and Investigations Act 1996 ('CPIA'). As those instructing me are aware, the defence is obliged to serve a Defence Statement within 14 days of prosecution disclosure, pursuant to s 5 of the CPIA. If there is any risk that the defence will not be ready to serve the statement within that time limit, then an application for an extension of time must be made *within* the 14-day period.

7 Conclusion

7.1 The following steps need to be taken at once:

7.1.1 further instructions on Mr Grant's allegation that Mrs Jones was responsible for the thefts;

7.1.2 serve the Defence Statement within 14 days of prosecution disclosure or apply within that period for an extension of time; and

7.1.3 an application for approval to seek expert assistance from an accountant.

CATHERINE PETERS

1 Prince's Buildings
Temple
London EC4
22nd March 2007

12.4 A more complex advice on evidence

THE QUEEN

v

JOHN LEAHY and MARGARET SQUIRES

ADVICE ON EVIDENCE

1 The preliminary hearing in this matter has now been fixed for 26th July 2007, and I am asked to advise on evidence, particularly in the light of the applications which the defence have indicated that they will be making.

2 The defendants appear jointly on the same indictment. Leahy is charged (counts 1 and 2) with possession with intent to supply (alternatively simple possession of) 1,021.2 grammes of cannabis resin, which, according to the statement of DC Trapp dated 28 February 2007, has a street value of £4,080. He is also charged (count 3) with possessing 440 mg of amphetamine sulphate. Mrs Squires is charged (counts 4 and 5) with possession with intent to supply (alternatively simple possession of) 179 grammes of cannabis resin, with a street value of £600.

3   On 1st February 2007 PCs Williamson and Hooper stopped a white Mini (registration number W841 PLE). The driver decamped before either officer could get a good look at his face. Their descriptions of him are fairly vague.

4   After an unsuccessful search for the driver, four police officers (PCs Williamson and Hooper, now joined by PS Craddock and PC Peel) returned to the Mini. PC Hooper found a plastic carrier-bag in the front driver's well. It contained two slabs of what he took to be cannabis and which indeed was 999 grammes of cannabis resin (DH/1).

5   PS Craddock found, on the floor in front of the passenger's seat, an insurance cover note in the name of Mrs Knightley of 22B Milton Road (MC/1), an envelope bearing the name of John Leahy of 36A Brick Road (MC/2) and five keys on a ring (MC/3). Although the documents are exhibits, there are no copies of them in my brief. I should be grateful if these could be provided. Copies must also be sent to the defence and sufficient made to distribute, in due course, to the jury.

6   PCs Williamson and Peel and PS Craddock then went to 22B Milton Road, where thaey hoped to find the driver of the Mini.

7   The door was answered by Mrs Squires. On entering the flat, the three officers went into the lounge. On a coffee table they found a number of bank notes (TW/1) and two cheques (TW/2). PC Williamson refers to a 'sum of money'; the other two officers say £300. I should be grateful if PC Williamson would make a further statement saying what happened to the money throughout and exhibiting it and stating how much was there and in what denominations. Photocopies of the cheques should be provided for the defence and, in due course, for the jury.

8   PC Williamson also found, on the floor behind the door to the junk room, a plastic bag containing what appeared to be cannabis resin: TW/3. The bag in fact contained 179 grammes of cannabis resin. As soon as he looked at the bag, PC Williamson (rightly) suspected that it was cannabis, and asked Mrs Squires what it was. He did not caution her and her answer to his question about it is therefore probably inadmissible under Code C (para C 10.1). She was then arrested and cautioned and everyone went back into the lounge.

9   The officers then asked her a number of questions. It is my opinion that these constituted an interview under the definition in para C 11.1A ('The questioning of a person regarding their involvement or suspected involvement in a criminal offence or offences which, under para C 10.1, must be carried out under caution'). As an interview, it took place in breach of para C 11.1 (it did not take place at a police station), para C 11.2 (Mrs Squires was not reminded of her entitlement to free legal advice), para C 11.7(c) (it was not recorded contemporaneously), para C 11.10 (the reasons for not recording it contemporaneously were not noted), para C 11.11 (Mrs Squires was not given the opportunity to read the interview record and to sign it as correct although she was in the police station for some time). There was also a breach of para C 6.6: although she said, 'I want a solicitor', the officers continued to question her. It is highly unlikely that anything said in the flat after the finding of TW/3 will be admissible.

10   In the meantime the Mini had been transported to the police station. There, later on in the evening, PC Hooper and PS Craddock searched the vehicle. They found a tobacco tin with cannabis (DH/2—later sealed in C306510) and two reefer-type cigarettes (DH/3—C306509). DH/2 was sent to the lab and analysed, and was found to contain 22.2 grammes of cannabis resin. At the lab, it was found also to contain a

folded piece of paper with 440 mg of amphetamine sulphate. That was seen by neither officer, and they naturally never refer to it. This is the entire subject matter of count 3. In the circumstances there is a strong probability that the jury will acquit on count 3. The defence are bound to suggest that the lack of continuity enables the jury to draw the inference that the amphetamine may have been added to the tin, either by the police or by the lab, either by accident or design. In the circumstances it may be difficult for them to be sure about the reliability of other evidence.

11   A computer check revealed that no current owner was shown for the Mini, which means that unless other evidence is forthcoming, the Crown cannot prove that the Mini belonged to Leahy.

12   While in the collator's office, PC Hooper happened to see, amongst several others on the wall, a photograph of a man whom he immediately recognised as the driver—a man he had described as having 'short grey hair, round face'. It is of course important to the prosecution case that this happened quite independently of PC Williamson making the same recognition at the flat with another photograph of Leahy. The defence have indicated that they will oppose the introduction of such evidence under *R v Lamb* (1980) 71 Cr App R 198.

13   In *R v Lamb* the witnesses first picked the defendant out from a police photo album of local villains. Lawton LJ said that this was equivalent to the prosecution leading, as part of their case, the fact that the accused had a criminal record. He did, however, refer to 'exceptional cases' where producing the photographs can be part of the prosecution case, namely, where the arrested suspect refuses to cooperate in any way and refuses to be put on an identification parade; where 'the prosecution may only be able to get their case going by revealing the fact that the witness was able to pick out the defendant from photographs'.

14   There was no formal identification under Code D in the case of Leahy, and the papers do not say why. The argument against producing the collator's photograph is a strong one under *R v Lamb*, particularly as PC Hooper had no opportunity to see Leahy's face save during the chase, which took place at night. PC Williamson, however, is in a better position, as he picked out a photograph which was in an ordinary family album, and he in fact went up to the driver in Baker Road. No doubt it can be said, though, that as he went to the flat intending to find Leahy, it is not surprising that he picked out a photograph of Mrs Squires's boyfriend.

15   Leahy was not interviewed until 22nd February, when he was interviewed twice, both interviews being taped and in the presence of a solicitor's representative. He admitted that he had lived at 22B Milton Road for about a year with Mrs Squires, and that it is the only place where they had lived together; that he used to live at 36A Brick Road; and that the cheques (TW/2) were his. I would like to listen to these tape recordings.

16   In short, the evidence against Leahy rests almost entirely on the identification by photographs. True, inside the Mini was an envelope addressed to him at his old address. There is no direct evidence of whose car it was or who had permission to drive it. Whoever was driving the car undoubtedly possessed such a large amount of cannabis that it could only have been intended for supply. Can it be proved that that person was Leahy? This is doubtful, having regard to the photograph evidence and the inevitable *Turnbull* direction.

17   Mrs Squires was interviewed as well, but on 16th February. The admissibility of this will be challenged on the grounds that she was only given half a caution, ie, 'First I must caution you that you do not have to answer any of my questions unless you wish to but it may harm your defence if you don't'. DC Trapp thus omits the warning that her answers could be used in evidence. Paragraph C 10.4 states that 'minor deviations' do not constitute a breach so long as the sense of the caution is preserved. Mrs Squires is of good character and so had heard the correct caution only once (when she was arrested). Nonetheless, the judge is likely to hold that the most important elements of the caution were administered by DC Trapp and so is likely to admit the evidence of the interview. Again, I need to hear the tape recording.

18   Mrs Squires admitted that the substances found in the flat were hers. She knew what they were worth. She insisted that they were for her sole use. She gave an excuse for having the £300 (to buy a car) although she does not say why it was on the floor or why it was mixed up with cheques made out to Leahy. She said that she buys and sells cars, but they are obviously of small value. She owes Barclays Bank £700, plus rent of £133.75 per week, and obviously has no means by which to buy cannabis of the quantity found. At the same time, no one asked her how much she smokes herself or how she uses it or how she breaks down a block of 179 grammes or whether she had already used any of it or how long she expected it to last.

19   If the interview is not admitted, then the evidence against her is that £600 worth of cannabis was found in her flat along with £300 loose on the floor and two cheques which did not belong to her. None of the tools of the trade was found: no scales, no small plastic bags, no cling film, no knives with stains, nothing packaged. At best it can be suggested that she was about to go into the drugs business but had not yet bought the necessary kit, or that she was somehow a wholesaler herself. The Crown cannot point to any evidence that she has benefited from the proceeds of drug trafficking: apparently some Abbey bank statements were seized in the flat, but the officers do not say so in their statements. I have seen copies of none of them, but in the interview it is said that the total credits amount to some £255.

20   Given the fact that the only evidence against Mrs Squires is what was found in the flat and the only evidence against Leahy relates to whether or not he was the driver of the Mini, a joint trial seems inappropriate. I therefore advise that the indictment be severed.

21   The defence statement served by Mr Leahy simply denies that he was the driver of the Mini stopped by the police and denies possession of any controlled drugs. He says that, at the time when the Mini was stopped by the police, he was in the company of one Michael Phillips. The statement served by Mrs Squires merely repeats what she said to the police in interview. Both statements are quite brief, but they appear to comply with the requirements of the Criminal Procedure and Investigations Act 1996.

22   Once the police have interviewed Mr Phillips, and assuming that Mr Phillips supports Mr Leahy's alibi, any record of that interview should be sent to the defence. It seems unlikely that there would be any material in the possession of the prosecution which would assist the case of Mrs Squires as disclosed in her defence statement, but those instructing should ensure that the list of unused material is checked carefully.

23   In the meantime, I should be grateful if the following could be dealt with:

(a) Sufficient photocopies of a plan or relevant page of the A–Z showing the route of the chase and including Milton Road.

(b) Sufficient photocopies of the insurance cover note, the envelope, the two cheques, and the Abbey bank statements.

(c) Copies of the custody record must be served. I should also like a copy. The originals must be brought to court.

(d) All the drugs and the money must be brought to court.

(e) PC Williamson must make a further statement relating to the money as set out above.

(f) The alibi witness Michael Phillips should have been interviewed.

(g) Full transcripts of the tape recorded interviews must be prepared and served on the defence. The transcripts and the tapes themselves must be brought to court.

24   Due to the time factor, it is essential that the CPS ensures that any memo has in fact been received and is being dealt with by the officer in the case.

JOHN BLOGGS

Gray's Inn Place
London WC1
3rd July 2007

13

Advice on evidence and quantum

13.1 Checklist for advice on evidence for assessment of damages in a personal injury case

13.1.1 Issues

List all issues which are likely to be before the court on the hearing of the assessment of damages to ensure that none are missed.

13.1.2 Case management

Which 'track' is the claim in or likely to be allocated to? Have the Pre-Action Protocols for Personal Injury Claims been complied with? Have the court's Case Management directions and orders been complied with? If not, how can the consequences of non-compliance be mitigated? At each stage below, consider how any further evidence required is to be fitted into the court's directions or whether further directions can or should be sought. Remember that applications should not be made piecemeal but all necessary directions should be sought at the same hearing, if possible (CPR, r 1.4(i)).

13.1.3 General damages for pain and suffering

1 Check medical reports

(a) Is the medical position stable?
If not—are the reports sufficiently up to date?
If not—advise a review.

(b) Have all aspects of claimant's condition been covered? Is a report required from another area of expertise, ie psychiatrist? Consider the claimant's complaints, if any, of inability to work. (Should it be from a single joint expert (CPR, r 35.8)?)

(c) Is this a case for provisional damages? Have they been claimed?

(d) Have reports been disclosed to other side? If not:
   (i) Should they now be disclosed?
   (ii) Is there non-medical prejudicial material to be edited out?
   (iii) Is there reference to material (and in particular privileged material) in respect of which the other side would be entitled to disclosure if the report is served as it stands?

(e) Have the other side's medical reports been disclosed? If so:

(i) Are there any questions for the experts required for clarification (CPR, r 35.6)?

(ii) Can they be agreed?

(iii) Should our expert be asked to comment on them first?

(f) Have the reports been verified with a statement of truth, etc, in accordance with CPR, r 35.10 and PD 35 (Experts and Assessors), paras 1.2, 1.3 and 1.4?

2   If acting for the claimant

(a) Does his/her witness statement deal with the medical position? Is it up to date? If not advise an addendum.

(b) Is it a case where evidence from family and friends will help to establish the extent of the changes in the claimant since the accident? Is there, for example, gross disability or personality change?

(c) Is a video needed, for example, to demonstrate the extent of the claimant's disability around the home? Or at work?

3   If acting for the defendant

Are there grounds for suspecting the claimant is exaggerating his/her disabilities? If so:

(a) Have we seen GP notes to check whether any relevant complaints were made before or after the accident?

(b) Are there proofs from witnesses, eg in the neighbourhood or at work, who can say what the true position is?

(c) Would a video help? Consider cost of enquiry agent against sum at stake.

4   Arrangements for disabled claimant to attend trial

In the case of a grossly disabled claimant, and where acting for claimant, remind solicitors of necessity for making suitable arrangements for the claimant to attend the trial.

5   Photographs

(a) Is it a scarring case? If the scars are in an embarrassing place (buttocks, breasts, abdomen, etc) are there up-to-date photographs? Colour is better than black and white. 7″ × 35″ should be the minimum size; 10″ × 38″ is better. Four booklets of photographs (or more if more than one defendant).

(b) In appropriate cases, are there any pre-accident photographs for comparison purposes?

(c) Have photographs been disclosed to the other side? If not—should they be?

(d) Have the other side's photographs (if any) been disclosed? If so—can they be agreed?

13.1.4 Damages for future loss and future care

1   <u>In a case where the claimant has not resumed his/her pre-accident or any employment</u>

(a) Did the medical reports deal with the claimant's prospects of being able to work again? If not, the omission should be covered.

(b) Is the evidence of future loss sufficiently full? Does it deal with the prospects of the claimant's promotion? Is evidence required from his/her former immediate superior as to his/her pre-accident abilities? If the claimant had only been in the pre-accident job for a short time, would evidence from a former employer help?

(c) In what financial state was/is the previous employer? Would the claimant have been made redundant?

2   In a case where the claimant has not resumed his/her pre-accident employment but has obtained less well-paid job

(a) Is there adequate evidence of the comparative earning rates?

(b) Is there adequate evidence of the claimant's abilities and promotional prospects in his/her present employment?

3   Claimant fit to resume work

If it is a case where the claimant is fit to resume work, his/her pre-accident job is not available but he/she is claiming that he/she has been unable to obtain alternative employment—is there documentary evidence of job seeking? Has it been disclosed? Can it be agreed?

4   Is there evidence of claimant attending a rehabilitation or retraining assessment course?

5   In a case where the claimant has resumed his/her pre-accident employment

(a) Is he/she likely to be at a disadvantage on the labour market, eg because of future disability (eg osteoarthritis) or present disability which does not prevent present work if he/she were to lose job?

(b) If so, is there evidence (1) as to the claimant's experience and qualifications and (2) of how secure his/her present job is likely to be?

6   Has the claimant lost pension rights?

If so:

(a) Have they been valued? (NB *Auty v National Coal Board* [1985] 1 WLR 784; and is accountancy help required?)

(b) Have/can the calculations be agreed?

7   In a case of gross disability

(a) Will there be a need for long-term care? If so, has it been properly costed? There should be an expert's report, if so can it be disclosed/agreed? If not, should there be a joint expert?

(b) Is this a case where a member of the claimant's family is providing the care? If so, is there a proof from the provider? Does it deal with his/her loss of earnings? This is to be taken into account when quantifying the value of his/her services. In general a court will apply a discount of 20 to 30 per cent to reflect the fact that care is provided by a non-commercial source. (*Donnelly v Joyce* [1974] QB 454 but note that the court may award only a gratuity rather than a 'wage': see *Housecroft v Burnett* [1986] 1 All ER 332 (CA) and *Hunt v Severs* [1994] 2 WLR 602.) Does the medical expert confirm the need for such care?

8 Is the loss of earnings supported by documentary evidence?

If not, it should be. If so, has it been disclosed? Can it be agreed?

9 Is further surgery likely?

If so, will it be performed privately? If so, has it been costed?

13.1.5 Special damages

1 Loss of earnings

Is this properly documented? Can the figures be agreed?

2 Additional benefits from employer

(a) Are these properly documented?

(b) Can the figures be agreed?

3 Other items

These can range from prescription charges and bus fares to specially adapted cars and even specially adapted accommodation. In the case of each major item:

(a) Does it require expert evidence to justify the expense? If so has a report been obtained/disclosed?

(b) Is item supported by documentary evidence? If so has it been disclosed?

If acting for the claimant

Has a schedule of past and future losses and expenses been prepared and served on the other parties in accordance with CPR, Part 16, PD 16, para 4.2? If not, advise solicitors that they should prepare the schedule or give instructions for counsel to do so.

Note that the following items need to be dealt with (where applicable):

(1) Loss of future earnings.

(2) Loss of future earning capacity.

(3) Medical or other expenses relating to or including the cost of care, attention, accommodation and appliances in the future.

(4) Loss of pension rights.

If acting for the defendant

(a) Have the items of special damages been agreed?

(b) If not, can they be?

(c) If not, can the documentary evidence supporting any item be agreed?

(d) Do the witness statements adequately cover the evidence which you intend to adduce in relation to special damages? If necessary advise solicitor to prepare supplementary witness statements.

13.1.6 Admissions and hearsay evidence

Is there any of your evidence that can properly be made the subject of a notice to admit facts or a notice to admit hearsay evidence under the Civil Evidence Act 1995 (see CPR, r 33.2)?

If the other side have served notice of intention to rely on hearsay evidence should an application be made for permission to cross-examine? (Note that CPR, r 33.4(2) allows only 14 days from the date of service of notice of intention to rely for the making of such an application.)

13.1.7 Witnesses

List:

(a) The witnesses whose attendance you will or *may* require at the trial in any event.

(b) The other witnesses who will have to attend if facts, documents or statements are not admitted by the other side.

(c) Have statements been taken from all relevant witnesses, and in a form suitable for disclosure? Consider each witness statement to see whether it contains embarrassing or contradictory material. Advise solicitor as appropriate, and check whether solicitor wishes you to prepare amendments.

13.1.8 Time estimate

A time estimate should be given, especially where acting for the claimant.

13.1.9 Part 36 offers and interest

If acting for the claimant:

- Have you made any Part 36 offer to settle? If not, should one be made and if so, how much?
- Have you remembered to take interest into account?

13.1.10 Skeleton argument

Prepare a skeleton argument for lodging with the court (and exchange with opponent) under the provisions of the *Practice Direction (Civil Litigation: Case Management)* [1995] 1 WLR 262 and any case management directions.

13.2 Sample advice on evidence on assessment of quantum

MARCUS ALLEN

v

SAMUEL WOOLF

ADVICE ON EVIDENCE

1 On 1st September 2004 the Claimant was travelling in his Vauxhall Astra motor car registration number A837 BJA in the direction of Macclesfield on the A34 in

Cheshire. The Defendant was driving a Jaguar XJS registration number ACE 1 on the opposite carriageway in the direction of Wilmslow. The Jaguar car veered out of control across the carriageway colliding with the Claimant's motor car. The Claimant sustained serious injuries as a result of the collision. He was taken to Macclesfield Royal Infirmary where examination revealed bruising to the head, fractures to the right wrist and ankle, and a soft tissue injury to the neck. Liability has been admitted by the Defendant's insurers. I am asked on behalf of the Claimant to advise on the evidence required for the assessment of damages.

2   The Claimant complains of a wide range of symptoms which are set out in some detail in the reports of Mr Kenneth Brand FRCS dated 4th October 2004 and 6th June 2005. In summary the Claimant continues to suffer from severe headaches which occur some two or three times a week, reduction in cognitive ability with poor short-term memory, pain and restricted movement in the neck, loss of grip and mobility in the right wrist, and extreme difficulty in walking as a result of the failure of the right ankle fracture to heal properly. The Claimant also complains of psychological trauma consequent on the accident and its aftermath. He is depressed and irritable and this is imposing a severe strain on his marriage. He and his wife have no children.

3   Mr Brand is an orthopaedic surgeon and, as he explains in his letter of 6th June 2005 which accompanied the report of that date, he cannot express confident opinions as to the Claimant's neurological or psychological condition. He is, however, a very experienced surgeon and forensic doctor, and his concern that the Claimant's symptoms may go somewhat further than the physiological evidence would substantiate have to be taken seriously. The financial consequences of the accident have been grave. The Claimant was born on 3rd July 1980 and at 24 years of age at the date of the accident had a promising and well-paid career as a North Sea diver with Dodd-Comex Limited. He has now been dismissed, and cannot find any suitable alternative employment.

4   In addition to his claim for general damages for pain, suffering, loss of amenity, and for loss of employment prospects, the following heads of claim may be advanced on behalf of the Claimant:

(1) loss of earnings and pension;

(2) loss of earnings for Mrs Allen;

(3) the excess on the Claimant's motor insurance policy;

(4) the value of personal effects damaged in the accident;

(5) the cost of adaptation to house and car;

(6) the cost of carrying out the maintenance, decorating and gardening tasks which the Claimant undertook before the accident;

(7) travel for treatment, cost of medication and miscellaneous expenses.

Medical evidence

5   It is essential that the Claimant's medical condition is properly investigated. Mr Brand refers to the findings of the Neurological Registrar at Macclesfield Royal Infirmary, but these are not sufficient for forensic purposes. Would my Instructing Solicitor please instruct both a consultant neurologist and a consultant psychiatrist to examine and report on the Claimant's present condition and prognosis. Additionally the Claimant's cognitive and memory abilities should be assessed by a clinical psychologist. The consultant experts should be asked to consider expressly how the Claimant's complaints

compare with the clinical findings and, if appropriate, the consultant psychiatrist should comment on the genuineness of the Claimant's complaints so far as they go beyond what would ordinarily be anticipated on the basis of the clinical findings. The Defendant's solicitors should be invited to agree to the instruction of joint experts in accordance with CPR, r 35.8.

6   In addition to this expert evidence my Instructing Solicitor should please take statements from Mrs Allen, and if possible one or two friends and the Claimant's former colleagues at work, explaining the type of person the Claimant was before the accident and how they have found him since.

Claimant's loss of earnings

7   A number of important issues arise in relation to this head of claim:

(a) the Claimant's ability as a diver and his future prospects at Dodd-Comex Limited;

(b) the Claimant's prospects of employment when his career as a diver ended;

(c) the Claimant's ability to find alternative employment following his injuries;

(d) the appropriate multiplier;

(e) loss of pension calculation.

8   *(a) Ability and future prospects*
In addition to the Claimant's own evidence I hope that it will be possible to obtain a statement from a director or senior manager of Dodd-Comex Limited covering the Claimant's ability as a diver, his prospects with the company or in the industry generally and the pay and other benefits which the Claimant could reasonably expect to earn. I understand that there was some ill feeling between himself and his employers on the termination of the Claimant's employment. If Dodd-Comex Limited will not cooperate the necessary evidence as to the Claimant's abilities and prospects can be given by Mr Phillips, the Claimant's diving instructor who appears to hold him in high regard, and the former colleague Mr Charles Jones to whom the Claimant refers in his recent letter.

(b) Prospects of employment after end of diving career
As I understand the position, few deep sea divers work as such after reaching the age of 40. However, there are considerable opportunities both in the UK and abroad for experienced deep sea divers as consultants or instructors. The Claimant needs to be in a position to adduce evidence both as to his prospects of further employment in the diving industry after he reached 40, and as to the remuneration which may be anticipated with that employment. Mr Phillips, and if they will assist a Dodd-Comex Limited witness, should be able to give the required evidence. Would my Instructing Solicitor please take draft proofs of evidence, and if appropriate ask Mr Phillips to introduce a further witness with the necessary experience to cover this part of the case.

(c) The Claimant's ability to obtain alternative employment
The Claimant's witness statement should cover his academic record and comment upon the areas of work in which, despite his injuries, he might obtain employment. I appreciate that the Claimant's sole ambition in life was to be a diver and that his academic record was poor. But while his opportunities following his accident may be limited the Claimant still has an obligation to seek alternative work. This is a suitable case for instructing an expert employment consultant to consider what, if any, work at what remuneration is available to the Claimant given his medical condition. If it is possible to find an employment consultant with experience of the diving industry

he could also assist the Claimant with evidence under point (b) above. Again, a joint expert should be instructed if possible.

(d) Appropriate multiplier

The Claimant is now almost 27 years of age and he will be 28 when the case comes to trial next year. The appropriate multiplier for loss of earnings to age 65, using a 2.5% discount rate would be 23.61 according to Ogden Table 9. However, it is necessary to make some reduction to this figure to reflect contingencies other than mortality. In this case the appropriate table is Table A: male loss of earnings to pension age 65. Since Mr Allen was working at the time of the accident and was educated to degree level the appropriate discount factor is 0.93. This reduces the multiplier to 21.96. Of this multiplier 10.39 will be attributable to the period to the Claimant's 40th birthday when his career as a deep sea diver would have ended. It remains to be seen (see (b) above) whether a different multiplicand will have to be used for the later period of the Claimant's employment.

(e) Loss of pension

The Claimant's employment was pensionable. A jointly instructed forensic accountant should be asked also to calculate the loss of pension (on *Auty v National Coal Board* principles) and provide the necessary tax and national insurance calculations for the remuneration figures under (b) and (c) above.

Mrs Allen's loss of earnings

9 Mrs Allen took time off work as a secretary and personal assistant at IFA plc to look after her husband after the accident. Her statement should cover this matter and explain what earnings she lost as a result. A statement should also be obtained from the Personnel Department of the company confirming the dates on which Mrs Allen was off work and the pay she lost as a result.

Excess on insurance policy, loss of personal effects

10 The Claimant must disclose his insurance documents which will show the relevant excess and set out a list of the personal effects damaged in the accident and their costs in his witness statement. Disclosure must be given of any receipts or vouchers of which the Claimant retains possession. The figures under these heads of claim should be capable of agreement with the Defendant's insurers. If any item is disputed and the relevant claim cannot be compromised, the Claimant will have to give evidence of the purchase of the item and its current replacement cost.

Cost of adaptations of car and home

11 My Instructions indicate the Claimant wishes to carry out a fair range of alterations to his present house in order to accommodate his difficulties in walking and moving his neck. He also wishes to have a specially adapted car. A joint report should be commissioned from a rehabilitation expert as to the alterations that may be appropriate and their capital and annual maintenance cost. I suggest that although the expert should be instructed now he or she should be asked not to finalise the report until the further medical evidence I have requested above is to hand.

Maintenance, decorating and gardening costs

12 The courts do regularly award damages for 'DIY claims' assessed on multiplicands of £500 and upwards. It is necessary however that the Claimant and Mrs Allen cover in their statements what it was that the Claimant did in fact do about the house before

his accident which he has been unable to do since, and comment on any expenditure they have in fact incurred on such items since the accident. The rehabilitation expert should be able to give evidence of the cost of assistance in the Claimant's locality, but it would also be advisable for my Instructing Solicitor to obtain letters from local decorators and gardeners as to the amounts they charge for their work. These letters should be forwarded to the Defendant's solicitors for their agreement and if and only if they cannot be agreed should witness statements be taken from the relevant witnesses.

Travel, medicines and miscellaneous costs

13   A list of these items should be prepared on the Claimant's instructions and agreed with the Defendant's solicitors.

Summary

14   Witness statements and experts' reports are to be obtained from the following witnesses.

Factual Witnesses

    (1) The Claimant

    (2) Mrs Allen

    (3) One or two friends/colleagues (see para 6 above)

    (4) Dodd-Comex Limited's witness

    (5) Mr Phillips

    (6) Mr C Jones

    (7) Local decorator/gardener (see para 12 above)

Expert Reports

    (1) Mr Kenneth Brand FRCS

    (2) Consultant Neurologist

    (3) Consultant Psychiatrist

    (4) Clinical Psychologist

    (5) Employment Consultant

    (6) Forensic Accountant

    (7) Rehabilitation Expert

15   I would be grateful for an opportunity to consider the witness statements and experts' reports before exchange. At the same time I will advise if required on the contents of the trial bundle. I leave it to my Instructing Solicitor to consider whether the Claimant should be warned that the Defendant's insurers may well instruct a firm of private investigators to carry out video surveillance of him.

JOHN DOE

1 Wilberforce Chambers
Temple
London EC4

14th June 2007

14

Assessment criteria

14.1 Assessment in opinion writing skills

14.1.1 The subject matter of assessments

All assessments in opinion writing will require you to write a full opinion. The content of the opinion may be any of the following, or a combination of them:

- Opinion on the merits.
- Opinion on liability.
- Advice on quantum.
- Advice on evidence.
- Advice on procedure.
- Advice on practical steps to be taken.
- Advice on specific issues.
- Advice on appeal.

The legal content of the opinion may be within a civil or a criminal case, at any stage from before commencement of proceedings until the hearing of an appeal. You may be asked to advise any party to the proceedings or matter in dispute.

14.1.2 The use of assessment criteria

Whenever you are assessed in opinion writing skills, you will be given the criteria according to which you will be assessed. These criteria can be used for self-assessment, and assessment of your fellow students. They will also be used by your tutor in giving you feedback (formal or informal) on your written work.

It is therefore important that you should familiarise yourself with the standard criteria used, and understand how the criteria are applied. The rest of this chapter sets out and explains the standard criteria used at the Inns of Court School of Law. Other teaching institutions probably use very similar criteria, because they are based on guidelines laid down by the Bar Council. You would be well advised to study the relevant criteria, and then to bear them in mind when practising your opinion writing.

The more you understand what will be required of you in assessments, the more you will appreciate the skill of opinion writing, and be able to practise it.

14.2 Criteria for a typical opinion

The usual criteria applied at the Inns of Court School of Law when you are being assessed on your opinion writing are set out below. They will be appropriate, with minor adaptations, to more or less any opinion on the merits, liability, quantum or procedure in a civil case.

In order to be graded competent or above, your opinion must satisfy these criteria:

(1) LANGUAGE (20%):
   (i) Is written in clear, grammatical English, correctly spelt and appropriately punctuated.
   (ii) Is written in language and in a style that is appropriate to an opinion.

(2) LAYOUT, STRUCTURE AND WEIGHT (20%)
   (i) Is properly and neatly laid out.
   (ii) Has a clear and appropriate structure in that it:
      (a) deals with the issues in a logical order;
      (b) is divided into an appropriate number of paragraphs;
      (c) makes appropriate use of subheadings; and
      (d) sets the conclusions out clearly and prominently.
   (iii) Gives each issue its due weight and significance.
   (iv) Is of suitable length overall.

(3) LAW AND ANALYSIS (60%)*
   This is sub-divided into three sections:
   (A) ISSUES, LAW AND FACT (20%)
      (i) Identifies and addresses the material issues and does not include immaterial issues.
      (ii) Identifies material facts accurately.
      (iii) Is based on a sound understanding and application of the correct relevant law.
   (B) CONCLUSIONS AND REASONING (20%)
      (i) Includes a justifiable overall conclusion.
      (ii) Includes a justifiable conclusion on every issue raised in the instructions either expressly or implicitly.
      (iii) Contains clear reasoning based on a sound understanding and practical application of the issues, law and facts.
      (iv) Contains reasoning which justifies the conclusions reached and explains, if necessary, why a definite conclusion cannot be reached.
   (C) PRACTICALITY (20%)
      (i) Addresses the needs and objectives of the client.
      (ii) Identifies and deals with gaps in the information which are material to the client's case.
      (iii) Deals with the evidence in a way which would assist the solicitor in preparing the case.
      (iv) Shows an awareness of the context in which the advice is given and deals appropriately with any practical and procedural matters.

*You cannot pass this assessment unless you obtain at least 30 marks out of 60 for criterion 3 (see Assessment Regulation 3.2.6) as well as at least 50% of all available marks.

We shall now break these down and explain in more detail what is involved in each.

14.2.1 Criterion (1)—Language

This criterion usually carries 20% of the marks. It is to do with the way you write.

Criterion (1)(i)

Is written in clear, grammatical English, correctly spelt and appropriately punctuated

The requirement is simply to produce an opinion which is written in clear English, without spelling mistakes, grammatical errors or incorrect punctuation. For example, verbs should be in the correct tense, nouns should have the appropriate article, every sentence should have a main verb and sentences should be separated by a full stop, not a comma. Spell names correctly.

Your English must be clear in the sense that the words you use must make sense. What you write must be comprehensible, and you should use words so that they have their correct meanings. So, for example, you would be penalised for muddling 'claimant' and 'defendant', for writing 'negligence' when you mean 'negligent', or for using the word 'imply' to mean 'infer'.

Criterion (1)(ii)

Is written in language and in a style appropriate to an opinion

Opinions are relatively formal documents, and so the language you use should not be too informal or loose and it should certainly not be colloquial. On the other hand, you should write in plain English, avoiding archaic, pompous or overly dense language. There is a difference between the kind of language that is appropriate in opinions and statements of case, for example. Your writing should be fluent—avoid note form, and if you use abbreviations make them sensible ones. Be polite both to your instructing solicitor and to your lay client. You will be rewarded for particularly elegant writing. The overall effect should be that your opinion is clear and easy to read, but has a professional and confident tone.

Use correct terminology. Refer to yourself in the first person, and to instructing solicitors and your client in the third person. Make sure you get case names and the names of statutes right. Use the correct words when referring to legal concepts: if they need to be explained in everyday language, do this as well. Don't write 'it is submitted that'. Don't be too judgmental about your client.

14.2.2 Criterion (2)—layout, structure and weight

This criterion usually carries 20% of the marks.

Criterion (2)(i)

Is properly and neatly laid out

As you can see, structure includes formalities and format. Your opinion should be properly headed, in accordance with your instructions, written in numbered paragraphs and signed (with a pseudonym for assessment purposes) at the end. Use capital letters when naming an Act, use italics or underlining for case names. Format is also important. If you are word-processing, you are strongly advised to take the time to ensure that the formatting is neat and consistent. Take care over line spacing and indents. Do not use very small or very large type. If you are writing by hand, as you will be in an unseen assessment, use space. Do not write into the margins, leave a space between paragraphs and generally ensure that the finished result looks neat. If you have planned your opinion properly, you should not need to write so fast that your handwriting deteriorates.

Criterion (2)(ii)(a)

Deals with the issues in a logical order

This is a very important requirement, and the one which, if not fulfilled, will do great damage to the clarity of your opinion. You cannot fulfil it if you have not also fulfilled the requirement to keep separate issues separate. You are strongly advised to have a skeleton plan for your opinion, and then to follow it, so as to ensure that what you write has a coherent structure and enables the reader to follow your reasoning. In most cases the logical order is that which coincides with conventional expectations. So in a case involving breach of contract, the reader would expect to see you deal with the issues in the order—contract, terms, breach, causation, loss. You may occasionally decide to deviate from this, but be careful, and be sure you know why you are doing so. Never deal with quantum before liability.

Criterion (2)(ii)(b)

Is divided into an appropriate number of paragraphs

The most important requirement here is not to muddle issues together, but to separate them clearly from each other. If you do not keep each issue distinct, you will have an incoherent opinion, which will be very hard to unravel, and which will almost certainly fail under this criterion.

If you are considering separate causes of action, deal with them in separate paragraphs, or sections of your opinion. If you are considering the liability of more than one potential defendant, deal with them separately as well. If there are several items of potential loss to be dealt with, take them separately, in separate paragraphs or sub-paragraphs, unless they can more conveniently be taken together (for example because the issues are identical).

The paragraphing in an opinion should follow the normal rules of good prose. Do not allow your paragraphs to get too long, or too short. Do not be afraid to have paragraphs of varying length. Ideally each paragraph should deal with one and only one segment of your reasoning, and each paragraph should tend to begin with a new issue or step in your reasoning. What is appropriate is what best puts over your opinion and explains the reasons for it. Paragraphs should be numbered.

Criterion (2)(ii)(c)

Makes appropriate use of subheadings

Subheadings are very useful, and it is most unlikely that an opinion without any subheadings will be as clear or as easy to read as it could be. But do not use too many—it is clumsy and unhelpful to have a subheading at the top of every paragraph or to label every small sub-issue in this way. Nevertheless, too few, and you are losing clarity. At the very least an assessor would expect to see an opinion divided into 'liability' and 'quantum'. When you do insert a subheading, make sure it is an accurate description of the content of the section that follows. It is misleading and unhelpful to head a section 'causation', for example, if what follows is to do with remoteness of damage.

Criterion (2)(ii)(d)

Sets the conclusions out clearly and prominently

Your conclusions should be quick and easy to find. You are encouraged to put the overall conclusions near the beginning of the opinion, but you do not have to do so. Wherever you put them, by the time the reader comes to the end of your opinion, they should be left with a very clear idea of what your conclusions are, and what advice you have given. Never leave your conclusions buried in the middle of a section or paragraph. Do not expect the reader to have to pull them together from several different places. This does indeed mean that there is an element of repetition in your opinion, but it is well worthwhile.

Criterion (2)(iii)

Gives each issue its due weight and significance

The requirement here is that you should not spend a lot of your time on peripheral issues at the expense of major ones. The longest sections of your opinion should be those dealing with the most important, or the most complex, issues. Deal with simple or relatively unimportant matters more briefly. Note that if you have dealt with matters that are irrelevant, you are not giving them their due significance (which is nil). Similarly, if you have missed out an important issue, you have not given it its due weight. In either case you will be penalised under this criterion as well as criterion (3)(A).

One of the most common faults in students' opinions is a poor introduction. When you set out the material facts and issues, you should ensure that you mention concisely anything of real importance, but do not go on at great length. It is not uncommon to see an unedited churning out of every fact, which takes up a page or more (typed) of the opinion. Be critical, analytical and selective.

It is also common for students, when setting out their overall conclusions near the beginning of the opinion (as you are encouraged to do) to go on at great length, beginning to explain the reasons for those conclusions, and so repeating what is about to follow. There is no need to do this.

Criterion (2)(iv)

Is of a suitable length overall

There is no correct length for an opinion, and what is suitable varies according to the complexity of the case and the style of the writer. But you will be penalised if your opinion is excessively short (in which case you have probably also failed to identify the issues, or not given them their due weight), or excessively long (in which case you may also have dealt with irrelevant issues, or given some issues too much weight). For further guidance, see **5.7.4**.

14.2.3 Criterion (3)—law and analysis

Criterion (3) consists of three criteria grouped together. This is to satisfy the Bar Council's requirement that you cannot pass the assessment overall unless you '(a) demonstrate adequate knowledge and comprehension of the law, and (b) adequately demonstrate the ability to manipulate and utilise such knowledge in the analysis and preparation of the case employed for the assessment'. So criterion (3) is the mandatory criterion on which you must pass, and it usually carries 60% of the marks in total.

14.2.3.1 Criterion (3A)—issues, law and fact

This part of criterion (3) requires you to identify and incorporate the correct subject matter for your opinion and usually carries 20% of the marks.

Criteria (3)(A)(i) and (3)(A)(ii)

(i) Identifies and addresses the material issues and does not include immaterial issues.
(ii) Identifies material facts accurately.

You cannot write a good opinion if you do not write about the right things. From your reading of the facts, you must apply the law and so identify what are the real issues that need to be dealt with. You should then deal with them. You will satisfy these criteria if you deal with all the right facts and issues and be penalised if you miss any important issues out, or deal with irrelevant facts and issues. It is the structured way of thinking that you have been taught that will enable you to identify the correct facts and issues. Muddled thinking, or an academic approach, will quite possibly lead you to deal with the wrong facts and issues.

You have a good opportunity in your introductory paragraph(s) to set out the facts you consider to be material. Take care over this. The first few paragraphs often signal very clearly what the quality of the opinion is going to be. If, when introducing the case, you ignore important facts, or get them wrong, it is likely to be because you are not going to address the right facts. If you churn out all the facts uncritically, you are signalling clearly that you have not worked out what is material and what is not.

Criterion (3)(A)(iii)

Is based on a sound understanding and application of the correct relevant law

In essence this means getting the law right, and it is inseparable from identifying the correct facts and issues, because you cannot do that if you do not apply the law correctly. Your careful analysis of the facts is what enables you to identify the relevant law. It is not enough to understand the law, you must apply it—in other words you must deal with the law in a practical, problem-solving way, not an academic way. You will fail badly under this criterion if you go off on a tangent and base your whole opinion on the wrong law.

Identifying the correct issues and getting the law right is fundamental to your assessment. If you fail under this criterion, then only too often it becomes inevitable that you will fail under criteria (2), (3)(B) and (3)(C) as well.

14.2.3.2 Criterion (3)(B)—Conclusions and reasoning

This part of criterion (3) is basically about delivering a clear and accurate answer and then justifying it. This does not, of course, necessarily mean a definite answer, but there must be sound reasons for the answer you give. The criterion usually carries 20% of the marks. Sometimes it is subdivided, eg 10% to the conclusions on liability and 10% to the conclusions on quantum.

Criterion (3)(B)(i)

Includes a justifiable overall conclusion

There is rarely only a single 'right' answer; but there may be any number of wrong answers. An answer is right if it is a justifiable conclusion to reach on the basis of the facts and the law, and is as far as possible in accordance with the client's needs. In other words, it is a conclusion which a competent practising barrister might reach in this case. You will be penalised under this criterion if your conclusion is not expressed. You must say what you think, not leave it to be deduced.

Your overall conclusion must be expressed in unambiguous terms. When it is vague or unclear, this is usually a sign that the writer is uncertain what conclusion he ought to be expressing and is trying to hedge his bets. This is a serious fault and it stands out a mile. Even worse is contradictory conclusions. It is by no means uncommon for one conclusion to be expressed at the beginning of an opinion (eg 'quite a strong case') and the opposite conclusion to appear later on (eg 'unlikely to succeed'). Such a contradiction would be very heavily penalised under this criterion.

As explained in **5.7.1**, it is important neither to be too definite nor too indefinite in your conclusion. Both are common faults in students' opinions. As well as expressing a sound conclusion, you need to be careful to get the strength of that conclusion right. It is not sound to advise a client there is a strong case, when the probability of success is only just better than even. It is useless to advise a client that a case may or may not succeed, if you give no indication of the chance of success. Take care over your choice of words when expressing your conclusion.

Criterion (3)(B)(ii)

Includes a justifiable conclusion on every issue raised in the instructions either expressly or implicitly

Of course you must answer every question you have been asked to deal with. If you do not do so, you will be penalised under this criterion, because your advice will be incomplete, or even misleading. If you do not even raise the question, you will also be penalised under criterion (3)(A). Remember that not all questions are asked expressly.

For example, instructions to advise 'whether Jane Smith has a claim in respect of her injuries' implicitly asks:

(a) how strong a claim?

(b) against whom?

(c) what would be the cause(s) of action?

(d) what might be recovered in such a claim?

(e) should proceedings be commenced?

And maybe other questions too, depending on the context.

Everything that has been said under criterion (3)(B)(i) above about reaching a justifiable overall conclusion and expressing it clearly of course applies equally to your conclusion on each subsidiary issue.

Criterion (3)(B)(iii)

Contains clear reasoning based on a sound understanding and practical application of the issues, laws and facts

It is not enough to reach conclusions, you must give reasons for those conclusions, and your reasoning must be clear. Sound reasoning involves careful and methodical construction of an argument, allowing the reader to see how your analysis of the issues, law and facts leads step by step to your conclusions. Your reasoning cannot be clear if your analysis is faulty in the first place, so if you fail under criterion (3)(A) you will very probably fail under this criterion too.

Criterion (3)(B)(iv)

Contains reasoning which justifies the conclusions reached and explains, if necessary, why a definite conclusion cannot be reached

The soundness of your conclusions has been tested under criterion (4). Now you must demonstrate that you have been able to justify those conclusions on the basis of the law and your analysis of the facts and issues. This will, of course, not be possible if your conclusions are unsound, or if your analysis is faulty, or if you simply fail to give reasons at all.

As you were reminded above, there is not often a definite conclusion that you can reach on any issue. If you express an indefinite conclusion, you must explain why you cannot be certain, and what the answer will eventually depend on. You may need to consider alternatives, and explain the circumstances in which each of those alternatives will be the right conclusion.

14.2.3.3 Criterion (3)(C)—practicality

This part of criterion (3) pulls together several different aspects of opinion writing, all of which are important in the process of giving sound advice to the client. It usually carries 20% of the marks.

Criterion (3)(C)(i)

Addresses the needs and objectives of the client

Addressing the needs and objectives of the client may not mean that you have to give any specific piece of advice, though sometimes you will. It is more to do with thinking practically and realistically. Always be aware of what your client is trying to achieve. Remember that your client is a real person, who will act on your advice. Be aware of what the consequences will be for the client. Identify any risks, and above all be aware of the cost implications of any step you have advised. If you have had to give the client bad news, still think what is the best advice you can give them in the circumstances. Any advice you give which is unhelpful, unwise or unethical will also be penalised under this criterion.

Criterion (3)(C)(ii)

Identifies and deals with gaps in the information which are material to the client's case

There are always gaps in the information you are provided with. The further information you need, because it will affect your conclusion, must be asked for, and put into context. Do not just ask for it, but explain why you need it and what difference it will make. If there are major gaps in your instructions, you will be penalised for failing to identify them and fill them. But do not ask for information that you do not need, or which cannot realistically be obtained. Think practically—if you ask for further information, be aware of who you are asking to do what.

Criterion (3)(C)(iii)

Deals with the evidence in a way which would assist the solicitor in preparing the case

Criterion (3)(C), as a whole, is basically measuring your ability to think and write like a practitioner rather than an academic. Central to this is your consideration of the evidence in a case. Even if you are not expressly asked to advise on evidence, your advice can never be practical if you do not think in terms of how a case can be proved. You must show an awareness of the evidence you know you have, because it is mentioned or included in your instructions, and the evidence that must be obtained before the case can succeed. Such evidence must be clearly identified to your instructing solicitor, and wherever possible you should indicate how and where it is to be obtained. It should also be apparent from your advice what purpose the evidence you have asked for will serve, so that the solicitor understands why it needs to be obtained. So clearly relate it to the issue that that evidence will go to prove.

Criterion (3)(C)(iv)

Shows an awareness of the context in which the advice is given and deals appropriately with any practical and procedural matters

The first point here is to be aware of the stage at which you are advising. If the case involves the possibility of court proceedings, think whether you need to give any relevant advice on procedure. For example, is the pre-action protocol being complied with? Should proceedings be commenced now or later? What steps should be taken before proceedings are commenced? If proceedings have already been commenced, then you are in the middle of a timetable, and there will most certainly be some procedural advice that needs to be given, if only to remind instructing solicitors of the next step required.

But in any event, there is always some practical step that needs to be taken, even if it is not a procedural step under the CPR. Having received your advice, who needs to do what next? This should be made clear in every opinion.

APPENDIX A
IMPROVING YOUR WRITING SKILLS

The importance of being able to write in good, clear, well-written English cannot be overestimated. Much of the work of a barrister involves writing. A solicitor who receives an opinion written in poor English will think twice before sending any more work to the barrister who wrote it.

It is said in *The Complete Plain Words* (Sir Ernest Gowers) that the 'test of good writing is whether you can convey to your readers exactly what you intend to convey'. It is therefore important that a barrister can write in a way that is intelligible to others.

If you write in poor English, there is a risk that you will fail to convey your intended meaning to your reader. Poor English is also likely to distract the attention of your reader.

The purpose of this appendix

The objective of the rules which relate to the construction of sentences (grammar and syntax) is to ensure that the same set of words means the same thing both to the writer and to the reader.

However, this appendix is not meant to be an exhaustive exposition of the 'rules' of English. Instead, its purpose is to try to identify mistakes which are commonly made and to show how those mistakes may be avoided.

How to improve your writing

(a) You must practise your writing. Fluency comes, in part, from familiarity with the skill of writing. The more of it you do, the easier it becomes.

(b) You should read the writings of others. If you spend some of your spare time reading novels, you should find that your own use of English becomes more fluent. If you come across a word which is unfamiliar to you, look it up in a dictionary: this is how to expand your vocabulary. If you read a sentence which is unclear, ask yourself why it is unclear; then make sure that you avoid writing something which is unclear for the same reason.

(c) You must make sure that you are familiar with the basic rules which govern the writing of the English language.

(d) Before starting to write a document, make sure that you know exactly what you want to say. The point is made in *The Complete Plain Words* (Sir Ernest Gowers) that 'loose thinking is bound to produce loose writing... It is wise therefore not to begin to write... until you are quite certain what you want to say'.

(e) If you are uncertain of the spelling of a particular word, use a dictionary. If you are using a word processor, remember that most spell check programs will only question words which are not in the program. This means that the misspelling of 'there' in the following sentence would not be highlighted: 'Their is one complaint about the defendant's work'. Proofread your work carefully to ensure that such errors are corrected.

(f) If you cannot think of the word which conveys precisely what you want to convey, use a thesaurus. Most word processors have a thesaurus function.

If you take these steps, you should improve your ability to write in a way which is clear and easy to read.

The sentence

Gowers, in *The Complete Plain Words*, writes: 'The two main things to be remembered about sentences by those who want to make their meaning plain is that they should be short and should have unity of thought'.

Ideally, a sentence should convey a single idea. It is sometimes said that, at its simplest, a sentence should include a subject, an object and a verb. For example, 'The barrister [subject] went [verb] into the courtroom [object]'. Most sentences will, of course, contain much more than these three elements, but you should check each sentence to ensure that a subject, object, and verb are all present. If a sentence does not contain all three elements, read it again to check that it makes sense.

Incomplete sentences

A common error is to write an incomplete sentence.

Take these words:

Although liability has been admitted. The question of the amount of damages has still to be decided.

The second sentence is complete, but the first is not.

The construction of a sentence often depends on the word with which the sentence begins. For example, when the word 'although' appears at the start of a sentence, it should be followed by two clauses. The structure of a sentence beginning with the word 'although' should be:

Although [something is/is not true], [something else is/is not true].

The phrase used in the example should therefore be written as follows:

Although liability has been admitted, the question of damages has still to be decided.

An alternative would be to write two sentences:

Liability has been admitted. However, the question of damages has still to be decided

or to create two clauses in a single sentence by means of a semicolon:

Liability has been admitted; however, the question of damages has still to be decided.

Conjunctions

It is permissible for two ideas to be linked in the same sentence, provided that appropriate punctuation or an appropriate conjunction is used. A conjunction is simply a 'joining' word.

Take this example, in which the conjunction is missing:

The claim form was issued on 1 April, it was not served until 30 June.

This sentence should be written as follows:

The claim form was issued on 1 April, but it was not served until 30 June.

In this example, the two clauses in the sentence are joined by the word 'but'.

Another option would be to use a single sentence, but to begin it with the word 'although':

Although the claim form was issued on 1 April, it was not served until 30 June.

Punctuation can also be used to solve the problem. In the example given, a semicolon would cure the defect:

The claim form was issued on 1 April; it was not served until 30 June.

The semicolon is effective in this instance because it is more emphatic than a comma and splits the sentence into two separate parts.

Yet another approach would be to use two sentences instead of one:

The claim form was issued on 1 April. However, it was not served until 30 June.

The words which follow a conjunction must 'harmonise' with the words which precede it.

So, in this example from Gowers, the sentence

A woman who is absent from work because of pregnancy or confinement has the right to return to work in the same grade <u>and working</u> the same hours...

is incorrect and should be rewritten because the clause 'to return to work' does not harmonise with the clause 'and working':

A woman who is absent from work because of pregnancy or confinement has the right to return to work in the same grade <u>and to work</u> the same hours...

Subject-verb agreement

The rule that the subject and the verb must 'agree' simply means that if the subject of the sentence (the doer) is plural, the plural form of the verb (the word which describes what is done) must be used. Similarly, if the subject is singular, the verb must also be singular.

Hence:

The claim form <u>was</u> served.
The claim forms <u>were</u> served.

A common reason for making a mistake is the distance between the noun and the verb. Gowers gives this example:

We regret that <u>assurances</u> given us twelve months ago that a sufficient supply of suitable local labour would be available to meet our requirements <u>has</u> not been fulfilled.

In this example, the verb 'has' (singular) does not agree with the noun 'assurances' (plural).

No doubt, the rule about subject-verb agreement seems very obvious. However, difficulties can arise where the subject of the sentence is a 'collective noun'.

Contrast

The witness statements <u>were</u> served three weeks before the trial

and

The bundle of witness statements <u>was</u> served three weeks before the trial.

In the sentence *'the witness statements were served...'*, the subject is plural (*'witness statements'*); in the sentence *'the bundle of witness statements was served...'*, the subject is a collective noun (*'bundle'*). The word *'bundle'* is singular (there is only one bundle), even though it consists of a number of objects.

The matter is confused by the fact that some collective nouns are treated as being plural:

A <u>number</u> of witnesses <u>are</u> available to give evidence for the claimant.

The contrast can be explained quite easily. In the sentence which refers to the *bundle of witness statements*, the emphasis is on the bundle (of which there is only one). In the sentence which refers to a *number of witnesses*, the emphasis is on the *witnesses* (of whom there are several).

A further complication is that some nouns may be regarded as being singular or plural. For example, a limited company may be referred to as singular or plural. Thus, the writer can choose between

Denby Ltd are manufacturers of widgets

and

Denby Ltd is a manufacturer of widgets.

The same is true of certain other collective nouns such as 'prosecution' and 'jury'.

Where you have a choice whether to regard a collective noun as singular or plural, make sure that you are consistent in your treatment of that noun throughout the document you are writing. For example it is wrong to write:

The Corporation <u>has</u> not asked for any advice...and I do not doubt <u>its</u> ability to deal with the immediate situation <u>themselves</u>.

The Corporation (which may be treated as either singular or plural) is treated as singular on two occasions ('has' and 'its') but then as plural ('themselves').

Another form of sentence construction which can trap the unwary is where there is a mixture of singular and plural nouns.

In the sentence

The claim form, the witness statements and the draft order <u>were</u> all handed to the judge

the correct form is, of course, plural. Several items *were* handed to the judge. However, it is possible to rewrite the sentence so that the emphasis is not on all the documents, but is on one particular document:

The draft order, together with the claim form and the witness statements, <u>was</u> handed to the judge.

In that case, the subject of the sentence is the draft order and so the verb is singular, not plural.

It should also be noted that where the subject is an 'indefinite pronoun', such as the word 'each', it is regarded as singular:

Each of the documents <u>has</u> been certified as being accurate.

Another complexity is the 'compound subject'. Essentially this is where the sentence has two subjects. The difficulty arises most frequently in the use of 'either' or 'neither'. Where both subjects are singular, the verb will be singular even though there are two subjects:

Neither the Particulars of Claim nor the Defence was served within the time limit prescribed by the rules.

Therefore, you should write:

Neither skill nor knowledge is needed

not

Neither skill or knowledge are needed.

Where one of the alternatives is plural, however, a plural verb is appropriate. For example:

Neither my letters nor my report on the case are in the file.

Subjunctive forms

The subjunctive form of a verb is often used in a phrase containing the word 'that' where the intention is to convey the idea that action is necessary. For example:

I would ask that Mr Jones deal with this in his report.
I suggest that this scheme go ahead.
I am not suggesting that such work be halted.

The subjunctive is also appropriate to express an idea which is conditional. For example:

If he were to be convicted, he would face a sentence of up to five years' imprisonment.
Should he have the chance, Mr Jones should obtain a copy of the letter.

Pronouns

A pronoun is a word which stands for a noun and is used to save repeating the noun.
   For example:

The offender's driving licence was endorsed and it was returned to him three weeks later.

This is much neater than writing:

The offender's driving licence was endorsed and the driving licence was returned to him three weeks later.

You must, however, take great care to avoid ambiguities when you use pronouns.
   Take this sentence:

If bicycles are chained to these railings, they will be removed.

What will be removed: the bicycles or the railings? To avoid this ambiguity, the sentence should be rephrased:

Any bicycles found chained to these railings will be removed.

Margot Costanzo in *Legal Writing* gives this example:

From the transcript of the evidence it is clear that the bank manager assisted the guarantor to execute the guarantee validly and then he left the room.

There is doubt as to who left the room: the bank manager or the guarantor. This sentence therefore needs to be re-drafted to eliminate the ambiguity.

Modifiers

As its name suggests, a modifier is a word or phrase which modifies (that is, restricts, limits or makes more exact) the meaning of another word or phrase.

For example, in the sentence

All barristers in private practice must be members of a circuit

the phrase *'in private practice'* modifies the phrase *'all barristers'*. The effect is that barristers only have to be members of a circuit if they are in private practice.

Care needs to be taken with the placing of a modifier to ensure that it only relates to the word or phrase to be modified.

For example, in the sentence

Only solicitors and barristers in private practice may appear as advocates in court

the phrase *'in private practice'* could modify either *'barristers'* or *'solicitors and barristers'*.

The sentence therefore has to be rewritten to remove this ambiguity. If the intention is that the modifier should apply only to barristers, the sentence should be written thus:

Only solicitors, and barristers in private practice, may appear in court as advocates.

The ambiguity is resolved by placing the modifier as close as possible to the word being modified, and by using commas to insulate the modified clause from the rest of the sentence.

If the intention is that the modifier (*'in private practice'*) should apply both to solicitors and barristers, the sentence should be written thus:

Solicitors and barristers may only appear as advocates in court if they are in private practice.

Gowers says that 'words...that are most closely related should be placed as near to each other as possible, so as to make clear their relationship'. He gives this example:

No child shall be employed on any weekday when the school is not open for a longer period than four hours.

The phrase *'for a longer period than four hours'* is intended to modify *'employed'*, not *'open'*, and so should be written:

No child shall be employed for a longer period than four hours on any weekday when the school is not open.

The position of a word like 'only' (which is one way of signifying a modifier) can have a dramatic effect on the meaning of the sentence. The following example is given by Gowers:

His disease can only be alleviated by a surgical operation

could mean

Only a surgical operation can alleviate his disease [ie the disease cannot be alleviated in any other way]

or

A surgical operation can only alleviate his disease [ie the operation cannot cure the disease].

Margot Costanzo in *Legal Writing* gives a further example of ambiguity caused by a misplaced modifier:

You could make a tax deductible gift to a school, hospital or community project within the definition of a charitable institution.

The ambiguity is whether it is only a 'community project' which has to fall within the definition of 'a charitable institution' or whether the school, the hospital and the community project must all fall within this definition.

If the intention is that the modifier should apply to all three, the sentence could be rewritten:

You could make a tax deductible gift to a charitable institution such as a hospital, school or community project.

The paragraph

A paragraph is merely a collection of sentences devoted to a single topic. Generally speaking, paragraphs which consist of only a single sentence should be avoided. On the other hand, long paragraphs are very difficult to read and so if you find that you have written a very long paragraph you should consider whether it could be split into two or more shorter paragraphs.

Each separate topic should be dealt with in a separate paragraph. Each paragraph should deal with only one topic.

Gowers writes, 'Every paragraph must be homogeneous in subject matter, and sequential in treatment of it. If a single sequence of treatment of a single subject goes on so long as to make an unreasonably long paragraph, it may be divided into more than one. But you must not do the opposite, and combine into a single paragraph passages that [do not have] this unity, even though each by itself may be below the average length of a paragraph.' In other words, a topic may be divided into a number of paragraphs if that topic is too long to be dealt with in a single paragraph, but a number of different topics should not be dealt with in one paragraph.

It is usually helpful if the opening sentence of the paragraphs sets out what the paragraph is about. For example:

<u>There can be little doubt that the defendant drove his car negligently</u>. He was driving at 50 mph on a stretch of road governed by a 30 mph speed limit. The road was icy, making it more difficult for the defendant to control his car.

Finally, related topics should be kept together in the same section of the document, in order to maintain the overall structure and coherence of what you are writing.

Punctuation

The full stop

The full stop is used to mark the end of a sentence.

When using a full stop, check that the sentence which precedes it is complete (see above).

The comma

The comma is used to mark breaks within a sentence. These breaks usually correspond with pauses which would be observed if the sentence were to be read out loud.

Commas are also used to write lists where the presentation of the list in the form of a table would not be appropriate. For example:

The agreement was to supply three photocopiers, a collator, a duplicator and various smaller items.

A comma may also be used after an introductory clause. For example:

Although the defendant admitted that he had been driving his car, he denied that he had consumed any alcohol that evening.

Another use for a comma is to introduce a quotation. For example:

Lord Denning said, 'It was bluebell time in Kent'.

In some instances, commas may also be used in place of brackets. For example:

The claimant's letter, which was received by the defendant on 1 April, sets out the details of the claimant's claim

instead of

The claimant's letter (which was received by the defendant on 1 April) sets out the details of the claimant's claim.

A common mistake in the use of the comma is to write a sentence like this:

A copy of the order made by the judge, must be served on the defendant by the claimant's solicitor.

The comma in that example should be deleted since it is inappropriate to place a comma between the subject and the verb which relates to that subject.

Another common error is to use a comma to link two independent clauses which are not linked together by a conjunction (such as 'and' or 'but'). For example, in this phrase:

On 1 May the company wrote to the engineers to ask them to service the boiler, this was followed up on 14 May by a telephone call repeating the request

the comma should either be preceded by the word 'and' or else should be replaced with a full stop or a semicolon.

Where the subject is followed by a phrase which is intended to modify the subject, the modifier will have to be placed between the subject and the verb. In that case, a comma is put before the modifier and a second comma is placed after the modifier.

For example:

A copy of the order, once it has been made by the judge, must be served on the defendant by the claimant's solicitor.

A common mistake is to omit the second comma. To give another example, in this sentence:

The claimant has, in my opinion a good claim against the defendant

there should be a comma after the word 'opinion'. A good way of remembering the need for two commas in this context is to think of the comma as a bracket. No one would think of writing

The claimant has (in my opinion a good claim against the defendant.

A slightly more complicated rule is explained by Sir Ernest Gowers. It is that a commenting clause should be placed within commas but a defining clause should not. A commenting clause is one like this: *'Mr Jones, who was here this morning, told me that...'*. A defining clause is one like this: *'The man who was here this morning told me that...'*. In the first case, the subject of the sentence (*'Mr Jones'*) is complete. This means that the sentence would be correct if it just read, *'Mr Jones told me that...'*. In the second case, the phrase *'who was here this morning'* is essential to the definition of *'the man'* and without it the subject is incompletely described.

Gowers gives this example:

Any expenditure incurred on major awards to students, who are not recognised for assistance from the Ministry, will rank for a grant.

The commas make the phrase *'who are not recognised'* a commenting clause. The implication is that no students are recognised for assistance from the Ministry. If the writer's intention is to say that only some students are not recognised, then the commas should be deleted.

Compare these two sentences:

Pilots, who are inattentive, do not usually live long.

This sentence means that all pilots are inattentive and therefore do not live long.

If it is written without the comma

Pilots who are inattentive do not usually live long

it means that only those pilots who are inattentive do not usually live long.

The semicolon

A semicolon is similar in effect to a full stop; it is used where a single idea (which could be conveyed in two separate sentences) is conveyed in a single sentence. The semicolon is a useful device where you want to convey two ideas in a single sentence because those two ideas are closely related to each other. It marks a break which is less emphatic than a full stop but more emphatic than a comma.

For example:

The claim form was issued on 1 April; however, it was not served until 30 June.

A very common error is to use a semicolon where a colon should be used. For example, in the following sentence a semicolon is wrongly used to introduce a list:

It was agreed that the following items would be supplied;

   (a) three photocopiers
   (b) one collator
   (c) one duplicator.

The colon

The colon is used to indicate that either a list or a direct quotation follows.

For example:

It was agreed that the following items would be supplied:

   (a) three photocopiers
   (b) one collator
   (c) one duplicator.

Or

Lord Denning said: 'It was bluebell time in Kent'.

In the latter case, a comma would serve equally well.

A common mistake is to use a semicolon (;) where a colon (:) should be used (for example to indicate that a list follows).

The apostrophe

The apostrophe has two main uses. The first is to indicate possession.

Where there is one possessor, the apostrophe precedes the s.

The claimant's house.

Where there is more than one possessor, the apostrophe comes after the s:

The claimants' house.

The second use of the apostrophe is to indicate that something has been omitted. Examples include *don't* and *isn't*. Such words are too colloquial to be used in a formal document such as an opinion or a statement of case.

Probably the most common mistake in the use of the apostrophe is made with the word *it's*:

it's can only mean it is.

Where the *it* connotes possession, then the word *its* is written without an apostrophe:

The company was convicted of manslaughter on the ground that its directors had been negligent.

The question mark

The only relatively common error is to use a question mark where a full stop would be appropriate. A question mark is used at the end of a *direct* question, such as:

Do you wish me to advise on this question?

Where the question is an *indirect* one, then the sentence should end with a full stop:

The claimant should be asked where he was standing just before the accident occurred.

Simplicity of language

You should always aim to write in plain English, that is 'in language which conveys its message clearly, simply and effectively' (De Groot and Maxwell, *Legal Letter Writing*).

You will improve your ability to write in plain English if you adopt the guidelines which follow.

Gowers proposes three rules which must be observed in order to write in plain English:

- Use no more words than are necessary to express your meaning.
- Use the familiar word rather than the far-fetched.
- Use words with a precise meaning rather than those which are vague.

However, there are several other principles to be borne in mind if you are to succeed in writing plain English.

Use the active voice rather than the passive voice

The 'active voice' is where the subject of the sentence does the action; the 'passive voice' is where the action is done to the subject of the sentence.

For example, it is better to write

The claimant sent a letter to the defendant

than

A letter was sent by the claimant to the defendant.

Using the active voice instead of the passive voice usually results in shorter sentences, which are therefore easier to read.

Use verbs rather than nouns based on verbs

It is clearer to write:

The defendant's lorry <u>collided</u> with the claimant's car

than

The defendant's lorry <u>was in collision</u> with the claimant's car.

Keep your sentences as short as possible

When someone is reading, they usually read sentence by sentence. All the information contained in a sentence is stored up in the memory until the reader reaches the end of the sentence. Only then can the information be processed and the whole message received. It is for this reason that short sentences are easier to read than long sentences. The longer the sentence, the more the reader has to remember before being able to work out what message the sentence is conveying. It follows that short sentences make it easier for the reader to take in the meaning of what is written.

Of course, in any piece of written work the sentences will vary in length. However, if you find yourself writing a long sentence, pause to ask yourself whether it could be split into two separate sentences (or whether it could be split into two parts by the use of a semicolon).

Margot Costanzo in *Legal Writing* gives this example of a sentence which, although not too long, could be split up in order to be more digestible:

Practice of the law today is difficult and successful practice is extremely challenging.

This sentence can be shortened by replacing the 'and' with a full stop:

Practice of the law today is difficult. Successful practice is extremely challenging.

Alternatively, a semicolon could be used:

Practice of the law today is difficult; successful practice is extremely challenging.

Sometimes, the only remedy is to rewrite an unduly long sentence. Take this example of an indigestible sentence taken from *The Complete Plain Words*:

Separate departments in the same premises are treated as separate premises for this purpose where separate branches of work which are commonly carried on as separate businesses in separate premises are carried on in separate departments in the same premises.

It is particularly easy to fall into the trap of writing this sort of nonsense when you are trying to paraphrase the words of a statute. The author suggests rewriting that particular nonsense by starting with the word 'if':

If branches of work commonly carried on as separate businesses are carried on in separate departments at the same premises, those departments will be treated as separate premises.

Put the words in a logical order

Ideally, the subject should be as close as possible to the verb and the verb should be as close as possible to the object. This keeps the 'action' in one place. Where a modifier is used, the words which constitute the modifier should be placed as close as possible to the word(s) being modified.

In Legal Letter Writing, De Groot and Maxwell (written at a time when a claimant was known as a plaintiff) give this example of a sentence which is difficult to assimilate because of a very long gap between the subject and the verb:

The lawyer, who previously acted for the plaintiff in these proceedings and, in all instances, can be said to have behaved in an exemplary manner (despite allegations to the contrary by the plaintiff), should be awarded her costs without delay.

The authors suggest that the sentence should be rewritten as follows:

This lawyer previously acted for the plaintiff in these proceedings. In all instances she can be said to have acted in an exemplary manner, despite allegations to the contrary by the plaintiff. Accordingly, she should be awarded her costs without delay.

Those three sentences are easier to read than the single, longer, sentence.

Sir Ernest Gowers, in *The Complete Plain Words*, gives this example:

The existing Immigration Regulations occasionally—only a very limited number of cases have come to my attention—produce undue hardship as a result of the very strict interpretation.

The reader is kept waiting because the flow of the sentence is interrupted by the comment about the number of cases which have come to the writer's attention.

Gowers suggests rewriting that sentence as follows:

The strict interpretation of the existing Immigration Regulations occasionally produces hardship, though I know of only a few cases.

Gowers gives a further example:

These proposals, which it is intended should be effected without requiring police authorities to increase manpower or expenditure although there may be some modest increase in expenditure by the Police Complaints Board, are described in Annex A to this paper.

It is much easier to read if written thus:

These proposals are described in Annex A to this paper. It is intended that they should be effected...

Another problem with the order of the words is that you can convey a meaning other than the one you intend if you do not get the order of the words right.

For example, the sentence:

When out of work, the state requires you to register as unemployed

suggests that the state is out of work.

It should be written:

When you are out of work, the state requires you to register as unemployed

or

The state requires you to register as unemployed when you are out of work.

Make sure that your use of terminology is consistent

You must be consistent in the names you give to things and to people. Otherwise, the reader will become confused. So, for example, decide whether you are going to identify a party as 'the respondent', 'the employer', 'the company' or 'Fiddlesticks Ltd' and use the same label throughout.

Do not use language which is too elaborate

An extensive vocabulary is a very useful asset to possess, since it enables you to find precisely the right word to convey the meaning which you intend. However, you should try to find the simplest word which says what you want to say. To write, *'The meteorological prognostications were unpropitious'* is pompous in the extreme. It means, *'The weather forecast was poor'*, or you might prefer, *'The weather forecast was unpromising'*.

In the drafting of documents such as contracts and statements of case, the language tends to be very formal. Phrases such as 'the said agreement' and 'hereinafter referred to as' often appear. However, such phrases have no place in documents such as opinions or in correspondence.

Avoid unnecessary words

In *The Complete Plain Words*, Sir Ernest Gowers complains about the use of 'padding', or 'verbiage' as it is sometimes called. He defines this as 'the use of words, phrases or even sentences that contribute nothing to the reader's perception of the writer's meaning'.

You should make sure that every word you write has a role to play in the sentence of which it forms part. Avoid putting in words which are simply padding. A common offender is the phrase 'as such'.

In the phrase:

The claimant has no claim against the defendant as such

the words '*as such*' are meaningless and so should be omitted.

Other offenders include '*it should be noted that*' or '*it should be pointed out that*': these phrases rarely add anything.

'During such time as' means 'while', 'in all probability' means 'probably', 'in close proximity' means 'near', 'on a temporary basis' means 'temporarily'.

Something else to be avoided is the 'double negative'. Usually two negatives cancel each other and produce an affirmative. To say that something is 'not uncommon' means that it is common. Perhaps the reason for saying 'not uncommon' is to try to convey that the thing is not very common; a better way of doing so would be to say that it is 'fairly common'. The reason for avoiding double negatives is that they can be difficult for the reader to understand. It is also easy for the writer to make a mistake and write the opposite of what is intended. Gowers gives this example:

There is no reason to doubt that what he says in his statement is not true.

What the writer was trying to say was

There is no reason to doubt that his statement is true.

Take care when using standard words and phrases

Care needs to be taken when using stock phrases. Examples of phrases which are often written incorrectly include: 'as regards', 'with regard to', 'consists of', 'comprises'.

You must not confuse the word 'counsel' (barrister) with the word 'council' (local authority). Remember that *'advice'* is a noun; *'advise'* is a verb.

Take care when using the word 'however' in the middle of a sentence. If the word 'however' introduces a new clause, then it should be preceded by a full stop or by a semi-colon. For example, do not write:

The claimant has a good case, however further evidence is needed to support the allegations that the defendant was negligent.

This should be written:

The claimant has a good case; however, further evidence is needed to support the allegations that the defendant was negligent

or

The claimant has a good case. However, further evidence is needed to support the allegations that the defendant was negligent.

Where the word 'however' is not introducing a new clause, it may be used thus:

I am of the opinion, however, that the claimant needs further evidence to support her allegation that the defendant was negligent.

Final example

Margot Costanzo in *Legal Writing* gives this example of a sentence which is too long, contains too many prepositions, and is written in the passive voice:

In these circumstances, it is appropriate for the legal profession to assert its right to determine the standards of prospective entrants to the profession by declining to recognise the adequacy of training offered by institutions which are inadequately resourced.

This unwieldy sentence could be written as follows:

In these circumstances, the legal profession should refuse to accept as adequate the training offered by institutions which are inadequately resourced. It is appropriate, after all, for the legal profession to determine the standard of its prospective entrants for itself.

Further reading

Costanzo, M, *Legal Writing*, Cavendish, 1993.
Gowers, Sir Ernest, *The Complete Plain Words*, 3rd edn, Sidney Greenbaum and Janet Whitcut (eds), Penguin, 2004.
Eastwood, J, *Oxford Guide to English Grammar*, Oxford University Press, 1994.
Trask, RL, *Mind the Gaffe—The Penguin Guide to Common Errors in English*, Penguin Books, 2002.

APPENDIX B
EXERCISES

Exercise 1
Consider these ten qualities of good writing from **Chapter 2:**

clarity,
logical structure,
spelling,
grammar,
punctuation,
precision,
non-ambiguity,
conciseness,
completeness,
style,
appearance.

Suppose these were the assessment criteria for marking a piece of writing. How many marks would you allocate to each if you had 100 marks to distribute:

- If you were assessing a letter from a lawyer to a lay client?
- If you were assessing a draft contract?

Exercise 2
Consider the following sentences. What is ambiguous, vague or inaccurate about them? How can that ambiguity or vagueness be removed or the inaccuracy corrected?

(1) Room 6 is for the use of barristers and their pupils.

(2) The landlord and his agent may enter the premises at any time.

(3) I gave £1,000 to John and Mary.

(4) This table is only to be used for reading and writing.

(5) My trustees may give the money to such benevolent and charitable institutions as they see fit.

(6) The defendant agreed to replace any units found to be defective within three months.

(7) No more than six books or files may be taken into the examination room.

(8) All prisoners with a conviction for theft on 31 January 2008 will be released.

(9) Students were deemed to have passed any examination they had failed to pass by 31 August 2007.

(10) The head of chambers shall be a member of the Bar Council.

(11) Money was to be paid to John only by Mary.

(12) No smoking, eating or drinking allowed.

(13) By a contract made on 10 December 2006 between the claimant and the defendant the claimant agreed to purchase 1,000 light bulbs at a price of 50 pence.

(14) The claimant was driving her Ford Sierra car in Piccadilly at 9 am on 13 April 2007 when she was struck by the defendant in a Vauxhall Astra car.

(15) The defendant denies that he was in breach of contract as alleged by the claimant.

(16) It is denied that the claimant's accident was caused by the defendant's negligence.

(17) The defendant does not owe the claimant £3,621.85.

(18) John Smith went to Leicester to start college on 30 September 2007.

(19) The claimant swerved to avoid the defendant who had strayed onto her side of the road and collided with a wall.

(20) The claimant was walking on a greasy marble floor when she slipped and fell over and was injured.

(21) The claimant did not deliver the goods to the defendant on 18 April 2007 as agreed.

(22) The defendant did not take adequate precautions to prevent the accident.

(23) The claimant claims damages for the death of John Smith for his dependants.

(24) The claimant seeks an injunction forbidding Mrs Jones from building her home extension on the claimant's land.

(25) Notice must be received between 13 and 15 January 2007.

(26) Replies must be received within 28 days of this notice.

(27) Notice may be delivered any weekday until 28 February 2007.

Exercise 3

Rewrite the following in plain English:

(a) Turning to the request which has been made by the claimant for the grant of injunctive relief. With respect to this request, the argument is put forward by the defendant that injunctive relief is not necessary because of the fact that the exclusionary clause is already null and void by reason of a prior judgment given in a similar case by the court. This being the case, the exclusionary clause can have no further force or effect, and the defendant argues that in such an instance the case can be fully and properly resolved without the issue of an injunction. For these reasons it is argued that injunctive relief is not suitable in this case.

(b) It shall be a breach of the terms of this agreement for any member to fail to post a notice in a prominent place that is in no way obscured from public view listing that member's retail prices for all items offered for sale, saving only that those items offered at a special sale price for a period not exceeding seven days need not be listed on the said notice.

(c) In consideration of the performance by the contractor of all the covenants and conditions contained herein and contained in the plans and specifications annexed hereto, the owners agree to pay to the said contractor an amount equal to the cost of all materials furnished by the contractor, and the cost of all labour furnished by the contractor, to include the cost of tax and insurance directly connected to such labour, together with the amounts payable to subcontractors properly employed by the said contractor in completion of his obligations herein set out. In addition to the amount hereinbefore specified, the owners agree to pay to the contractor a sum equal to 10% of the value of the construction on completion, the total amount payable to fall due only on satisfactory completion of the said construction. It is specifically agreed by the parties hereto that notwithstanding this term the owners shall not be required under the terms of this agreement to pay to the contractor an amount in excess of the sum of Five Hundred Thousand Pounds.

(d) It shall be and is hereby declared to be unlawful for any person to expel, discharge, or expectorate any mucus, spittle, saliva or other such substance from the mouth of the said person in or on or onto any public pavement, street, road or highway, or in or on or onto any railway train, bus, taxicab or other public conveyance, or in or on or onto any other public place of whatsoever kind or description, and any person who does so expel, discharge or expectorate any such substance as defined above in any place herein delineated shall be guilty of an offence.

Exercise 4

Humpty Dumpty sat on a wall,
Humpty Dumpty had a great fall;
All the King's Horses,
And all the King's Men,
Couldn't put Humpty together again.

(a) Ask Humpty and your instructing solicitor a series of questions which will elicit the further information required for you to determine whether he has an action for damages for personal injury and if so against whom and on what basis.

Compose your questions on the basis that the specific question you ask will be answered, not any question you may think you are asking—your questions must be precise.

(b) Having acquired all the information you need, state the facts of the case in such a way that if they are proved, then whoever you consider to be liable must be found liable.

Exercise 5

The following figure shows two different building techniques for a stone wall. Write a paragraph or two explaining the difference between coursed random rubble and squared uncoursed rubble.

quoins

coursed random rubble   squared uncoursed rubble

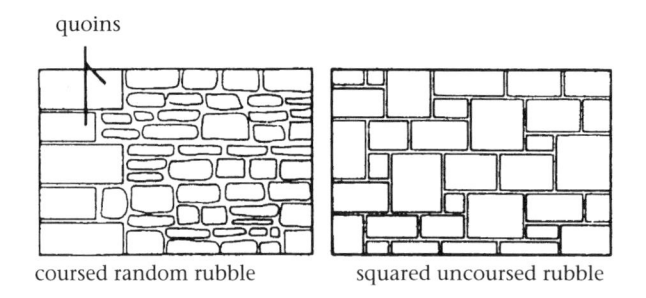

Exercise 6

Describe in writing the design and construction of a spiral staircase, being as concise and clear as possible.

Exercise 7

Rewrite the following particulars of claim so as to state the facts more clearly and remove ambiguities. If in doubt as to the sense intended, make a sensible choice.

(1) The claimant rents the first floor flat of 24 Lockwood Grove, London W17. The defendant is on the floor above.

(2) The defendant is always making a lot of noise day and night. It started in December 2006. It gets into the flat below and the claimant cannot bear it.

(3) He plays loud music all night four or five days a week and when he was asked to turn it down he refused. He was asked three times but the defendant turned it up.

(4) When he was asked to turn it down the defendant deliberately stamped on the floor for about half an hour, all five of them.

(5) They sang as well several times, in the early hours.

(6) It is disturbing the claimant's family which is a nuisance and he will go on doing it unless he is stopped.

(7) The claimant cannot sleep and has suffered damages.

Exercise 8

You are instructed by Homewood Garden Centre Ltd. As part of its business Homewood undertakes the service and repair of motor mowers. Recently it repaired and serviced a mower on behalf of a long-standing customer. A few days later the mower's throttle return spring came adrift, with the result that the mower was stuck at full throttle, ran out of control and smashed into a greenhouse causing damage to the greenhouse itself and to the plants inside, which were being grown for sale. Homewood was obliged to settle a claim by the customer for the cost of repairing the mower, damage to the greenhouse, damage to plants and loss of profit.

The company now wishes to incorporate into all its service and repair contracts a standard term which would prevent it being liable to such an extent again. It feels that it was reasonable that it should be liable for the cost of repairing the mower, but not for any of the other damage or loss. You are asked to draft a suitable clause to be inserted into your client's standard-form contract which will limit its liability in the way it wishes. It should cover the service and repair not only of motor mowers, but any other mains-, battery-, petrol-, or diesel-driven garden tool. It should be written in plain intelligible language to comply with reg 7 of the Unfair Terms in Consumer Contracts Regulations 1999.

APPENDIX C
FURTHER EXERCISES

Exercise 1

Consider these instructions and the opinion which follows. Identify the faults in the opinion. How could these be put right? What omissions are there in the opinion? Discuss.

Instructions

<u>RE: SUSANNA AND EMMA WILLIAMS DECEASED</u>

Counsel has herewith:

(a) Statement of Michael Morley.

(b) Letter dated 20th July 2007 from Clifford Thwaite.

Counsel is instructed by Gatwicks on behalf of Mr Michael Morley, the executor of the estate of his late cohabitee, Susanna Williams, who died on 6th February last in the circumstances explained in Mr Morley's statement. Probate of Miss Williams's estate was granted to Mr Morley out of the Brighton District Probate Registry on 29th July 2007. Your instructing solicitor has sent letters before action to both Mr Thwaite, the owner of 24 Eastside, and Benedict Brutus, the estate agents. Mr Thwaite's reply is enclosed with these instructions. Benedict Brutus have responded only by telephone asserting that they can have no responsibility for this accident.

Counsel is requested to advise whether a claim may be brought in respect of this tragic accident and, if so, against whom, and whether it would be worthwhile bringing a claim in respect of Emma Williams's death. Counsel's advice on quantum is not required at this stage.

Would Counsel therefore please advise on liability.

MICHAEL MORLEY of 18 Carlton Terrace, London SW1 will say:

I was born on 21st November 1977 and have since 2001 been living with Susanna Williams at the above address. We considered ourselves to have a stable relationship, but we never married. We had two children, Mark, who was born on 3rd March 2000, and Emma who was born on 12th October 2006. I am presently unemployed, having been dismissed from my job as an investment analyst at the Biological Bank on 1st November 2006. Susanna Williams was born on 14th October 1977 and worked as a commodity broker.

On 6th February 2007 Susanna and I went to inspect 24 Eastside, Clapham Common with a view to purchasing it. This was a fine Victorian six-storey property overlooking the Common and was offered for sale at £1,250,000. It had a nice paved patio and an ornate wrought iron balcony on the fourth floor. We went with our children and met Miss Jackie Welland of Benedict Brutus, the estate agents, at about 10.00 am at the property. She opened up and showed us round. She was very enthusiastic about the property's potential not least, perhaps, because she could not enthuse about the existing state of the property which was dilapidated. She did indeed warn us to take care as we went about the property in case, as she laughingly put it, we fell through the floor. In the event her joking turned very sour. When we reached the fourth floor front room Susanna asked if she could go out on to the balcony from which there were fine views of the Common. Miss Welland produced a key and opened the door. Susanna went out on to the balcony holding Emma in her arms. I turned to say something to Mark and as I did so heard a crash and a scream. A large section of the balcony was rotten and it had given way under Susanna's weight. She and Emma fell to the patio area below and both were killed in the fall.

Messrs Gatwicks
42 Cheapside
London EC

42 Burley Street
York

20th July 2007

Dear Sirs

Re: Susanna and Emma Williams Decd

I was sorry to learn of the death of your clients while inspecting my property at 24 Eastside, Clapham earlier this year. As requested I have passed your letter on to my insurers. However, I would like to point out that since inheriting the property from my aunt last year I only visited it on one occasion, sometime in January 2007. I instructed Benedict Brutus to sell the property for me and I went with Miss Busby of that firm to look it over. It was evident that the property was not in good repair and she suggested that I had it done up before sale. I was not too keen on this idea, but agreed that Benedict Brutus should draw up a specification of work and obtain tenders, while at the same time putting the property on the market at a good price.

On 11th February 2007 I received a specification from Mr Johnson of Benedict Brutus following his inspection on 4th February, which showed amongst other matters that the balcony was in urgent need of substantial repair. I do not feel that I am to blame for this tragic accident.

Yours faithfully
Clifford Thwaite

Opinion

RE: MICHAEL MORLEY

COUNSEL'S ADVICE

The facts

Mr Clifford Thwaite inherited a house at 24 Eastside, Clapham Common, from his aunt in 2006. He only visited it once, in January 2007, when he instructed Estate Agents, Benedict Brutus, to sell it for him. They advised him to have it done up before sale. He was not keen, but agreed that Benedict Brutus should draw up a specification of work and obtain tenders, while at the same time putting the property on the market at a good price.

On 6th February 2007 Susanna Williams and Michael Morley, who had been living together in a stable unmarried relationship since 2001, went to inspect 24 Eastside, Clapham Common with a view to purchasing it for £650,000. It was a fine Victorian six-storey property overlooking the Common with (inter alia) an ornate wrought iron balcony on the fourth floor. They went with their children, Mark, aged 6, and Emma, aged 4 months. They were shown around by Miss Jackie Welland of Benedict Brutus. She was very enthusiastic about the property's potential and warned them to take care as they went about the property in case, as she laughingly put it, they fell through the floor.

In the event, this joke turned very sour, for when they reached the fourth floor front room, Susanna asked if she could go out on the balcony from where there were fine views of the Common. Miss Welland produced a key and opened the door. Susanna went out on to the balcony holding Emma in her arms. Mr Morley turned to say something to Mark and as he did so he heard a crash and a scream. A large section of the balcony was rotten and it had given way, causing both Susanna and Emma to fall and be killed on the nice paved patio beneath.

A week later, Mr Thwaite received a specification from Benedict Brutus, which showed amongst other matters that the balcony was in urgent need of substantial repair.

Mr Morley obtained probate of Susanna Williams's estate on 29th July 2007, and Instructing Solicitors have written letters of claim to Mr Thwaite and Benedict Brutus, both of whom have denied liability, Mr Thwaite by a letter dated 20th July 2007 and Benedict Brutus by telephone.

Counsel is asked to advise whether a claim may be brought in respect of this tragic accident and, if so, against whom, and whether it would be worth bringing a claim in respect of Emma's death.

Conclusion

In my opinion Benedict Brutus are liable but Clifford Thwaite may not be. Instructing Solicitors should therefore sue Benedict Brutus and recover substantial damages (although I am not asked to advise on quantum at this stage). In my opinion the claim will be brought under the Fatal Accidents Act 1976.

By s 1(1) of this Act, if death is caused by any wrongful act, neglect or default which is such as would (if death had not ensued) have entitled the person injured to maintain an action and recover damages in respect thereof, the person who would have been liable if death had not ensued shall be liable to an action for damages, notwithstanding the death of the person injured. By s 1(2) the action shall be for the benefit of the dependants of the deceased. By s 1(3) both Mr Morley and Mark are dependants. By s 2 Mr Morley can therefore bring a successful action against whoever is liable in law.

The law

The relevant law in this case is set out in the Occupiers' Liability Acts 1957 and 1984. The 1957 Act deals with liability if the claimant was a lawful visitor of the occupier, while the 1984 Act applies if he was a trespasser or other non-visitor. Under the 1957 Act, an occupier owes a common duty of care to all his visitors to take such care as in all the circumstances of the case is reasonable to see that the visitor will be reasonably safe in using the premises for the purposes for which he is invited or permitted to be there. On the other hand, the duty under the 1984 Act is a lesser one, which only arises in limited circumstances. However, in my opinion, since Susanna Williams was being shown around the house by Benedict Brutus with Mr Thwaite's permission, there can be no doubt that she was a lawful visitor and so there is no need to consider the Occupiers' Liability Act 1984 any further.

We must therefore consider who was the occupier of the house at the material time and whether they were negligent. If so, they will be liable to Mr Morley.

Who was the occupier

The occupier is the person who has a sufficient degree of control over the premises to impose upon him a duty of care to those who enter the premises. Mr Thwaite is the owner, but he was not in actual occupation of the premises at the time. He may or may not therefore be the occupier (*Harris v Birkenhead Corporation* [1976] 1 WLR 279). He would not be if he had effectively given control over to Benedict Brutus. I would ask Instructing Solicitors for further information on how much control he had over the premises, and for a copy of any contract he may have made with the Estate Agents.

However, I submit that Benedict Brutus are occupiers at the same time (*Wheat v Lacon & Co Ltd* [1966] AC 552), because they actually opened up the premises on the fateful day.

Negligence

It seems that Benedict Brutus were aware that the balcony was unsafe on the 4th (of February, not floor!), because Mr Johnson made an inspection on that date as a result of which he reported the need for repair. They therefore should not have been showing clients around on the 6th, even if the appointment was made before the 4th (will Instructing Solicitors please ascertain how, when and where the appointment was made). It follows that Benedict Brutus have been negligent.

In the case of Mr Thwaite his negligence is less clear. He was aware that the property was not in good repair and he had been advised that he ought to have the property done up before selling it. Therefore it may well have been reasonably foreseeable that parts of the property were in a dangerous condition, but he nevertheless allowed Benedict Brutus to show prospective purchasers around. It is certainly a possibility that this was in breach of his duty of care as an occupier, because it is arguable that the reasonable occupier would not allow visitors to enter until he was satisfied that all necessary repairs had taken place. If this can be established, then in my submission, Mr Thwaite would also be liable.

Alternatively, and this is a much stronger cause of action, Mr Thwaite is liable for employing negligent agents. I have already advised that Benedict Brutus were negligent, and in these circumstances a reasonable owner would not have employed them. They are by definition his agents and as such he must be vicariously liable for their actions. In my opinion therefore both Benedict Brutus and Mr Thwaite are likely to be found liable in this claim.

Contributory negligence

There remains the question of whether there is any contributory negligence on the part of Susanna, Emma or Mr Morley. In the case of Emma, since she was only 4 months old at the time of her death, I think that it is most unlikely that the court would find her to have been contributorily negligent. But in the case of Mr Morley and Susanna, I foresee that the defendants may argue that they should have taken greater care for their own safety, and that Susanna should not have gone onto the balcony following

Miss Welland's express warning, and that Mr Morley should have tried to prevent her doing so. Instructing Solicitors should be prepared for this possibility, and I would like more information on this issue.

Further information required

Will Instructing Solicitors please provide me with the following:

(a) A copy of the grant of probate.

(b) A copy of Mr Johnson's report and specification.

JOHN DOE

Boswell Chambers
Temple EC4

Exercise 2

Consider the following instructions. Draw up a skeleton plan for your opinion, identifying the issues and stating your conclusions.

RE: SOUTHERN FRUIT GROWERS LTD

Instructing solicitors act for Southern Fruit Growers Ltd (the 'Company') which owns extensive orchards in Kent. Fruit is usually picked in September or October of each year, stored in refrigerated storage chambers over the winter and marketed in the following spring to take advantage of the more favourable prices prevailing then. The Company insures with the Greenwich Insurance Co Ltd (the 'Insurers') against loss, including loss of profit on premature sale of fruit stored, caused by mechanical failure of the refrigeration plant. The policy of insurance dated 18 April 2006 is subject to certain special conditions, set out in enclosure 1 herewith. The Company employs (see enclosure 2) Refrigeration Systems (the 'Engineers') to carry out the inspection, do the work and provide the certificate required by special conditions 1 and 2 of the insurance policy.

In accordance with clause 1 of the maintenance contract the Company paid the Engineers £1,500 on 2 July 2006. In accordance with clause 2 of the contract, the Company notified the Engineers by letter (see enclosure 3) of its intention to start loading the storage chambers on 28 September 2006. The Engineers acknowledged receipt of that letter but despite frequent reminders by telephone and letter failed to inspect the plant. By 1 October, the storage chambers had been loaded with pears to their full capacity (50 tonnes). The refrigeration plant was then operating normally. On 21 October, however, a valve stuck in the heat exchanger causing a complete breakdown of the refrigeration plant. This took two weeks to repair. No notification of the breakdown was given to the Insurers until the plant had been completely repaired. Due to the sudden rise in temperature in the storage chambers, the pears had to be sold. The Company's labour force which at that time was engaged on picking Bramley drops (apples) had to be redeployed on grading and packing pears. The Bramley drops deteriorated and became completely unsaleable.

The pears were sold for £100,000. If they had been kept until the following spring, the figure would have been in the region of £150,000. The Bramley drops would have realised around £21,000. The Company submitted a claim to its Insurers for the loss it had suffered as a result of the breakdown. The Insurers, however, repudiated liability on the grounds that there had been a breach of special conditions 2 and 3 of the insurance policy.

Counsel is asked:

(a) to advise the Company whether it can recover its loss from the Engineers; and

(b) to advise on quantum.

Enclosure 1: special conditions

1 The Company shall before the commencement of each storage season engage a firm of competent refrigeration engineers to inspect the refrigeration plant, put the same into good operating condition and provide a certificate that the plant is in such condition.

2 Insurance cover shall be suspended during any storage season in respect of which no such certificate has been obtained.

3 The Company shall notify the Insurers of any breakdown at the time it occurs. Such notification shall be a condition precedent to the liability of the Insurers for any loss ensuing.

Enclosure 2: maintenance contract

Dated: 2 July 2005

Between: Refrigeration Systems (the Engineers) and Southern Fruit Growers Ltd (the Company).

1 The Company agrees to pay to the Engineers £1,500 a year on 2 July in each year during the continuance of this contract.

2 The Engineers agree on receiving from the Company at least three weeks' notification in writing of intention to load to inspect the Company's refrigeration plant and put the same into good operating condition and provide a certificate that the plant is in such condition within three weeks of receiving such notification.

3 This contract may be terminated on 1 July in any year by three months' previous notice in writing.

Enclosure 3: letter

3rd September 2006

Dear Sirs,

We hereby give you notice in accordance with clause 2 of the maintenance contract that we intend to start loading on 28 September 2006.

Yours faithfully,

Southern Fruit Growers Ltd

The following Exercises 3–16 are 'mini-opinion' exercises, designed to enable you to practise some of the sub-skills that are part of the skill of opinion writing. In each case try to advise clearly and fully, with reasons, in a concise way: a few short paragraphs will do. There is no need to set out what you are asked to advise about or to summarise the facts (as you would in a full opinion).

Exercise 3

At 11.00 am on 1st March 2007 Mr Robbie Nutt was riding his motor cycle along Sandy Road in Westbury at about 55 mph when he struck a ramp, or 'sleeping policeman', and was thrown from his motor cycle and injured.

Sandy Road is on land owned by the Duke of Westland and leased for the past five years to the Westbury District Council. There are six ramps on Sandy Road, which were put there by the Duke of Westland more than five years ago. They were painted with yellow stripes at the time of the lease, but the paint has long since worn off. The ramps were not marked in any other way. There was, however, a small sign placed by the district council at the entrance to Sandy Road which said 'Westland Estate. Private Road to Sandy Beach. No right of way. Public enter at their own risk. Caution: Ramps: Max speed 20 mph'. Mr Nutt, who was on his way to the beach, saw neither the sign nor the ramp.

Advise Mr Nutt whether the Duke of Westland and/or Westbury District Council is liable to him for his injuries.

Exercise 4

On 2 January 2007 at about 8.15 am, a cold and icy morning, Mr John Dedham was driving at about 45 mph along Castle Street in Faverstock, up a moderately steep hill, when a car driven by Mr Stephen Tribe came over the brow of the hill, also travelling at about 45 mph, started down the hill, skidded on a patch of black ice, veered on to the wrong side of the road, and struck Mr Dedham's car on the driver's door. Castle Street is subject to a 30 mph speed restriction. The road becomes derestricted at the top of the hill.

Advise Mr Dedham, who was injured in the accident, whether Mr Tribe is liable to him and whether there was any contributory negligence on his part, and if so how much.

Exercise 5

On 1 May 2007 at about 9.00 pm, Mr Underwood was driving along Offchurch Lane. It was dusk but not yet fully dark. It was not raining but the road was wet from an earlier downpour. He had his headlights on. He stopped at the junction with the A45, intending to turn right. The road seemed clear, so he moved forward about 4 or 5 feet but saw a car approaching from his right and stopped again. This car was driven by Mr Willis, and was travelling at about 60 mph with its sidelights but not headlights on. As Mr Willis's car approached, a third car driven by Mr Gatting struck the rear of Mr Underwood's car and pushed it forward into the path of Mr Willis's car causing a collision.

Mr Willis and Mr Underwood were injured. Mr Willis's car had damage to the front end, and Mr Underwood's car had damage to its rear end and its front end. It is not clear whether Mr Underwood's injuries were caused by the collision between his car and Mr Gatting's, or his car and Mr Willis's, or both.

Mr Willis has brought a claim against Mr Underwood, who has counterclaimed against Mr Willis and made an additional claim against Mr Gatting claiming contribution or indemnity in respect of Mr Willis's claim and damages in respect of his own injury and loss.

Advise Mr Underwood how liability will be apportioned in respect of Mr Willis's claim and his own claim and counterclaim.

Exercise 6

Mr James Salmon suffered an injury to his leg as a result of the negligence of his employer, Teviot Decorations Ltd. Six months later, while crossing the road on the way to visit the hospital for physiotherapy treatment to his injured leg, he was struck by a lorry and suffered a further injury to his leg, as a result of which it was amputated. The driver of the lorry was not prosecuted.

Advise Mr Salmon whether his employer is liable for his loss on a continuing basis, whether it is liable for the increased loss caused by the amputation, or whether its liability is limited to the six months prior to the second accident.

Exercise 7

On 28th April 2007 Mrs Jenkins was chopping onions in the kitchen of her house when Mr Wates negligently drove his car into the front wall of the house. This so frightened Mrs Jenkins's dog that it ran between her legs, causing her to fall and injure herself with the chopping knife. Advise Mrs Jenkins whether Mr Wates is liable for her injury.

Exercise 8

Dreamy Travel Ltd is a package holiday operator, whose managing director is Mr Dream. Greed Hotels Ltd owns and operates holiday hotels. According to Mr Dream in December 2006 Mr Greed, the managing director of Greed Hotels Ltd, had a private business lunch with Mr Dream and told him that Greed Hotels Ltd had just completed a new luxury hotel in Brighton, which would be available in the 2007 summer season. He described the facilities in great detail and provided Mr Dream with photographs, including one of what Mr Dream took to be the swimming pool.

Acting in reliance on these representations, Dreamy Travel booked accommodation at the new hotel and sold holidays to its customers at the hotel. In fact it turned out that the hotel was unfinished. The swimming pool was not ready and the photograph was obviously not of the swimming pool at that hotel. Dreamy Travel had to compensate its customers and suffered heavy losses.

Advise Dreamy Travel Ltd whether it would be appropriate to allege fraud on the part of Greed Hotels Ltd.

Exercise 9

Captain Brassbound was employed as sales director at a salary of £96,000 pa by Undershaft Ltd, which is an arms manufacturer, on a ten-year contract commencing 1 November 2003. The contract contained the following clauses:

4   The employee agrees that during the period of five years following the determination of this contract he will not solicit any of the customers of Undershaft Ltd.

5   The employee agrees that during a period of one year following the determination of this contract he will not accept employment with any firm or body that manufactures or sells armaments.

Captain Brassbound has recently handed in his notice, and intends to become employed by Wonderweapons Ltd, another arms manufacturer, and a direct competitor of Undershaft Ltd.

Advise Undershaft Ltd whether clauses 4 and 5 are enforceable against Captain Brassbound.

Exercise 10

Captain Brassbound was employed as sales director at a salary of £96,000 pa by Undershaft Ltd, on a ten-year contract commencing 1 November 2003, without any provision for early determination. The contract contained the following clauses:

2 The employer agrees to reimburse the employee for any legitimate expense incurred by the employee in the performance of his duties.

3 The employee agrees to perform all duties which are assigned to him by the board of directors.

6 The employer and employee agree that in the event of any breach of any term, whether express or implied, of this agreement, the party at fault will pay to the other party as liquidated damages a sum equivalent to one month's salary of the employee.

Undershaft Ltd recently repudiated the contract without cause and with six and a quarter years still to run. Advise Captain Brassbound whether his damages will be limited to one month's salary under clause 6.

Exercise 11

Daphne decided to attend a 'gourmet weekend' at a 4-star hotel. She took her favourite diamond necklace (value £20,000) with her. On arriving at the hotel Daphne asked the receptionist if it would be possible to leave her necklace in the hotel's safe when she was not wearing it. The receptionist replied that it was all part of the service and then gave Daphne a form to sign. Daphne did not bother to read the form but signed it and gave it back to the receptionist along with the diamond necklace.

During the weekend the necklace was stolen after the safe door was left open by the receptionist who had been distracted by one of the thieves.

When Daphne claimed against the hotel for the loss of the necklace the hotel's manager drew her attention to an exclusion clause on the form, which she had signed, which disclaimed all liability for thefts from the hotel other than those committed by the hotel's employees.

The exclusion clause is printed clearly and visibly and is written in plain English. Advise Daphne whether the hotel can rely upon it.

Exercise 12

Tactile Ltd, a company of roofing contractors, entered into a contract with Lord Blunder for the re-roofing of his ancestral home in Buckinghamshire (which is his private residence). One of the terms in the contract provided as follows:

Tactile Ltd's liability for any damage, howsoever caused, whether by reason of the negligence of Tactile Ltd its servants or agents or otherwise, occurring to the premises or to movable property (including *all* furnishings and valuables) during the period of the contract to be limited to £1,000.

During a storm one of the temporary canopies covering the roof was displaced and rain caused £5,000 worth of damage to the plasterwork in the room below and also caused approximately £3,000 worth of damage to an antique four-poster bed and carpets worth £25,000 were ruined.

Advise Tactile Ltd whether it may be liable for the full extent of the damage. The company concedes that the canopy was not properly fixed to the roof.

Exercise 13

Mrs Albert left her green Mini parked outside her house on 28 June 2007. When she returned home she found it had been seriously damaged, apparently by another car. Flakes of red paint were found on her car, which forensic examination shows to be a paint used by Ford on Escorts and Mondeos. There are twice as many Escorts as Mondeos in this country painted in this colour.

Mrs Albert's neighbour, Mr George, owns a Ford Mondeo painted this colour. It was undamaged on 27 June, but on 28 June, when Mrs Albert found her car damaged, it had damage to its front nearside wing, consistent with having struck Mrs Albert's car.

However, there was no sign of green paint on Mr George's car. Mr George denies having damaged Mrs Albert's car, and alleges his car was also damaged while parked outside his house on 28 June.

Another neighbour, Miss Fry, says that she heard a bang at about 3.00 pm on 28 June and looked outside, where she saw a red Ford Escort with a damaged front nearside wing speeding away. She then saw Mrs Albert's car had been damaged, but Mr George's car was not outside his house.

Advise Mrs Albert as to her chances of establishing that her car was damaged by Mr George.

Exercise 14

On 7 June 2007 Thomas Boulder knocked on the door of Mr Charles Muffett's house and told Mr Muffett that his name was John Tulip, that he was an experienced roofer and that Mr Muffett's roof needed mending. He said he could mend the roof for £5,000. Mr Muffett wrote out a cheque, payable to John Tulip, in the sum of £5,000 and gave it to him. Boulder said that he would start the work within two weeks.

The next day Boulder opened a bank account in the name of John Tulip, depositing Mr Muffett's cheque into the new account. A week later he wrote out a cheque for £4,999 drawn on the John Tulip account and payable to Thomas Boulder. He paid this cheque into another account in his own name.

On 22 June he withdrew £4,999 in cash from the Boulder account. The cashier says he was suspicious, but since Boulder was able to establish his identity and since there were sufficient funds in the account, he had no option but to pay the cash.

A week later Boulder was arrested and confessed that he had no intention of repairing the roof.

Advise the prosecution with what offence or offences Boulder should be charged.

Exercise 15

Simbad Jones was stopped by the police driving a Ford Orion car which had been reported stolen. He attempted to run away when challenged, and was found to be in possession of a stolen cheque book belonging to Elsie Evans and personalised in her name which had been stolen two weeks earlier. Two days after the cheque book was stolen, a cheque from the book was used to purchase the Orion car from James White, a car dealer. The person who wrote out the cheque, which bounced, was described by

Mr White and the description matches the appearance of Simbad Jones; however, Mr White failed to pick Jones out at an identification parade. Jones says that he bought the car from a man in a pub car park and found the cheque book in the glove compartment. The car is still registered at DVLA in the name of James White.

Jones made no answer when asked why the car was not registered in his name.

Advise the prosecution whether the evidence is sufficiently strong for a jury to convict Jones of stealing or receiving the cheque book and obtaining the car by deception.

Exercise 16

Advise as to the likely sentence in each of the following cases:

(a) *Manslaughter* In an argument with X, aged 62, whom D had met by chance, D struck X in the eye, causing him to fall, hit his head and sustain injuries from which he died three months later. D was initially charged with common assault, which was increased to manslaughter when X died.

(b) *Rape* Victim, who had known D for one year, came to D's house looking for her friend, D's cousin. D made sexual advances, which were rejected, and then raped her. D had previous convictions for indecent assault on a boy of five and indecent assault and incest.

(c) *Theft* D was a hospital porter who stole $1,000 from a tourist injured in a road traffic accident whom D was wheeling. Currently under a three-month suspended sentence for theft from a customer at a restaurant where he had worked, D had many previous convictions and custodial sentences.

APPENDIX D
RE MR AND MRS ROBERTS

<u>RE MR AND MRS ROBERTS</u>

Summary of facts

1. At the beginning of March 2007, Mrs Roberts engaged Mr Cork, a painter and decorator, to re-decorate the flat which comprises the top floor of the house owned by Mrs Roberts and her husband for £1,500. The flat was due to be let to a Mrs Heller for 6 months from 1st April 2007 at a rent of £200 pw. The price for the re-decoration was £1,500. Mr and Mrs Roberts say that Mr Cork carried out the work so poorly that Mrs Heller refused to move into the flat and went to live somewhere else. Mr and Mrs Roberts had to get the flat re-decorated (at a cost of £1,200) and had to find a new tenant. They had to instruct an agent to find a new tenant. Eventually, a new tenant was found; he moved into the flat on 1st September 2007.
2. I am asked to advise Mr and Mrs Roberts whether they have a good claim against Mr Cork and, if so, what damages they can expect to recover.

Summary of advice

3. In summary, I would advise that Mr and Mrs Roberts have a strong case against Mr Cork provided that they can prove that Mr Cork's work fell below the acceptable standard. In order to recover the full cost of re-decoration, it will have to be shown that re-decoration was necessary and that the price paid was reasonable. In order for the lost rent to be recovered, it will have to be established that Mr Cork knew that Mr and Mrs Roberts intended to let the flat to a tenant.

Breach of contract

4. I am not told whether the contract was oral or written. If it was in writing (or if there is any written evidence of its terms), my Instructing Solicitor should check to see if there is any term as to the standard of workmanship or any clause which purports to exclude or limit Mr Cork's liability.
5. It was an implied term of the agreement between Mr and Mrs Roberts and Mr Cork that he would carry out the re-decoration of the flat with reasonable care and skill (s 13 of the Supply of Goods and Services Act 1982). To establish breach of this term, evidence will have to be adduced to show that the standard of Mr Cork's work fell below that to be expected of a reasonable decorator.

6. Mr and Mrs Roberts should provide a proof of evidence setting out, in as much detail as they can, the defects in Mr Cork's work. They should include any photographs that happen to be available.
7. The fact that Mrs Heller rejected the flat because of its condition is useful evidence and a statement should be taken from her if she can be traced and is willing to provide one. If she is not available as a witness, Mr and Mrs Roberts will be the only source of evidence of the fact of, and her reasons for, refusing to rent the flat.
8. More crucially, a statement should be taken from the person who re-decorated the flat after Mr Cork. Assuming he or she is willing to provide a statement, this would be an invaluable source of evidence both of the state of the flat before the remedial work was carried out, and of the standard of the work done by Mr Cork. A detailed statement should be sought, setting out all the defects in the work done by Mr Cork.

Damages

9. If liability is established, the cost of re-decoration (£1,200) is recoverable, provided that full re-decoration (rather than something less drastic) was required and provided that the sum charged was reasonable for the work done. The person who re-decorated the flat should be asked to comment on this specifically.
10. The remaining losses (loss of rent and the agent's fee) can only be recovered if Mr Cork was aware that the flat was to be let to a tenant. Otherwise, the loss could not fairly be said to be within his contemplation when the contract was made, and so will be held too remote. Mrs Roberts should include in her proof of evidence details of what they told Mr Cork about the intended use of the flat and/or whether it is obvious from the appearance of the flat that it was to be let.
11. Assuming that it can be established that Mr Cork realised that the flat was to be let, the loss of rent will be recoverable for the entire period from the date when Mrs Heller should have moved in to the date when the tenant moved in. This loss clearly flows from Mr Cork's breach of contract and, in my opinion, it cannot be said that Mr and Mrs Roberts failed to mitigate their loss: by instructing an agent, they acted reasonably. It follows that the agent's fees must also be recoverable.
12. If Mr Cork argues that it took Mr and Mrs Roberts too long to find a new tenant (in other words, that they failed to mitigate their loss), evidence from the agent of the attempts to find a tenant, and the state of the market for rented accommodation at the relevant time, would be required.

Next steps

13. The damages likely to be recoverable in this case are at the bottom end of the value of cases allocated to the fast-track. Expenditure in pursuing the claim must reflect its likely value. At this stage, I would advise that the following steps be taken:
    (i) if there is a written contract, or written evidence of the contract, this should be inspected to check for the existence of any terms relating to the standard of workmanship or which seek to exclude or restrict liability;
    (ii) a full proof of evidence should be obtained from Mr and Mrs Roberts (dealing with the state of the flat after Mr Cork had finished work on it and also indicating whether anything was said which would have made it clear to Mr Cork that the flat was to be let to a tenant);

(iii) attempts should be made to see if the second decorator would be prepared to provide a witness statement setting out the shortcomings in Mr Cork's work and how those defects were put right;

(iv) attempts should be made to locate Mrs Heller and to see if she would be willing to provide a statement about her reasons for rejecting the flat;

(v) a letter should be sent to Mr Cork by those instructing me explaining the nature of the allegations made by Mr and Mrs Roberts, setting out the full extent of their losses, and inviting him to make an open admission of liability;

(vi) it would be worth checking whether Mr Cork is a member of a trade association and, if so, whether it offers an arbitration scheme as an alternative to court proceedings (if this is so, it should be established whether the award could include consequential losses and legal costs that would be recoverable in court proceedings).

PETER NORVIC

City Chambers WC1
[date]

NOTE: This opinion relates to a case which is comparatively straightforward—there is very little law in it as the issues are largely factual ones. An opinion in a case involving more complex legal or factual issues would look very different.

Index

A
academic approach 25
admissibility of evidence 137–8
advice
  next steps 64, 65
  see also individual types eg **criminal advice on evidence**
advisory character (of opinion) 24–5
analytical process
  breach of contract 59–60
  cause of action 57
  evidence 60–1, 65
  existence of contract 57
  losses 61–4
  next steps advice 64, 65
  parties 57
  proof 59–60
  structure 56–7
  terms of contract
    breach 59–60
    express 58
    implied 58–9
apostrophe 178
argument
  no place in opinion 34
  skeleton 155
assessment criteria
  advice 160
  conclusions 161, 165–7
  content 160, 161, 164–5
  language 161, 162
  law and analysis 161, 164–8
  length 164
  practicality 161, 167–8
  structure 161, 162–4
  use 160
authorities *see* **citation of authorities**

B
brief 55–6

C
case management 151
cases *see* **citation of cases**
citation of authorities 43
  choice of material 52
  points of law 47–8
  statutory materials 51–2
citation of cases 43, 47–8
  choice of cases 50–1
  facts and judgment 49

neutral 48
  relevance 50
civil advice on evidence
  content 117–18
  documentary evidence 123, 125–6, 129, 133
  evidence available on each issue 122–4
  examination of statements of case 120–1, 130
  exchange of statements 124–5
  expert evidence 122–3, 125
  final considerations 126
  formalities 118
  hearsay evidence 124, 126
  issues
    evidence available on each 122–4
    listing 122
  oral evidence 122, 124, 127–8, 132
  potential police evidence 129
  purpose of advice 117
  reading the brief 119–20
  sample advice 127–34
  selection of evidence 124–6
  step-by-step approach 119–27
  structure 118
  timing of instructions 118
  writing 126–7
client
  opinion written for 34–5
Code of Conduct 21
colon 177–8
comma 176–7
communication
  word skills 2
Community Legal Service 106
Community Legal Service Partnerships 106
conclusions 53
conditional fee agreements 108
conjunctions 170–1
content of opinion
  citation *see* **citation of authorities; citation of cases**
  civil advice on evidence 117–18
  lack of information 43–4, 93–5
  length 44, 82
  public funding 112–13
  questions with no definite answer 41–3
  uncertainties 41–3
contract action
  breach 59–60
  causation 61, 62
  cause of action 57
  losses 61–4
  mitigation 61, 62, 63
  parties 57

contract action (*cont.*)
   privity of contract 57
   proof of breach 59–60
   remoteness 61, 62
   structure of analysis 56–7
   terms of contract
      express 58
      implied 58–9
costs
   cost benefit 112
   layout 40
   public funding proceedings 112
criminal advice on evidence
   admissibility 137–8
   charge 135–6
   continuity 142
   disclosure 140–1
   evidence in light of charges 136
   expert evidence 139
   further statements required 136
   marking exhibits 142
   no admissions by defence 137
   photographs 139
   plans 139
   sample advice
      for defence 144–6
      for prosecution 142–3
   service by defence on prosecution 141
   submissions of law 138–9
   witnesses
      attendance at court 140
      further 140
      police and civilian 137

D

defence statement 141
disclosure 140–1
dissenting judgments 53

E

employment tribunals
   public funding exclusion 107
English language 5
   see also **plain English**
essay
   opinion is not 34
evidence
   admissibility 137–8
   admissions 154–5
   advice on *see* civil advice on; criminal advice on
   analysis 60–1, 65
   civil advice on
   content 117–18
      documentary evidence 123, 125–6, 129, 133
      evidence, available on each issue 122–4
      examination of statements of case 120–1, 130
      exchange of statements 124–5
      expert evidence 122–3, 125
      final considerations 126
      formalities 118
      hearsay evidence 124, 126
      issues
         evidence available on each 122–4
         listing 122
      oral evidence 122, 124, 127–8, 132
      potential police evidence 129
      purpose of advice 117
      reading the brief 119–20
      sample advice 127–34
      selection of evidence 124–6
      step-by-step approach 119–27
      structure 118
      timing of instructions 118
      writing 126–7
   complex advice 146–50
   conflicts 32
   continuity 142
   criminal advice on
      admissibility 137–8
      charge 135–6
      continuity 142
      disclosure 140–1
      evidence in light of charges 136
      expert evidence 139
      further statements required 136
      marking exhibits 142
      no admissions by defence 137
      photographs 139
      plans 139
      sample advice
         for defence 144–6
         for prosecution 142–3
      service by defence on prosecution 141
      submissions of law 138–9
      witnesses
         attendance at court 140
         further 140
         police and civilian 137
   disclosure 140–1
   documentary 123, 125–6, 129, 133
   exchange of statements 124–5
   expert 122–3, 125, 139
   hearsay 124, 126, 154–5
   marking exhibits 142
   oral 122, 124, 127–8, 132
   photographs 139
   plans 139
   police evidence 129
   of quantum
      admissions 154–5
      future loss and future care 152–4
      hearsay evidence 154–5
      issues 151
      loss of earnings 154
      pain and suffering 151–2
      Part 36 offers 155
      payment into court 155
      sample 155–9
      skeleton argument 155
      special damages 154
      time estimates 155
      witnesses 155
   refreshment of memory 137
   service by defence on prosecution 141
   witnesses
      attendance at court 140
      criminal advice 137, 140
      evidence on quantum 155
      police and civilian 137
exercises 183–98

F

facts
  application of law to 52–3
  disputed 32
  organisation during preparation 28–9
  sample analysis 69–72
  as starting point 26
family help 107
family mediation 107
formalities 44–5, 118
full stop 175
funding
  conditional fee agreements 108
  insurance 107
  legal aid *see* **public funding**
  private 107

G

grammar 6–7, 16

H

hearings
  plea and case management 138–9, 141
  pre-trial 138–9
  preparatory 138

I

incomplete sentences 170
instructing solicitor
  conflicting view of 32
  opinion written for 34–5
  sending opinion to 45
instructions 24
  content 24
  endorsement of backsheet 45
  example 67–9
  implied questions 40
  lack of information 43–4, 93–5
  questions 24
    on receiving instructions 26
    to be answered 27, 28
  read and digest 27–8
  timing 118
insurance for legal costs 107
irrelevance 38–9

L

lack of information 43–4, 93–5
language
  legal language
    court order 14–15
    lease 13
    letter 13
    problems 12
    recognising and rewriting 12–15
    statute 14
  plain English *see* **plain English**
  simplicity of 178–82
  standard words or phrases 181–2
  terminology use 181
  verbiage 181
  see also **writing**
law
  application to facts 52–3
  citation of authorities 43
    choice of material 52
    points of law 47–8
    statutory materials 51–2
  citation of cases 43, 47–8
    choice of cases 50–1
    facts and judgment 49
    neutral 48
    relevance 50
  conclusions 53
  criminal advice on evidence 138–9
  dissenting judgments 53
  important sources 48–9
  lecture not required 46–7
  legal framework construction 29–31
  as means to end 26–7
  minor points 48
  opinion based on 46–54, 99–102
  sample analysis 72–3
  statutory materials 51–2
  use in opinion 46–54, 99–102
  well known principles 47
layout
  backsheet 36
  basic facts and key issues 36
  conclusion 41
  costs 40
  framework 75–6
  further advice 40–1
  heading 36
  irrelevance 38–9
  length 44, 82
  liability 39
  opening paragraphs 36–7
  procedural points 40
  quantum 39
  reasoning 37–9
  rules of structure 39–40
  separate parties 39–40
  signature of counsel 41
  skeleton plan 35–6
  subsequent paragraphs 37–9
  subsidiary points 40
  variations in practice 41
leases 102–5
legal aid 106
legal authorities, citation *see* **citation of authorities**
legal costs insurances 107
legal language *see* **language**
legal research
  opinion following 102–5
  preparation of opinion 73
Legal Services Commission 106
  duty of barrister 109
  see also **public funding**
length of opinion 44, 82
liability and damages
  insufficient information 93–5
  layout 39
  personal injury 89–93

M

marking exhibits 142
modes of address 45
modifiers 174–5

O

opinion
    assessment *see* **assessment criteria**
    content *see* **content of opinion**
    law in *see* **law**
    not argument, essay, submission or instruction 34
    purpose 33–4
    sample 77–105, 199–201
    sending to instructing solicitor 45
    setting out *see* **layout**
    for solicitor or client 34–5
    style 44–5
    uncertainty 41–3
opinion writing
    advisory character 24–5
    attitude to *see* **practitioner approach**
    citations *see* **citation of authorities**; **citation of cases**
    instructions *see* **instructions**
    meaning 23
    paperwork 23
    planning *see* **preparation**
    reason for learning 23
    thinking process *see* **preparation**

P

paperwork 23
paragraphs 175
Part 36 offers/payment into court
    advice on 155
    interest 155
personal injuries
    admissions 154–5
    advice on quantum 95–9, 151–9
    future loss and future care 152–4
    hearsay evidence 154–5
    issues 151
    loss of earnings 154
    pain and suffering 151–2
    payment into court 155
    Pre-Action Protocol 151
    sample 155–9
    sample opinion 89–93
    skeleton argument 155
    special damages 154
    time estimates 155
    'track' 151
    witnesses 155
plain English 5, 178
    basic rules 16–18
    legal language
        problems 12
        recognising and rewriting 12–15
    meaning 11
    promotion of 12
    reasons for use 11
    writing in 15–16
planning *see* **preparation**

plea and case management hearing 138–9, 141
police
    evidence in civil case 129
    witnesses 137
practitioner approach
    academic approach abandoned 25
    answering the question 27, 28
    facts as starting point 26
    law as means to end 26–7
    real situation 26
Pre-Action Protocol
    personal injuries 151
pre-trial disclosure 140–1
pre-trial hearing 138–9
preparation
    advice consideration 32–3
    case against 73
    clarification of objectives 69
    consider case as whole 31
    example 69–76
    facts
        absorbed and organised 28–9
        sample analysis 69–72
        as starting point 26
    framework for layout 75–6
    law analysis, sample 72–3
    legal framework construction 29–31
    questions to be answered 26, 27, 28
        all questions 31–2
    reading the brief 27–8, 69, 119–20
    research 73, 102–5
    skeleton opinion 35–6, 75–6, 155
    using professional judgment 74
preparatory hearings 138
professional conduct 21–2
pronouns 173–4
public funding
    advising for purpose of 106–16
    certificates 108
    Community Legal Service 106
    content of opinion 112–13
    current scheme 106–8
    duty to Legal Services Commission 109
    excluded categories 107
    family mediation 107
    financial eligibility 110
    franchise holders 106
    Funding Code 107, 109
    general family help 107
    help at court 107
    help with mediation 107
    legal aid 106
    legal help 107
    legal representation 107
    legal services certificate 108
    merits of the case 111–12
    privately paying client test 113
    professional conduct 108–9
    prospect of success 109, 111
    restrictions 108
    risk analysis 107–8
    sample of opinions 114–16
    specific directions 107
    statutory charge 113
    unquantifiable claims 113

punctuation 7, 16–17
  apostrophe 178
  colon 177–8
  comma 176–7
  full stop 175
  question mark 178
  semicolon 177

Q

quantum
  admissions 154–5
  future loss and future care 152–4
  hearsay evidence 154–5
  issues 151
  layout 39
  loss of earnings 154
  pain and suffering 151–2
  payment into court 155
  personal injuries 95–9
  sample 155–9
  skeleton argument 155
  special damages 154
  time estimates 155
  witnesses 155
question mark 178
questions
  implied 40
  in instructions 27, 28
  with no definite answer 41–3
  preparation 26, 28, 31–2

R

refreshment of memory 137
research
  opinion following 102–5
  preparation of opinion 73

S

semicolon 177
sentences
  conjunctions 170–1
  incomplete 170
  modifiers 174–5
  pronouns 173–4
  short as possible 16, 179–80
  subject-verb agreement 171–3
  subjunctives 173
separate parties 39–40
skeleton opinion 35–6, 75–6, 155
spelling 6
statements of case 120–1, 130
statutory charge 113
statutory materials 51–2
style of opinion
  formality 44–5
  modes of address 45
subject-verb agreement 171–3
subjunctives 173
submission
  opinion is not 34

T

thinking process *see* preparation
typographical errors 10

U

uncertainties 41–3

W

witnesses
  attendance at court 140
  criminal advice 137, 140
  evidence on quantum 155
  police and civilian 137
word skills
  barristers and 1–3
  communication 2
  spoken 2
  standards 2–3
  written 1
  see also **language; plain English; writing**
writing
  active voice 179
  appearance 9
  choices 4–5
  clarity 5
  completeness 8–9
  conciseness 8–9
  elegance 9
  English language 5
    everyday English 17
    plain English 15–16
  first and second person use 17
  grammar 6–7, 16
  improving skills 169–82
  layout 18
  logical structure 6
  non-ambiguity 8
  order of words 17–18, 180
  paragraphs 175
  passive voice 179
  precision 7–8
  punctuation 7, 16–17
    apostrophe 178
    colon 177–8
    comma 176–7
    full stop 175
    question mark 178
    semicolon 177
  readers 10
  reading over and correcting 10
  sentences
    conjunctions 170–1
    incomplete 170
    modifiers 174–5
    pronouns 173–4
    short as possible 16, 179–80
    subject-verb agreement 171–3
    subjunctives 173
  simple structures 17
  simplicity of language 178–82
  spelling 6
  standard words or phrases 181–2

writing (*cont.*)
  structure 64–5
  terminology use 181
  typographical errors 10
  unnecessary words 181
  verbiage 181
  verbs preferred to nouns based on verbs 179
  word order 17–18, 180
  written word skills 1, 2
  see also **language**
Written Standards for the Conduct of Professional Work 21–2